A WOMAN ON TOP

A WOMAN ON TOP

MY JOURNEY OF SELF-DISCOVERY
THROUGH LOVE AND MONEY

Suzanne Leydecker

STRONGPrint
PUBLISHING

Published and distributed by STRONGPrint Publishing
Colorado, USA
Library of Congress Control Number: 2023917481
Leydecker, Suzanne

A Woman on Top:
My Journey of Self-Discovery through Love and Money

ISBN: 978-1-962074-00-1 (Paperback)
ISBN: 978-1-962074-01-8 (Casebound)

If we know how to use it, then money can help us pass through this earthly existence with more ease. However, if we don't know how to deal with it, then money can destroy us.

SRI PREM BABA

CONTENTS

Foreword

When I began reading this book early one night, the last thing I imagined was that I would stay up as long as it took to finish it, which turned out to be sometime early the next morning.

"Why might you do that?" you may ask. The answer, of course, is, "I just couldn't put it down."

I had to see where it would lead, and what I discovered was that the unfolding continued all the way through to the end of the book. And the end itself, along with Suzanne's learnings and the way she is using what she's learned, is highly inspirational for those I might refer to as "Seekers of the Light." And thus, the unfolding continues, and continues, and continues—as endless as time itself.

As Suzanne points out, we are living at a time when change in an upward direction is the order of the day. *A Woman on Top* is certainly what I would call an "instructional manual" for those seeking a path leading to the same destination, which I refer to as "awakening into the emerging Light, consistent with the evolution of consciousness we are all involved in at this time."

I don't recall ever starting a book and reading it cover to cover because someone, or something within me, just had to follow the thread to see where it was going. I am pleased I chose to follow Suzanne's path and see that it led her higher and higher into what I like to identify and refer to as "the workings of the Earth School."

May this journey lead you to your own path of awakening and evolution.

Now I think I'll go take a nap.

H. RONALD HULNICK, PHD
President, University of Santa Monica

The Elephant in the Room

The truth knocks on the door and you say, "Go away, I'm looking for the truth," and so it goes away. Puzzling.

—ROBERT M. PIRSIG

You may be wondering why this book is called *A Woman on Top*.

One of its early titles was *Women on Top*. At the time, if you Googled "Women on Top," you got, well, women on top, and then you got me.

Wait a minute—is this a sex book?

I hate to disappoint you. This isn't a book about sex.

It's about a topic even more taboo than sex. Money. And more specifically, how money, relationships, and sex are intertwined.

I remember watching an interview with Eckhart Tolle, author of *The Power of Now* and one of today's great spiritual teachers.

A man in the audience asked Tolle, "Do you *really* believe in reincarnation?"

Tolle answered the man with complete confidence, "Really, I have no idea."

As Tolle said in his thick German accent, and I paraphrase, *choosing to believe in reincarnation makes it easier for me to understand what is going on in the here and now, but it's up to you. It doesn't matter whether you believe in it or not.*

For the record, I do believe in reincarnation, but no matter what *you* believe, I think we can agree that during the course of our lives we tend to encounter the same kind of challenges again and again and again.

In fact, some believe that on an unconscious level we choose our parents, families, and life experiences—including our experiences with money—*before* we get here. And then upon the arduous journey through the birth canal, we agree to forget what we know—and forget we have chosen everything we experience in our lifetime. Some (including me) call the life challenges we face our spiritual curriculum, which we chose before we were born in order to learn what we need to learn.

I might have lost some of you here, but why couldn't it be true?

However, on a conscious level, I didn't get to choose if I was going to incarnate as male or female, black or white, gay or straight—or anything in between. I did not get to choose whether I would be born in a remote village of Uganda or in Ross, California. I just arrived.

If we knew what our life challenges were going to be and how to handle them, they wouldn't be challenges. Life would be, as they say, a bowl of cherries. We could sit around and rest on our laurels. We could bask in our successes, spend our time pursuing leisure activities, experience financial freedom, and eat all the dessert we want with no negative consequences. We would know how to handle setbacks, divorce, disappointments, and serious illness.

This is the fantasy.

Instead, the reality is we work, we struggle, and we ponder whether the job or partner we choose will lead us to nirvana. We ponder over which lifestyles and choices will lead us toward the good life.

Some are luckier than others. Most would say I am in the "lucky" category, and I am. I have lived an unbelievably magical 63 years. If I die tomorrow, I can say I have lived the fullest life imaginable.

In 2007, after my second parent passed away, I inherited more money than I had ever imagined, but that's not why my life has been magical. Many times since, I have wished I never inherited it. Every bit of security and opportunity it offered was matched by the chaos it created in my relationships.

Even with all I have going for me, I have my challenges on this journey of navigating the calm—and the not-so-calm—seas. I am a woman, and women come with our own unique set of challenges. Maybe that's why we give boats female names.

What *has* been magical is the inner journey created by receiving the money. While I thought I was on an outer journey of mastering money and relationships, the truth was I was on an inner journey, and money was just the catalyst. My inner journey became about discovering what true self-worth, self-care, and love without the entanglement of money really looked like.

I have had many conversations with many women over the course of my life that went something like this.

Me: "[Name of latest guy] isn't calling me back. I think he's so great, and I just don't understand." I pause, feeling sorry for myself. "I mean, we had such a good time last night. I thought he really liked me."

My girlfriend(s): "Come on, you're great. He's the one who is losing out. I (we) don't get it either, but I (we) think it's because you come across as too powerful, and men are intimidated by strong, powerful women."

I hated those conversations.

I've been told many times that because I come off as powerful, or tough, or strong, men feel "intimidated" by me.

Intimidated by me?

That sounded ridiculous.

I knew my friends were just trying to make me feel better and pay me a compliment, but either it was true (which didn't really inspire me to stand up and be powerful), or it wasn't—meaning there was something wrong with me.

Neither felt good.

The cold, hard truth was I looked tough on the outside, but in reality I was a soft pile of mush on the inside—which is not a particularly powerful way of being.

I got the problem but didn't have the solution.

After inheriting the money, this one question would become the major question of my lifetime:

What happens in a heterosexual relationship when a woman makes more?

My particular challenges have been the following:

1. Being a woman on top, or a woman who has more resources than most (for me it is money, but it could just as easily be intelligence, talent, connections, or any other resource).
2. Habitually saying and thinking things that keep me stuck—even when I know better.
3. Being without a soulmate in a world that seems obsessed with finding "the one."

If any of these sound familiar, I wrote this book for you.

So, I'm supposed to be the expert who will provide the "secret answer," right?

I was inspired a few years back by Lynne Twist, who states in the introduction of her book *The Soul of Money* that her intention in writing her book was about "finding a new freedom, truth, and joy in our relationship with money." She goes on to say she is "not an economist or a banker or an investment advisor."

"I have no degrees in finance or business," she states. "I do, however, have a deep and special knowledge, experience, and understanding of money. My education in money has come through direct and intimate experiences."

This is how I feel about being a so-called breadwinning woman in intimate relationships. I'm not a money or relationship expert and I don't have an MBA. I do hold a master's degree in Marriage and Family Counseling and a certificate in Spiritual Psychology. Like Lynne Twist, my education has come from direct and intimate experiences.

However, since I travel a great deal, I've had the opportunity to hear stories from around the globe. Each story is different, but they are all the same. When a woman has more or makes more than her male partner, relationships often suffer.

I have heard stories from a female taxicab driver in France, schoolteachers in New York City, a front desk clerk in South Africa, and some of the wealthiest women and men in the world. As I continued to meet women from all financial backgrounds with varying levels of education from many corners of the planet, my biggest surprise was that, even though I was in the financial top one percent of people alive today, women all over the world were grappling with the very same questions I was.

This "Woman on Top" problem isn't just my problem, or a rich woman's problem, or a first-world problem; it's a global problem.

It's not related to age, economics, education, or location; it was everywhere I looked.

If you identify as a woman who feels you must sacrifice your success to have a relationship—or sacrifice a relationship to have success—I want you to know you are not alone.

I often wonder about the idioms we hear and say without thinking about them. We grow up hearing them repeated to us over and over again, and if we don't question them, they can become the scripts for our lives.

But just because we believe them and use them doesn't mean they're true or applicable.

See if any of these sayings sound familiar:

- The apple doesn't fall far from the tree.
- She wears the pants in the family.
- Money is the root of all evil.
- He who makes the gold makes the rules.
- The grass is always greener on the other side.

Put into today's language, they might sound like:

- My mom stayed at home with us kids, so I should too.
- She's in control of the relationship, which means he is completely emasculated.
- Rich women are bitches.
- Stay-at-home dads are losers.
- My life would be so much better if my husband made more money and I could stay home with the kids. (Or my life would be so much better if I could work instead of staying home with the kids.)

If we really want women to be successful—and if we really want men to want us to succeed—let's begin by looking at our current assumptions and choose whether they still have value for us. And if they don't, let's replace them.

I invite all of us to *question everything*—including the idioms and references we use—and consider what will serve ourselves and society best in this new world.

———————

It's time to talk about the elephant in the room. We can no longer ignore the dynamic that happens over and over, usually behind closed doors. When women are outearning men, women feel they must diminish themselves.

To have viable conversations that actually produce solutions, we can practice calmly and directly speaking about it. Maybe if we start talking about it together, we'll better understand how big the elephant is, whether it's hostile or friendly, and what to do with it.

So, with this book, I'm breaking the ice. I'm sharing my raw, vulnerable, imperfect story of facing my own inherited beliefs about men, money, and sex.

Although I am in no way an expert, I believe my whole life was perfectly designed to lead me to this task. Our planet is in the midst of a major transition, and it is time for us all to examine our beliefs regarding money and relationships, no matter what gender we are.

If you are a woman on top and want to fully embrace your purpose and passions while engaging in a healthy relationship, my hope is that my story will inspire you to embrace your own empowerment and stop feeling ashamed of your gifts—and begin to feel more comfortable sharing them.

If you are a wealthy woman, chances are you're going to date a man with less money than you. If you are a woman with a lot of *any* resource, chances are you're going to date a man who has less of that resource than you. Rather than a curse, my life story shows that wealth—and everything that comes with wealth—is an opportunity for spiritual growth.

We're all born with gifts we don't necessarily deserve. None of us got to choose where we were born, or how much money our family of origin had, or our athletic ability, or level of beauty.

We are all also born with the opportunity to awaken into whatever we were given and use it to benefit our life experiences and the life experiences of others. Although I still have things to work on, I have finally reached the point where I feel blessed to have this gift of money.

I may not have all the answers, but I do have a story. My hope is that my story will invite you to examine your beliefs, see the lessons in your own story, and continue the conversation.

CHAPTER 1

The Apple Doesn't Fall Far from the Tree

Perhaps home is not a place
but simply an irrevocable condition.

–JAMES BALDWIN

I grew up in Ross, California, an affluent community in Marin County, twenty minutes north of San Francisco across the Golden Gate Bridge. In 1959, the year I was born, my parents—Patricia Lute and John Huge Robinson—bought a plot of land and built their house in Ross for $27,000. Today, that same amount of money wouldn't buy you a driveway in Marin County. Over time, it became one of the more desirable locations to live, but back then it was quiet.

My world and family seemed normal as a child. Our home and lifestyle were basic but adequate. Others had more (and much fancier) homes and things than we did, but my family's life was simple. We went skiing for a weekend in the winter every year and spent two weeks in the summer at a camp in the mountains. Otherwise, we stuck around home. We played hide-and-seek in the neighborhood and kickball in the field near our house with friends. Ross was a great place to grow up, and I appreciated our rural lifestyle and community—and it was all I knew.

My parents grew up in the aftermath of the Depression, which I'm sure affected their views about money. My mother was born in a small apartment in San Francisco on Van Ness Avenue, and my father in Piedmont, a suburb of Oakland, California. As a young woman, my mother worked at KGO radio station until she got married. My father worked for the Harper Group, which eventually became a branch of Circle Freight International. The Harper Group was the family freight-forwarding business my father's father had acquired in 1940 from Mr. Harper after working there since the early 1900s.

My father was always a hard worker, even as a boy. He, along with his younger brother, started off in the mailroom of the Harper Group sorting and stacking the incoming mail shortly after he turned twelve years old. My father eventually took over the company as president at age forty. His brother became vice president shortly after.

From that point on, there was always friction between my father and the rest of his family over the business. His parents and only brother did not want the company to grow. They wanted the business to remain a small family operation with its ten employees and moderate profits. Over time, my father saw the company's potential as a successful global business. Money, wealth, and loyalty within his family of origin were big conversations in our house.

Before taking over the business, my father was very close to his family. He spent a great deal of time with his brother hunting and skiing, among other things, and they loved each other dearly. As young children, our family spent most Saturdays at my grandparents' house in

Piedmont with my uncle, my aunt, and their five children. Those were happy times. As a child I felt loved and included in my extended family.

As my father fought with his parents and brother over the growth of the company, these wonderful Saturdays simply stopped happening. By attempting to grow the company, my father was seen as going against the family. We became estranged from our grandparents and cousins. I was sad about no longer being included, but there was no room for negotiation or discussion.

When I went to my uncle's funeral forty years later, I discovered there were lingering hurt feelings. My aunt still believed my father chose money and the success of the company over love and loyalty. The story that my father broke up the family for his own personal gain continued to thrive.

Based on the sadness I saw my father carry, I don't believe he did not love his family. I believe he made the choice to follow his dream of growing the business, and they wanted nothing to do with it. No one was wrong; it was just how it happened.

In 1977, when I was seventeen, my father took Circle Freight International public. Due to his vision and hard work, he built from next to nothing a worldwide shipping business—one of the most successful of its kind globally.

My bedroom was next to my parents', so I know he worked hard. His alarm went off at 4:30 a.m. every morning Monday through Friday—and at 6 a.m. on Saturdays—so he could go running and then to work when he wasn't traveling. He was about as quiet as a herd of elephants well before the sun came up. I spent many mornings with a pillow over my head as he hit the road.

My father started running when he was 50, about the same age as most people stop. He was obsessive about everything, and running was no different. He ran seven days a week until he could no longer walk.

My father traveled nine months out of the year—every year—when I was growing up. I didn't see him much. I'm quite sure he sacrificed our family's life—and love—to create something successful, but unlike his family of origin, I didn't feel resentful about his work ethic. Again, it was all I knew.

At home, the connection between love and money was cemented in my mind from a young age. Strangely enough, in many ways, my father couldn't have cared less about money. His mission was to be successful. I believe he was trying to impress his mother, his father, and his brother with his success and earn back their love. Unfortunately, and ironically, they were far from proud of him and more or less disowned him— equating the company's success with betrayal of the family.

I saw my father as an unusual and eclectic man. His messages about money were always mixed. When I was a teenager, it became apparent he was building a successful company—but he walked around in shirts with holes and outdated suits.

He did *not* like spending money.

Yet sometimes money was no issue. Christmas Eve was one example. From the age of eight and into my twenties, after our obligatory visit to my father's aging father—on our way home from our traditional family lunch in San Francisco—we would make a stop at Gump's, a high-end jewelry store in the city. We would all pile out of the car, and my father would buy my mother—and me as I got older—a beautiful piece of jewelry. It wasn't Tiffany's, but it was expensive, and I saw the price tags grow on each piece of jewelry as time went on. Looking back on our annual stop, I realized the price of the gifts increased in line with his business success.

Similarly, when I was eighteen, my father decided to get a limousine and driver. He didn't buy it for the status. He just wasn't a very good driver, and because he worked so hard, he was always tired. No one wanted him falling asleep at the wheel. He embraced his commute to and from work so he could squeeze in a bit more work time.

Because his messages about money were always mixed, as I grew older I never knew what any given financial discussion might bring—about business, buying things, or anything else for that matter. I found it odd that he would spend money on expensive jewelry but not on basic necessities—other than at the hardware store, where we made another regular stop every Sunday after church when he was home.

I think he loved the hardware store because he could buy lots of goodies to tinker with around the house for next to nothing. He wasn't very good at tinkering, but he enjoyed his Sundays away from the office when my mother, brother, and I were forced to work alongside him in the garden and around the house. We pruned, we raked the gravel driveway to perfection, and we painted the strips of wood that ran through the egg timer-shaped piece of concrete we called a backyard.

What he bought at the hardware store wasn't important. He once took a trip to the hardware store with my mother because he wanted to buy a lawn mower—not an unusual purchase for most people. The salesman, of course, tried to sell them the best—and most expensive—lawn mower in the store.

My mother looked at the salesman and said, "We really don't need the *best* lawn mower you have. We just need a basic lawn mower."

The salesman looked at her, slightly confused, and responded, "Is there a reason you just want a basic lawn mower? Our higher-end lawn mowers make mowing the lawn much easier."

"Yes," she said with a completely straight face, "We don't need a fancy lawnmower because we don't have a lawn."

The salesman was shocked, I'm sure. We had a Japanese garden. It didn't have *any* grass whatsoever. My father just wanted a lawn mower. I still laugh out loud when I think of this story.

When I was in high school, my father wanted to teach me the value of money. Together, we worked out an allowance of exactly $62.50 a month—an odd figure that stands out in my memory. He arrived at that number after adding up precisely how much it would cost me to take the bus to and from school, the cost of school lunch on average, and other monthly expenses—like movie nights with friends or the occasional trip to my favorite clothing store. His math added up to a grand total of $62.50, so that is how much I was given each month.

To receive my monthly allowance, I had chores to do. An allowance was far from necessary; I made my own money babysitting and didn't have real expenses, but he wanted the allowance to teach me the value of money—a concept I genuinely appreciated and still do to this day.

My father was generous when he wanted to be—but always on his terms. The problem was his terms changed without me—or anyone else—ever knowing why or when. Money and love were interconnected and interchanged at will. As a young child, I had no way to know where one began and the other ended. It confused me—and I hated it.

After my father became successful, I think he was fearful as many people are of losing what he had made—or of someone taking it away—so he was protective of his wealth. He made list after list of his net worth. After his death, I found an unusually large number of lists calculating his monetary holdings scattered throughout his paperwork.

My mother also had a simple upbringing, just like my father, but she had a completely different perspective on money. She was a "do whatever you need to do to get what you want when you want it" type of woman. She was a survivor and then some. My mother was very social and enjoyed going out, playing bridge with her friends, and shopping when my father was working or out of town. She was also generous to others with her money, her time, and more importantly, her spirit. She was a wonderful soul and well-loved by many.

When I was seventeen, my parents began making plans to remodel our simple home. The transformation took our house from being nothing special to a magnificent, contemporary home. As usual, there was a tremendous amount of fighting over the cost of everything. The house came out beautifully, but there were some terrible arguments along the way—mostly between my father and Francois, the French decorator—but certainly between my parents as well. As with most of their disagreements, my mother just smiled and nodded.

After the remodel, my mother had her own dressing area with plenty of closet space that—of course—needed to be filled. Her favorite activity was shopping. Her addiction was shopping. Her avoidance of reality was shopping. She bought things nonstop not only to adorn the closet but to fill a hole that could never be filled. When she died years later, I packed up bags and bags of clothes with the price tags still on them. Shopping was her salvation from the chaos created by my father. The more she could buy, the better.

Throughout her life, my mother was a fashion queen and often dressed in high heels and gorgeous outfits. She was an important figure in San Francisco and was regularly mentioned on the society page of the *San Francisco Chronicle*.

Somewhere along the line, she met Phillipe and Juan, who were high-end designers of custom clothing. Phillipe and Juan were a dream come true for my mother. They were purveyors of customized outfits who absolutely adored her. She was easy to adore—and I'm also sure they loved having such a good client.

Over the years, she took me with her many times to see their latest and greatest collection. I ended up with a baby pink taffeta skirt that wasn't flattering at all, several long gowns, floppy skirts, and a black silk bustier that I just recently managed to part with. My mother's shopping habits both delighted and bothered me at the same time. But I never asked how she was paying for any of it.

When I was twenty-one, my grandmother on my mother's side passed away. She was a good, kind, loving soul. She lived nearby and took care of my brother and me when my mother traveled abroad with my father. My grandmother was a little woman—only 5'2"—but feisty and opinionated. I adored her. When she died, her house was her only real asset. After my mother and I spent weeks cleaning out her thirty years of things, we sold it.

My grandmother had left a will stating that my brother, mother, and I were to get equal shares of the proceeds from the sale of her house—close to $250,000 for each of us. Because I was just twenty-one and my brother was nineteen, we never questioned where the money went. As a matter of fact, we had no idea our grandmother had even left us any money.

When I was twenty-three, my mother decided she wanted a new car—a cute little Jaguar. This was way beyond what she could afford, but she wanted it anyway. So, she bought it.

She never mentioned buying the car to my father, and he never acknowledged the purchase. No words were *ever* exchanged over the new swishy vehicle parked in the garage one day. She didn't talk about it because she thought he would get mad—and he just ignored it.

The fact that my mother bought this expensive car without any discussion before or after was another lasting memory for me. How could they never have talked about an $80,000 car? How did she pay for it? My takeaway was that money could mean secrets between a husband and a wife.

It wasn't until I was twenty-six, when I was busy starting my own life and taking care of myself, that I finally asked my mother about my share of my grandmother's money.

My mother nonchalantly informed me that she had spent the $250,000 my grandmother had left me. I didn't know what to say.

"What did you spend it on?" I asked.

"Well," she said hesitating, "how do you think I paid for all those clothes?"

She had spent all the money on clothing—including the unflattering baby pink taffeta skirt. I was devastated.

To spend $250,000 on clothes I did not realize I was buying for myself—and for her—really made me mad. It was unfair. I wanted control of my own money, and I wanted to make choices about how it was spent.

I quickly figured out where the Jaguar had come from.

My father was a walking contradiction about money, and my mother was a spendaholic.

I was confused. Were we rich? Were we poor?

I had no idea. Growing up with such different and inconsistent role models caused both me and my brother massive confusion about how to handle finances.

Over time I realized my "normal" childhood wasn't very normal after all.

CHAPTER 2

He Wears the Pants in the Family

We realize the importance of our voices
only when we are silenced.

–MALALA YOUSAFZAI

My father was successful, but he was also a control freak. His company probably could have grown to twice its size, but as his managers said (mostly behind his back), he was like a "human bottleneck." They hated his need to be involved in making decisions, but he didn't care what they thought. Policy, company changes, acquisitions, and outstanding bills had to go through him in a way that often slowed down the process. Luckily, he had an enormous amount of insight and vision coupled with a hard-working, loyal team behind him that led to the company's overall success.

My father not only made all the money in our family, he also controlled all the money. Nothing was in my mother's name, and I don't recall her knowing anything about how to access his wealth. This was a common arrangement between husbands and wives back then, and she willingly accepted the way things were.

My mother got an allowance that she used to pay the household bills—with very little left over at the end of each month (or so she said). My father didn't just give her the allowance; she had to ask for it every month. If she needed more, she had to beg for it. Her allowance was the way my father manipulated and controlled her. He seemed to enjoy making her squirm. Watching their dynamic and interactions around money was upsetting to me as a child.

I still remember feeling bad for her and cringing every time the subject came up. My mother was supposed to get her allowance on the first of every month. There was no such thing as direct deposit back then, so she relied on my father to write her a check. Most months the check was late—sometimes weeks late. Since my father traveled intermittently nine months out of the year, he was not home often, making it even more challenging for her to get the money.

My mother was always ready for my father's arrival from work around 8 p.m. when he was home. She would dress in a long skirt and cute top. My brother and I would be in our pajamas with teeth brushed and homework done. Our simple kitchen had the lights turned down low, the fire crackling, and romantic music playing.

She was not much of a cook, but there would be cheese and crackers out, a bottle of cheap white wine cracked open, and chicken ready to "pop in the oven," as she put it. My father liked inexpensive wine and simple food—nothing fancy or elegant. He was proud of his frugality.

When my father was traveling, my mother, brother, and I had a more flexible lifestyle. I loved my mother, but I was always telling her she got an "F" in motherhood. She was a horrible cook and didn't like to clean. I recall many breakfasts consisting of cold, burnt scrambled eggs—complete with shells—before school and a lot of wilted celery in the fridge. She often paid me a dollar to clean the kitchen for her. I was a neatnik even back then, so I didn't mind. Even when she didn't ask me to, I did it anyway. Maybe I thought order and cleanliness would make our home more normal.

There was no strict bedtime or curfew when my father was gone. In fact, there wasn't much of a schedule at all. With few rules, there wasn't a lot to be upset over, but I knew in my heart this was not the healthiest way to raise children—and it was so different from any of my friends' upbringing.

I remember playing sports, watching *My Favorite Martian* on Thursday evenings, endlessly throwing a tennis ball for our black lab Missy, and the occasional trip to Taco Bell with a neighbor's father. All the kids in the neighborhood piled into the back of his old pickup truck to go to the next town for dinner. I don't think my mother even knew where we were.

My brother and I were always fighting when we were home, and my mother ignored it. I spent most of my time at the neighbors' houses. No one cared—or missed me—and I was happier being on my own.

Things were different when my father was home. Life was more rigid and not nearly as much fun. He was only home for an hour or so before we went to bed, but the dynamics were different and more stressful. I would wait for his car to come up the driveway, wondering what would happen that night.

The evenings' events varied anywhere from playing Clue as a family and having him put me to bed with a loving back rub, to salad and salad bowl being tossed up in the air in a fit of rage—leaving a permanent mark on the ceiling. I prayed for peace, but there was no guarantee. Many of those nights were disturbing and sometimes scary.

Partially, I think my father's temper came from him always being so tired. Working long hours took a toll on him, and he often fell asleep at the dinner table. Frequently, he had his eyes closed before the meal was over. He would go from a slumped position as he fell into a deep sleep and then back to his perfect posture—while still sleeping. It was impressive, honestly. We all knew he thought perfect posture was a discipline *necessary* for success.

He would occasionally reach for a spoon or fork, hunting for something to scoop into his mouth while he was asleep. I saw him eat pats of butter, chicken bones, or anything else left that was nearby. He would sit up in his chair at the dinner table straight as an arrow and smile (a practice he had also mastered in his sleep). One time at a dinner party, I saw a friend save him from eating cigarette butts and ashes with a spoon.

He probably wouldn't have noticed.

When he was home in the evening, it was the only time of day my mother had to ask for her allowance. The subject came up month after month. I never recall my father volunteering a check.

In a soft, loving voice, she would say: "John, can you please give me my allowance?"

Those words were sometimes met with, "Yes, I can," often followed by: "I will get it to you tomorrow. I left my checkbook at the office." When he felt like it, he might even write her a check right then and there.

But sometimes the conversation didn't go so well.

"How dare you ask for money?" he would say. "Who do you think you are?"

My father's comments aimed at my mother—about her inability to handle the family finances—were degrading and difficult to hear, even though they were sometimes true.

After that, the evening usually went downhill in a hurry—with screaming and yelling directed toward my mother, or my brother or me. It wasn't a pleasant experience—and it was extra difficult not knowing when it would happen or how bad it would be.

In our house, money was talked about all the time: If you were good, money was promised to you—though the promises were usually forgotten. And if you dared to assume the promise from the night before was a reality, there was hell to pay. As a young adult, until the day my father got sick, I was demoralized over and over and over, thinking he was going to help me with some form of business or financial enterprise—before he backed out or accused me of making up the conversation.

There was no talk of my brother or me ever working at the family company. He had a strong belief about children *not* getting involved in the family business—even though he had done just that. He was anti-nepotism and made his opinion very clear to both me and my brother.

Little girl was one of my father's favorite demoralizing expressions he resorted to when he wanted to ensure I knew my place. He used it often, and I struggled a great deal over the sting of his tone and implication as to my lack of ability. I do not believe he really meant to hurt me. I think he was just acting with me the way his parents acted with him. My father was as abusive with our family as his family of origin had been to him. Regardless of why he did it, his comments chipped away at my self-esteem.

My mother was supportive of my father and always knew her place. She tailored her life around doing what a good wife should. She stayed home when he was there and did whatever she felt inclined to do when he was gone.

In 1972, when I was twelve, my mother decided our family needed some help, so as a group and individually, we started seeing Dr. Jerry Jampolsky, who had a psychiatric practice in Tiburon, California. In 1975, Jerry founded the Center for Attitudinal Healing. Both of my parents were instrumental in starting the Center, a place where people with life-threatening illnesses could come and get support—and practice seeing their situation in a positive, loving, peaceful way. The Center provided a nurturing environment for those with an illness as well as their family members. My mother was a facilitator of many groups, her favorite being one held weekly on Tuesday evenings.

From my perspective, her involvement with Jerry and the Center was the first time my mother had a sense of purpose outside the family. She spent nearly every day at the Center, but when my father was home, she always skipped her favorite meeting on Tuesday nights. I know she hated missing those meetings, but she did it anyway. As we got older, she started to become more independent and went to her Tuesday night meetings, leaving my father to fend for himself. His ability to control her was waning.

My dad was often upset over her not being home Tuesday evenings, and he threw more than one temper tantrum, but she no longer cared. My father still tried to use money to control and manipulate her, but she was becoming less easily controlled. For him, their relationship did not work as well as she became more independent. My father always knew he held the purse strings, and it made him feel powerful. He wore the pants in the family—or at least he tried.

My father abused my mother mentally and emotionally. And on many occasions, she stood around and watched him abuse both me and my brother as well, without doing anything to protect us. Later in life—when I understood the severity of her father's alcoholism—I realized why she didn't stand up for us.

She had grown up in an alcoholic family where her role as the only child was to keep the peace. She didn't want any conflict, yet she chose a similar chaotic environment in her marriage full of degradation and torment. I had a great deal of sadness around this as a child. Sometimes it felt like she was fighting for her survival at the expense of anything else.

When I was a young adult, I asked her why she had stayed in the marriage. She looked around our home and said: "Why would I leave all this?"

She was referring to the money, the travel, and the things. I certainly didn't think it was worth it, but she did. She loved her lifestyle, and she loved her husband. He did have a gentle, kind, lovable heart, sometimes. Unfortunately, it was often superseded by his need to succeed and control those around him.

His behavior didn't end with the family. I witnessed him at work many times—and in social situations—using his skill to attack and demoralize people, and he was quite proficient at it.

Twice a year, my mother joined my father on a two-week trip to somewhere in the world. They covered every continent together over the years, and for whatever reason, they traveled quite well together. My father kept his hectic sixteen-cities-in-fourteen-days kind of schedule—even when my mother was with him— and she was always up for the next adventure. She was patient and didn't mind the frantic pace. These two-week excursions seemed to make it possible for them to stay married for all those years.

They always departed for their fall trip the Friday after Thanksgiving. Pat Steiger, who crafted the society column for the *San Francisco Chronicle,* wrote more than once how Patsy and John Robinson were again enjoying their time over the Thanksgiving weekend in Paris—or some other exotic place.

Because my birthday is December 2, the only two birthdays my parents were ever present for were my first birthday (I know because I have seen Polaroid pictures) and my twentieth. They were only around for my twentieth birthday because I was studying in Switzerland. They magnificently surprised me and showed up at my school for dinner.

Most parents show up for their children's birthday—and most kids expect them to—but in my case, I never expected them to be there, nor do I remember feeling upset about them *not* being there. Again, it was all I knew.

My father paid for the big stuff, including the travel—although he often complained about paying to the point of nausea. Other times, he paid willingly. He always wanted to get the best deal out of everyone and not pay one penny more than he needed to. That's certainly not a bad or unusual trait, except when it becomes a detriment to your happiness and the happiness of everyone around you.

My opinions were controlled as much as my finances. I remember being in seventh grade and coming home to share what I had learned about India in school. I was trying to show off by sharing my opinions and hoping for a lively discussion. My father proceeded to tell me how stupid I was and how what I was saying was nonsense.

I was devastated and slunk back to my room where I cried my eyes out and vowed to never express my thoughts about anything ever again. I'm not one to keep my thoughts to myself, so I repeated the same mistake many times, over many years, always expecting a different outcome—and usually re-living my sadness.

I remember the first time I was old enough to vote. I was home from college during the 1980 presidential election. I voted in our local church: Ronald Reagan was running against Jimmy Carter. Being the staunch conservative Republican that he was, my father marched down to the church afterward to ensure I had voted Republican.

It didn't really matter who was running; the only thing that counted was being loyal to your party and to your family. My father was a businessman opposed to paying taxes, and he could not have cared less about any other issues. He was *not* going to have any child of his voting anything other than Republican.

If I had, I'm not sure he would have let me back in the house. I laugh at it now, but at the time I was left with a feeling of not being valued for my choices. And yet, I never would have done anything to upset him. At least I tried not to. I loved him and wanted him to love me—and I knew the consequences of going against him could be severe.

If my mother hid behind shopping, I hid behind food and used it for comfort from the time I went to high school at thirteen until after having my first child at thirty-one. Food protected me and kept me safe. I just couldn't control my weight. All the shopping, the therapy, and the love I did receive over those many years could not quiet the hunger inside.

My father hated me being heavy. It was the worst thing I could ever have done to him. He was trim and fit, as was my mother and brother. I was the one in the family who stood out. On the surface I wanted so badly to be thin to please him—and myself—but my inner being was not cooperating.

My father tried everything—mostly degrading comments—to get me to lose weight and look like *he* thought I should. Posture was also a big deal for him, and I was forced to stand against the kitchen wall when I was a teenager. He was trying to build my self-confidence, and so it was hard to take offense to his comments, but I still struggled.

"Knockers out, girls!" my father would say as I stood against that kitchen wall.

He said it not only to me but to many women, young and old. His comment was intended to encourage good posture in what he considered to be a humorous sort of way. He was clearly disciplined about his own posture, as indicated by his sitting up straight while sleeping at the dinner table.

Who sits up straight while sleeping?

My father did.

"Knockers out, girls" wasn't really meant in a sexist way. I think he thought it was endearing. Looking back, it was definitely sexist, and I cringed every time it came out of his mouth.

Yet I would do anything to please him. I stood against that wall proudly, adoring the attention—still fat and still lacking self-confidence.

CHAPTER 3

Dumbing Myself Down

Never be so focused on what you're looking for that you overlook the thing you actually find.

–ANN PATCHETT

I went off to college at seventeen at the same time my parents began the remodel of their home in Ross. My bedroom growing up was just off the living room.

As I was packing for college, my father came into my room, shook my hand vigorously, and literally said to me: "Have a nice life. We are turning your bedroom into a bar."

I am still laughing about it, but he was serious. My bedroom became the bar off the living room.

I didn't go home much after that.

———————————

Nobody told me I should apply to such-and-such college. Nobody took me to look at colleges. My parents both went to college, and they expected me to as well, but there was no guidance. I made it up as I went along. I applied to several schools, including the University of Colorado in Boulder, for one primary reason: I wanted to ski and live in the mountains.

I got in, so I went—simple as that.

I was ten days late for school because of our first international family trip to Africa. I had only left the United States once before, when I was twelve, and my father decided the August before I started college was the perfect time to take a family vacation, so off we went.

Neither parent seemed too concerned I was missing freshman orientation and class at a huge, completely unfamiliar university I had never stepped foot on. No one called to say I would be late—it just didn't seem to matter.

We arrived home from Africa, and off I went with a friend from home to drive the 1,200 miles from Ross, California to Boulder, Colorado, in a car my parents had given me.

There were no big, long goodbyes. The words "We are going to miss you" never crossed anyone's lips. It wasn't mean. We were all just used to each other coming and going. There were no tears when one or both parents left *ever*—just a casual goodbye. This was one aspect of my family that seemed healthy. Traveling was part of our reality, and we were together when we were together.

I arrived late with not one friend among thousands of students. I was shy as a child, and that trait returned with so many unfamiliar faces. I tried to come off as confident and independent, which my classmates mostly interpreted as arrogant and aloof, but inside I was scared—and lonely. There were no cell phones back then, so I had little communication with my parents, except for an occasional pay phone call. I was on my own.

In high school, I had an enormous group of friends, and we did outlandish things and partied like rock stars. With my parents gone so much of the time, my friends ended up at my house a lot. By the time I was seventeen, I had been on my own for years. I thought college was going to be a breeze. I was a cool kid. But my lack of self-confidence overshadowed my experience. I wanted to fit in but didn't find it all that easy.

I got placed in the only all-girls dorm on campus, Hallett Hall, with no friends and the weirdest roommate possible. I made a few friends—whom I love dearly to this day—but we were the outcasts and certainly *not* the popular girls. I wondered where my life in California had gone.

What was I doing in Boulder?

I was not with the kids I wanted to be with. I was not in a sorority. I had missed the opportunity to rush with the other girls because of our trip to Africa and my late arrival to school. Other than the skiing, I felt lost in this enormous new world.

After a frightful semester in Hallett Hall, I moved to a co-ed dorm, figuring it would enhance the social aspects of my college life—and help me find a boyfriend. Just my luck—or destiny—I got put at the end of the hall in my new dorm on the second floor with some other strange girls. I still felt shy and uncomfortable. The cool kids still seemed out of reach.

Plus, there was the issue of the car I had brought from California. I felt fortunate to have a car in college, but back then it was a bit out of the ordinary. I made many day trips to the mountains to go skiing in the winter. During my freshman year, I often wondered if the boys I was taking wanted to go skiing with me, or whether they just liked the ride—and my father's company gas card that came with it.

I took them because I wanted their company and it's no fun to go skiing by yourself. I liked them and I think they liked me, but would they have invited me to go skiing if they had to give *me* a ride?

Then, during the end of my freshman year, I was lucky enough to meet Spike. Spike was handsome and charming, and he approached me one day in the cafeteria. I could see him coming, and I was tickled pink.

He leaned over me and said smugly, "What, are you afraid you'll forget to do something?"

He was referring to the fact that I had notes all over the back of my hand. Ever since I can remember, I have been writing important things on my hand.

I looked up, smiling, and said, "Well, I can lose a piece of paper very easily, but the chance of losing my hand is very slim."

And that was it. Our fate in college was sealed. Spike and I had an extraordinary time together over the next three years. I adored him— and he adored me. During college, he had his own car as well. He took *me* skiing. He wanted me to come with him—and I wanted to go.

When I was twenty, I received the first inkling there may be some family money in my future. At that time, three years after Circle Freight International's initial public offering (IPO) in 1977, my father was able to sell his first shares of stock on the open market.

He set up a trust for me and my brother that provided an allowance of $500 per month for each of us. It certainly was a lot more than the $62.50 I got in high school. The trust had strict guidelines and was not accessible to us without a trustee's involvement. My father strongly believed—as many do—that second generations of wealth tend to spend all the money and end up with nothing to pass on. He reminded us of this over and over again, and he wanted to ensure it would not happen.

His goal was to create a family fortune that would extend through many generations. The bulk of the money wasn't for his use—or for my generation's use—it was meant to extend into many future generations as the lasting legacy of his brilliance and financial achievements.

He regularly reminded me: "I want to be just like John D. Rockefeller and create a family fortune that will last an eternity."

I spent most of my time trying to prove he was wrong about second-generation wealth and that I was different. Given the chance, I was determined I would not only keep the money but make even more. I bought what I needed or wanted, but I wasn't a big spender. My father didn't seem to notice.

One morning during the summer of my junior year, my father called me and said: "Suzanne, go to Chase Bank tomorrow and sign the check they give you. It's made out to you. You are to deposit it into the trust account the bankers have set up. Call me when you're finished."

I vividly remember that first check, in my name, for $150,000. The money came from the proceeds of my father's first opportunity to sell stock. I had a feeling of importance as I entered the bank, and I loved it. I had no idea what was going on. I was just doing what I was told. In theory, my financial situation had changed forever. In reality, there was little change at all. At the time, I was only twenty, so I really didn't understand what was going on, but over the course of more than twenty years, my father included me in all investment decisions involving the trust.

During college, I worked hard and studied Environmental Design and Planning with an emphasis on Landscape Architecture. I enjoyed it. I was receiving the $500 from the trust to pay for my expenses, which was a generous amount. I was expected to pay for everything minus room and board, and I never asked for more. I spent the money on school supplies and extras like food, drinks, and skiing. Life was simple.

I don't recall issues around money when I was with Spike. Neither of us had a lot, but it was enough for us to have fun in college—and take a vagabond trip through Europe one summer after a school year abroad in Switzerland. I never felt he was there for money. There really wasn't any money to be there for.

My mother adored Spike. She and her friends called him "Our Spike."

My father tolerated him. Spike's father was a trader on the Pacific Coast Stock Exchange. He was fun, charismatic, loving, and had a babe of a wife. Even though my mother was quite the party girl, Spike's parents were younger and a lot more fun than mine.

I think my father was slightly jealous of Spike's father's light-hearted, fun-loving personality. Spike's father was a successful trader and made a good living but nothing elaborate. Although my father never said it out loud, I knew he felt Spike was not going to be *good enough* for me in a financial sense. My father attached Spike's future earning ability to Spike's father's success—and he was not impressed.

My father said to me in a stern voice as he slapped his palm on some table more than once while I was dating Spike (and until the day he died), "Don't marry *anyone* if they don't have at least five million dollars in their bank account."

Ironically, most of the men I had dated were poor—sometimes the poorer, the better. Oddly enough, other than the man I eventually married, Spike was *by far* the most successful and still is.

Spike and I stayed together until shortly after college, and then we went our separate ways. I wonder now whether my father's stern opinion influenced my decision to part company with Spike. At the time, I believed I wasn't ready to continue such a serious relationship at such a young age. That said, my father's opinions always seeped into my thoughts—and still do today.

My parents bought a second home in Lake Tahoe just after I left for college. I was over-the-moon excited—*finally*, a home in the mountains. It felt like mine from the first moment I walked through the front door. It had orange shag carpet, multiple levels, and other bizarre elements, but it was perfect and I loved it.

My parents buying that house was the most amazing thing that had ever happened to me. Tahoe was my happy place. My parents went there occasionally, but mostly it was just me and my friends on our breaks from college and after I graduated. I felt like an adult when I went there.

I broke up with Spike for the last time on the deck of that home and took up gallivanting around the North Shore of Lake Tahoe—single and wild. I finally felt independent and cool again.

I spent one summer as a hostess at a local restaurant. Because I was living at my parents' second home in Tahoe, it was obvious to anyone who knew me that my family had money—though I tried desperately to hide it. I was twenty-two and hanging around people who had much less than me. I remember *not* wanting to be seen as the rich girl. My family's wealth—although it was not extraordinary and not really mine—made me feel different than my peers.

As a young, independent, twenty-something-year-old, this was really the first time I remember feeling different from my friends because of my family's money. I wanted to be normal—and loved—but money made me feel different, and I was always questioning my ability to fit in.

After my summer hosting job, I found more serious work with a landscape architect where I could use my hard-earned degree in design and planning from the University of Colorado. I worked on landscape projects in the field during the summer and had a less serious job selling timeshares for The Inn at Squaw Valley during the winter. I did this for a year and loved it, but I knew I wasn't living up to my abilities. I didn't make much money selling timeshares in a parking lot, but I wanted to be average, to work hard to get by.

During that winter of 1982 in Lake Tahoe, I so longed to be like everyone else. I drove around in a beat-up Toyota pickup truck even though I had a brand-new BMW 520i sitting idle in the garage. My father had bought me the BMW when I was twenty-two, and the pickup truck shortly thereafter for my landscaping business.

The BMW was super cool and I loved it, but I felt embarrassed to drive it. The pickup felt much more like who I was—or at least who I wanted to be. I hid the BMW from my peers the same way my mother hid the Jaguar from my father. We did it for different reasons, but I had learned from my mother's example to hide expensive things I didn't want anyone to see.

I felt embarrassed about the house. I felt embarrassed about the car. I even felt embarrassed about the truck. Sometimes, I went to the extent of leaving the beat-up pickup truck in the parking lot of Albertson's in town so I could hitchhike from there to Squaw Valley. Some of those winter mornings were dreadfully cold, and still I would drive the 2.5 miles from my parents' house to town, ditch my truck in the parking lot, and hitchhike from there. I didn't like being cold, but that's how badly I wanted to fit in.

It reminded me of another time I played small and dumbed myself down so people would like me. I was living at home with my parents in Ross and was just about to go out one summer afternoon to play tennis with Dave. I had a crush on Dave, and I wanted him to like me.

Just as I was about to leave the house, my mother shouted out to me over her shoulder: "Don't forget, sweetheart. Make sure you don't win."

Dave and I scampered off to the local tennis court. My game was on fire. Then I heard my mother's voice in my head, and even though I was clearly going to win, I let Dave beat me.

At the time, I was relieved. I had followed my mother's instructions and thrown the game. Of course, I never told Dave. I felt strangely triumphant knowing I *could* have won, but I lost so he would like me—and ask me out to dinner.

He did ask me out after that first match, but later I felt angry at myself for giving up my chance at victory. We played many other times, and I never won a match against Dave again—not because I didn't want to, but because my game was never as good as it had been that first day.

The concept of losing on purpose in order to be adored by a man stuck with me. I knew in my heart I had thrown away a chance to take a stand and play my best. Here I was again, dumbing myself down and hiding what I had, just to be liked.

During my time in Lake Tahoe, I made my own money, but since I lived in my family's house for free, I felt ashamed. I was a rich girl who wanted to be poor. Isn't that silly?

On the other hand, my father was not pleased by my choice to live in Tahoe and yelled and screamed about my unworthiness many times. "Little girl…" he would begin, and then went on from there until my eyes filled with tears, my chest tightened, and a deep sadness seeped into my heart.

In order to defend myself against him (even though I still don't know why he was so upset with me)—and simultaneously free myself of the burden of having more than my friends—I came up with a brilliant plan to pay *all* the household expenses I was incurring by living in *my parents'* house.

I still have the letter I wrote him that winter outlining all the household expenses and my plan to pay for them myself. He was not impressed by my letter, nor did he ever respond to it—and on top of that, none of my friends could have cared less.

After that first year in the mountains, I took a job with a landscape architecture firm in San Francisco for the opportunity to work in the city part-time, while also continuing several projects in Tahoe. I moved in with two friends in a not-so-glamorous neighborhood in San Francisco and commuted in the pickup truck back and forth between Lake Tahoe and San Francisco.

I love nature, plant material, and working with my hands in the soil. I was a hard worker. I still am. I put my heart and soul into my job and whatever project I happened to be working on.

I continued to pretend to live from paycheck to paycheck as most of my friends were, but the truth was I never had any true concerns about how I was going to eat or pay rent. I was still receiving money from the trust, and I relied on the fact that if I really got in trouble financially, my parents would bail me out—probably with a lot of screaming—but I knew they would. Plus, I had signed that big check at the bank, so I knew there was some financial cushion if I ever needed it.

For the next couple of years, I continued to go back and forth between San Francisco during the week and Tahoe on the weekends. Life was good, but my father was still unimpressed. And as far as most of my peers were concerned, I was a rich girl who shouldn't have a care in the world and had no reason to *ever* possibly feel badly about anything.

Looking back, I don't understand why I felt so much shame around money—it was not as if I had stolen it or done anything wrong. I was just born into it.

CHAPTER 4

He Who Makes the Gold Makes the Rules

We can relax and float in the direction that the water flows, or we can swim hard against it. If we go with the river, the energy of a thousand mountain streams will be with us.

–ELIZABETH LESSER

While I was still living in Lake Tahoe, I went to a party at the house of a young man I was dating. A girl spotted me from across the room.

She looked at me inquisitively and asked: "Are you Suzanne Robinson?"

"Yes, I am," I replied, not thinking too much about it.

She was all excited and said with a big smile: "I'm Criss Leydecker."

When my brother and I were children, our mother took us to the Belvedere Tennis Club every day of every summer for four years. Belvedere was often cold and gloomy from the fog that rolled in from the ocean side of the Golden Gate Bridge. Sometimes as a young child

I would ask my mother, why were we leaving sunny, beautiful Ross to go to rainy, cloudy, foggy Belvedere?

My mother's answer: "Get in the car."

I decided at a young age the reason she took us to the club was for guilt-free childcare for me and my brother while she played tennis and lunched with her friends.

Criss's mom was doing the same with Criss and her brother Mark. I don't blame our mothers for finding ways to entertain us because I have done it myself with my children. And there wasn't much for us to complain about at the club. There was tennis and swimming, burgers, and mint chocolate chip milkshakes.

That first summer I was eight and Mark was six. We became fast friends. After the summer I turned twelve, Mark and I went our separate ways. Even though we lived only a few miles apart, we went to different high schools and colleges, and somehow our paths never cross.

That night in Tahoe was the first time I had seen Criss since I was twelve. We spoke for a while, and finally I got up the nerve to ask timidly: "Where's your brother?"

"He's upstairs," she responded gleefully.

I went upstairs feeling a bit nervous. I was excited to see him after such a long time, but during our initial conversation, I quickly realized he was a good friend of the man I was dating *and* he had a girlfriend. After that night, we saw each other several times but he was always with his girlfriend, and so our interactions were friendly but brief.

One brisk Saturday morning, on December 22, 1984, I was out skiing in Tahoe by myself. I had just turned twenty-five. I was gearing up to ride the KT-22 chairlift in Squaw Valley. As I was putting on my skis, I glanced up the hill and noticed two men coming off the mountain. It was Mark and his new stepfather, who happened to be exactly his age. They stopped at the bottom of the chairlift I was about to get on.

Mark turned to me—barely recognizing who I was—but soon figured it out after our initial greeting. I learned his stepfather was on his way to work, and Mark asked me if I wanted to ski with him.

"Absolutely," I said. "Let's go."

We skied for the rest of the day, and before leaving the mountain, Mark asked if I wanted to go skiing again the following weekend. The next Saturday we met and wandered around the mountain, having a blast. After a few runs, we ended up back on the KT-22 chairlift.

If you know anything about Squaw Valley ski resort in Lake Tahoe (now Palisades Tahoe), you know the KT-22 chairlift passes over some enormous cliffs. I personally am not a big fan of chairlifts; they honestly kind of scare me. As Mark and I went over the cliffs—me with my arm tucked around the back of the swinging chair—we had our first kiss. My heart beat rapidly over the kiss—and the cliffs below.

Our courtship took off from there. We spent several weekends together over the winter while I was in Tahoe. In the spring, I moved to San Francisco for my job—and so did Mark. We spent even more time together. One night, we were sitting at a bar in San Francisco called Tar and Feathers, and as I was sipping my drink, Mark assured me in no uncertain terms that we *would* be getting married. He wasn't asking me that night, but he was very clear.

I don't think even three months had gone by since the infamous chairlift ride. I nearly spit my drink across the bar and said, "Have you lost your mind? There's no way we're getting married."

Prior to meeting Mark and his declaration in the bar, I had decided I wanted to build a life abroad. After working in landscape architecture for a few years, I was no longer as inspired by my career path. I wanted to travel and see the world. I thought it would be fun to live in Australia for a couple of years and find work there.

Once I came up with the idea to follow my heart, a man came entered the picture. After much debate with Mark as to whether I should go, I packed my bags and headed down under. I stayed for only one year, but I was proud of myself for going. Although I was afraid of losing Mark if I went and I felt guilty for leaving, I did it anyway.

Mark was still waiting for me when I got back.

Once I returned home, I felt myself pulled in the direction of healing and psychology. Like my mother at the Center for Attitudinal Healing, I became a facilitator and started a group for women with eating disorders—applying the twelve principles of Attitudinal Healing gleaned from the Course in Miracles. I loved what I was doing so much, I applied to graduate school in San Francisco at the California Institute for Integral Studies. I was accepted and began my formal training in Marriage and Family Counseling shortly after I returned from Australia.

My father, although he still always included me in decisions about my trust and his business, was keen on me getting a graduate degree only if it seemed "appropriate" for a woman. No need to go into the family business. My father encouraged me to be great—to a point.

Both landscape architecture and counseling were fields acceptable for a young woman because they didn't threaten the status quo (or *his* status quo). I could work in either field, make a nice living, and ultimately rely on the man I was going to marry to support me.

While I was going to graduate school, Mark landed a job as an assistant trader at a securities firm in San Francisco. We rented our first apartment together in Marin County and began to share our rent and bills equally. I don't recall any issues over money. I was still getting some money from the trust, and Mark was making money at his new job.

Every weekend we went to Lake Tahoe and stayed at my parents' house on the lake *and* drove the BMW I had kept hidden in the garage when I was single. Mark knew everything about my life, and there no longer seemed to be a reason to feel uncomfortable about the wealth of my family—or myself. My family had more financial resources than his, but Mark grew up in a very sophisticated environment, so my family's wealth was nothing new for him.

Although Mark and I got along quite well, a couple of years into our relationship, I confessed to my mother my concerns about dating him. Although he fit the picture of what my parents had in mind as an ideal husband, I was not sure I was completely in love with him. I was used to wild boys and not used to such a proper gentleman. It all seemed strange to me and far from exciting.

My mother's advice to me at the time in her worldly way was to *practice*.

"Well, if you aren't sure about Mark," she said, "why don't you *practice* with him so that when the right man does come along, you will know how to accept him with open arms?"

She said this knowing all too well that over time I would learn to love and accept Mark's kindness and become accustomed to being treated well. She adored him and thought he was a good choice.

After Mark and I had lived together for over a year, my father offered to buy me a house—quite an offer, to say the least. He was adamant, and for one of the only times I remember, he followed through on his word. The realtor was the wife of one of his managers at Circle Freight, and I think he knew if he backed out of his promise, he would not have impressed many people. My mother and I immediately started looking.

Mark resisted my father's offer. Mark was driven to make his own way and did not like the idea of my father buying me a home. Mark wanted no help from anyone, and he thought I should feel the same. We fought over whether it was okay for my father to buy me a house, but in the end—with my mother on my side—I was the proud owner of a beautiful home in Ross.

After all, who was I going to disappoint—my mother and father, or my boyfriend? My father put the house in my name. This amazing, heartfelt gift from my parents made me feel loved, protected, and cared for.

Mark and I moved into the house shortly after closing. We had no mortgage, but we evenly split all of our living costs.

After three years of dating, naturally the question of marriage was on the table. I had my own personal concept of engagement protocol. As women, we typically wait and wait and wait. We do *all* the perfect things, and act in *all* the perfect ways so our knight in shining armor will come and rescue us—i.e., marry us—and we will run off into the sunset living happily ever after.

I decided if Mark—or anyone—asked for my hand in marriage after I had waited patiently on my best behavior for a number of years, I would let him know I would be getting back to him in no less than two weeks with my answer. I thought two weeks sounded like a reasonable amount of time. I wait three years, and he waits two weeks—a very clever and empowering goal.

Or so I thought.

On the night of December 22, 1987, exactly three years after we met, Mark got down on his knee—after a challenging dinner conversation about how I didn't think our relationship was working—and showered me with an expression of love I was not expecting. He told me all the reasons he loved me. He reminded me he had always planned to ask for my hand in marriage since that night at Tar and Feathers three years before.

When he asked, I didn't wait two weeks.

I barely waited two minutes before "Yes" came out of my mouth.

Everything I had planned flew out the window. I was overjoyed. I called my parents immediately. They were thrilled. Before Mark, I had made what they considered to be poor choices in relationships. Mark was one of my only prospects who had the possibility of meeting my father's requirements of being a suitable husband *and* becoming a big money-earner.

The very next day, I found out my parents already knew Mark was going to propose. Mark had met with them a few evenings before and told them of his plan. Mark was old-fashioned and wanted to do the proper thing, which meant asking my parents for my hand in marriage.

I also discovered when Mark asked my parents that evening, he asked if my father wanted him to sign a prenuptial agreement. My father was so excited about the idea of me marrying, he adamantly answered—for the both of us—that a prenuptial agreement was not necessary.

Mark and I were married nine months later, on September 24, 1988. We had a beautiful wedding—paid for by my parents—so there were no squabbles between the two of us over cost.

As we were planning the wedding, I was thankful we weren't paying for it, or for the rehearsal dinner, which his parents generously paid for. Mark didn't like spending money unnecessarily, even though he grew up with a more elaborate taste for elegance than I did.

Mark's problem wasn't paying. His problem was an ongoing concern about the value of the item in question. If he brought it up once, he brought up a thousand times how a screw—or some other simple item—was "ridiculously overpriced." I did not enjoy these discussions. I definitely would *not* have enjoyed haggling over expenses around our wedding and was grateful those conversations were not necessary.

My father had given me and my mother an ample budget for my special day, but his ample but strict budget did not fit my mother's expensive tastes.

As the day was rapidly approaching, my mother looked at me and said: "Suzanne, we are going to need to add to the floral and decor budget. It's not big enough, and I just can't have it.

"The colored umbrellas at the reception site just don't work. I have arranged for white umbrellas to be brought over for the day."

All I said was: "Okay."

What I was really thinking was, *How is all this going to be paid for?*

But I didn't complain about her expensive taste, and in the end, it was a beautiful day.

Later I found out how the "extras" were paid for. My grandfather on my father's side had died earlier that spring, leaving me and my brother $80,000 each in his will, a huge sum of money to me. Just like the money from my grandmother, I not only never saw that money, I also didn't know it existed until years later.

After the wedding and honeymoon, Mark and I returned to our lives. We were newly married and living in a beautiful home. Mark had a good job as a trader in San Francisco, and I was completing graduate school. We had an adorable golden retriever named Teaka, who we referred to as our first child. All of it was a dream come true.

Just prior to graduating from my two-year program, Mark lost his job. He was good at what he did, but his firm shut down his division a year or so after he was hired. Mark had always wanted to move to New York City, so that is where he set his sights on finding a new employer.

I never thought it would happen. I was a California girl through and through. I had been to New York City many times, and although I enjoyed my visits there, I was not prepared to move from my comfortable and predictable world.

In early 1990, just after I turned thirty, Mark accepted a trading position at Goldman Sachs in New York City. I threw a temper tantrum. I didn't want to leave my new home, which I considered "ours," my budding career in counseling, or my friends and family.

I finally agreed to try it for eighteen months. We took our precious golden retriever, and the three of us moved into a small fifth-floor walk-up apartment on the Upper West Side.

Eighteen months turned into ten years.

With his new job, Mark's salary skyrocketed from roughly $30,000 to over $100,000 a year—a good salary for a twenty-eight-year-old, especially at that time. But my fate was less assured. Because there was no reciprocity between New York and California, the master's in Marriage and Family Counseling I had just spent over two years working for was not a valid, recognizable degree in the state of New York.

After six months in New York City with no possibility of working in my chosen field, we decided it was time to have a baby. I became pregnant immediately. And after waddling up and down those five flights of stairs for eight months, I made the decision to fly home to California during my last month of pregnancy to deliver our baby in the comfort of familiar surroundings.

Being a new mother didn't go exactly as I had envisioned—but whatever does? Mark barely made the birth of Alexandra because of weather delays and canceled planes, but he did make it. We had seven glorious days together as new parents before Mark had to return to work in New York City while I stayed in Ross. Much to my dismay, my mother jetted off to Europe after only ten days. I was left alone at my parents' house—entirely unprepared for the daunting task of taking care of a newborn.

Like most new mothers, I loved my daughter, but I had no idea what I was doing—particularly without the help of another caring adult. Alexandra and I had many sleepless, teary-eyed nights—for her and for me—as I lay in the darkness on the hard tile kitchen floor, wondering what I had gotten myself into.

After five weeks, Alexandra and I flew home to New York City to reunite as a family. The following months were beautiful, challenging, frustrating, and complicated all at once.

When Alexandra was six months old, we moved from our fifth-floor walk-up apartment to the two-bedroom apartment we would stay in for the duration of our time in New York. Despite my harrowing experience with Alexandra, our other two children, Carson and Derek, were born in New York City over the next six years. Mark was, of course, as happy with the children as I was and stepped up to the plate as a good father, doting on his children sometimes more than I did.

Mark continued to do well at Goldman Sachs, and I stayed home. I had a strong work ethic but never considered working for money, which is something I feel strange about now. Instead of finding a way to practice counseling professionally, I spent much of my free time away from the children volunteering with the New York Junior League by working in a minimum-security all-women's prison on the Lower West Side, among other volunteer positions, and eventually running the New York Junior League's Arts for Children Program.

While I was on the stay-at-home mom track, other women were making different choices. I became aware there were a few women at Goldman Sachs at the time. I could count them on one hand. I'm talking about women traders and high-level management, rather than back-office employees and assistants, who were mostly female.

The majority of these high-level women had a solid reputation with their male associates as competent coworkers. They were go-getters. They were tough. They were the forerunners of powerful women in the workplace.

Never should a tear flow out of their eyes, or any seemingly female emotion come over their face—or swim around in their thoughts. This relatively small group of women lived up to the work standards expected of them. They were well respected, and I admired that.

What intrigued me were the occasional comments from their male coworkers expressed outside of work and behind their backs.

If I heard it once, I heard it a dozen times from Mark's male peers: "She's great at what she does. She is tough—and sometimes a real bitch."

"I love working with her," I would hear, followed by, "But I certainly wouldn't want to be married to her. She'd definitely wear the pants in the family."

Everyone chuckled.

I wasn't shocked at their comments. These women were tough, and I could understand why the men talked about them in that way. It didn't seem right to me, but they were part of a societal shift where women were starting to pursue jobs in power roles in high-paying companies. No one had much experience with this paradigm shift—neither me, nor Mark, nor his male *or* female colleagues.

Just like no one gives you a rulebook on how to succeed as a woman in a male-dominated career, no one gives you a rulebook on how to be married with children, either. I wanted Mark to help out more, but he had a job that required more attention than I would have liked. I struggled to adapt to my new life. It was also not lost on me that I grew up with a father who made the money and a mother who stayed home, volunteered for the Junior League, and played bridge with her friends.

Now I had moved across the country for Mark's job, and although I enjoyed my time in New York, I had lost my opportunity to practice my chosen profession and had left behind my friends, my family, and my beautiful home in Ross.

The apple hadn't fallen far from the tree, and he who was making the gold was making the rules. And I reluctantly agreed.

CHAPTER 5

House of Cards

Doubt is an uncomfortable condition, but
certainty is a ridiculous one.

–VOLTAIRE

I was home with young children, struggling a bit and not having much of an adult life beyond my work with the New York Junior League and our weekly date nights. In contrast, Mark was out working long hours and often entertaining at night. I was sometimes lonely. I certainly had moments of being thrilled to stay home with my children—along with moments of complete boredom over playing Hot Wheels (which I honestly did kind of enjoy) or dressing Barbie in her pink outfit, complete with tiny matching shoes, for the hundredth time.

I was still receiving my trusty monthly income, which had increased over time from the original $500 to $8,000 per month, so I always felt I was contributing monetarily to our marriage, and the money gave me some financial freedom. As I remember, my money was primarily what we lived on, while Mark's income went into a savings account and to buy larger ticket items.

Neither Mark nor I were huge spenders, so we lived a relatively frugal existence within our means. I paid the bills and was comfortable with our finances. I was a typical wife and did what I thought a typical wife did.

I was continuing to rent out my house in California. It was my responsibility, so I took care of most details. Over time, Mark became more and more upset that this asset was not owned jointly, but I wouldn't give in to putting his name on the deed. I wouldn't even discuss it. I felt a bit guilty as he was bringing in most of the money, but I didn't back down. It was out of character for me, but I did it anyways.

After seven years of living in New York City, Mark and I decided to buy a weekend home in the Berkshire mountains of Massachusetts. By then, I was tired of taking care of my house in California, and I finally offered to sell it and put the money into purchasing our vacation home. It felt like the right time to put that money into our marital joint venture, and I felt good about my decision.

We spent the next two years remodeling our new country house. It was composed of three old barns, originally transported from upstate New York, with lots of problems—and lots of wildlife—both inside and outside the house, including copious numbers of mice, snakes, and the biggest snapping turtles you have ever seen. Our "new" house was due for a total overhaul.

I had to be involved 110 percent in the remodel of our home in a way that spoke fully to my soul. I loved our new country house, and Mark did as well. It was rustic and had a personality that touched our souls. The three barns that formed the backbone of the house sat on top of a ridge overlooking miles and miles of open space to the south. The vistas were spectacular.

Somewhere toward the end of our two-year remodeling project came my personal Black Thursday: April 28, 1999.

Tuesdays and Thursdays were our date nights. On this particular Thursday, Mark and I had our date at a local Sushi restaurant. The dinner had a strange feeling to it. When we arrived home, Mark sent the babysitter home and confessed he was in love with one of his co-workers. She was his "soulmate"—a word a wife so hates to hear about another woman.

Never in my wildest dreams would I have thought Mark—the one who was so "good" and "suitable" compared to the other men I had dated—would be the one to have an affair. I was devastated *and* overwhelmed *and* confused.

I hit him hard with my fists on his back after he told me. He buried his face, protecting it with his hands, and let me haul off and whack him over and over. Eventually, I stopped long enough for him to leave for the airport to pick up his mother. He had planned to have his mother arrive shortly after breaking the news to me, so I would have someone to talk to. Looking back at this, I find his plan to be incredibly strange, putting both his mother and me in a unique situation.

I sank to my knees, sobbing. It felt like I had been socked in the gut.

The next morning, after a long run through Central Park, I found a marriage counselor. I purposely picked a man so Mark wouldn't feel intimidated. Within our first few meetings, the therapist suggested I stay in New York City that summer. Normally, I would leave with the children to go to the Berkshires and Lake Tahoe to get out of the heat of the city, and Mark would join us on the weekends. But the therapist was adamant this would be a poor decision that summer, given our failing marriage.

After much debate—and Mark's reassurance that there was no need to worry—off I went with the children, against the therapist's advice. Mark's affair continued. He was seeing his soulmate while still living at home. I honestly don't think he knew what to do—or where he would be happier—but this was a disaster for our marriage.

When I *was* at home that summer, Mark and I spent many, many hours sitting on our tiny terrace in New York discussing the fate of our marriage. During those conversations all kinds of things came to light. I realized why his eight-minute late-night dog walks had recently begun taking twenty minutes, and then thirty minutes. Turns out, he was talking on the phone to his soulmate while walking the dog.

I think Mark wanted me to tell him how much I loved him and how much I wanted him. I wanted to tell him to stay, but I just couldn't do it. He didn't believe I loved him enough—and maybe I didn't.

What I did tell him was: "Follow your heart."

In hindsight, this might have been a mistake, but I was upset—and in some ways looking forward to moving on, despite my fear of the unknown. I wanted him to be happy with his choice to stay or to go. And I wanted to be happy with my choice. I wanted a note from God signed, notarized, and in triplicate telling me what to do.

During that summer of 1999, three months after my Black Thursday, we were scheduled to go on a family vacation to Nantucket. To the best of my recollection, Mark wanted his soulmate to come, and I agreed apprehensively. Mark and I, the three children, and the girlfriend would all go to Nantucket together for ten days to stay with Mark's sister, Criss.

As I was sharing my apprehension about the vacation with my friend Jill, she stopped me mid-conversation.

"Are you kidding me?" she said. "No, no, no, you're *not* doing that."

Our conversation stalled for a moment and then she continued: "I have a suggestion. You go for the first five days, and let the girlfriend go for the last five days."

My mind started going crazy. I had no clue how to respond to her idea. I wanted to do the right thing. Up until that moment, I thought the right thing was to go on the family vacation and endure whatever was going to happen. I was curious as to how ten days together would unfold.

Jill continued with her idea: "Let's go to New Orleans. Let's go to Mexico. Let's go to Aspen. It's Ruggerfest in Aspen. There will be a lot of boys there," she said enticingly.

Her last comment piqued my interest. As many of us do, I wanted to find a man to immediately fill the void I felt—and sow a few wild oats along the way.

Our vacation to Nantucket was scheduled for August. I started thinking to myself: August in New Orleans or Mexico? They both sounded really hot.

I called Jill back on the phone later that day and said: "I pick Aspen."

I remember arriving in Aspen with Jill and our friend Christina. Tom, a friend of Jill's from college (whom I barely knew), picked us up from the airport. It was early evening, and the four of us made our way to the Sardi House, a charming hotel in Aspen, overlooking Paepcke Park with its beautiful gazebo in the middle of the spacious green grass at the base of Shadow Mountain.

I sat on the porch happily sipping my margarita with no salt, served to me by a man who had the bluest eyes I had ever seen, and said, "I could definitely live here."

Jill, Christina, and I had an amazing time. We hiked, we biked, we ate, we went to bars, we flirted, we talked, we slept. We even went to church to pray one morning. But even though I had said I could live in Aspen, it was just a passing thought. Only four months had gone by since my Black Thursday, and I wasn't ready to kill off my marriage.

It became clear shortly after the vacation in Nantucket that Mark intended to continue living with me and keep seeing the soulmate.

Finally, after months of late-night conversations about what we should do, I asked him to move out. Not long after, Mark announced he was moving to London with his soul mate.

There was no going back.

For my entire life I have been drawn to the mountains, but I always had to live near a city for one reason or another. Now for the first time I did not. It was critical for me to pick a place to live that would serve us all, especially the children. They were so young—only three, five, and eight at the time.

I knew Mark would miss the children, but moving to London for me and the children was not a viable option at that point. He was building a new life with someone else, and that picture did not include his soon-to-be ex-wife and children. I had the freedom to move wherever I wanted.

After investigating several mountain towns including Tahoe, Sun Valley, and Aspen; the possibility of staying in New York City; and moving back to Marin County, where I grew up—I ended up asking my angels for guidance, and I chose Aspen, Colorado, as our new home.

Aspen is a small community rich in culture and diversity that sets it apart from other mountain towns in the world. Lake Tahoe would have been the most logical mountain community for us to join, but my father was not mentally sound at that point (more on that later) and refused to let us live in the family home. I didn't want a second home in Tahoe, so moving there wasn't a particularly good option. The idea of moving to Aspen and knowing just one person there (Jill's college friend, Tom) was a bold move on my part, but after exploring all my options, Aspen felt like the perfect solution.

Mark wanted us to live in our country house in the Berkshires. I refused. It's a beautiful area, but I wanted to move where I would have a life and hopefully find *my* soulmate. After all, I was only forty years old.

Once we had a plan, both Mark and I set about separating mentally and physically. There was an entire country house to empty, as well as our small but full apartment in the city. Some things went to London, some to Aspen, and some to Goodwill. It was an enormous, heart-breaking undertaking.

Of course, I was upset about our relationship—but I was seriously pissed about the country house. I often wondered why Mark waited to tell me until *after* we bought a home mostly financed with the money from the sale of my house in California *and* after just completing a complicated remodel.

I vividly remember our final moments at our country house. It was a beautiful afternoon in June. Everything was packed, and some of the newly renovated rooms were filled ceiling-high with cardboard boxes. I looked around, eyeing the spectacular remodel I would never be able to enjoy.

The children were headed to London for three weeks with their dad and his girlfriend to allow me time to move us to Aspen. I was sitting on the stoop of the front door of our country house—my head resting in the palms of my hands, boxes behind me—as I watched Mark, the soulmate who had come up to meet him, and the three children climb into his Porsche and drive off.

It was a surreal moment as I sat there watching the five of them pull out of the driveway. I felt sheer terror and bewilderment over what was to come, sprinkled with relief that *finally* a choice had been made. I could look to the future rather than swirling in the sewage of the past.

Shortly after they pulled out, I got in my car and left as well. I was headed back to New York City to deal with the next set of boxes and empty rooms. As we had never owned our apartment there, leaving was slightly less upsetting, but I still cried a few tears as I finished packing the last of our things and said goodbye to our decade in New York City.

It was the summer of 2000. I realized my time in New York was coming to an end without my husband and without the security of married life. A new decade was unfolding.

The rules had changed forever.

CHAPTER 6

The Grass Is Always Greener on the Other Side

Stress is caused by being "here"
but wanting to be "there."

—ECKHART TOLLE

After I finished packing up our apartment, I climbed into the family car and drove myself across the country from New York City to Aspen. I had a lot of quiet time to think along the way, but even after my 2,000-mile journey, I wasn't clear on where I was headed in life. All I could do was follow the road map that led me west.

An 18-wheeler holding 27,000 pounds of household items, including an ungodly number of children's toys, arrived in Aspen shortly after I did. Ten years, three kids, and two homes add up to a lot of Barbies, train sets, and an assortment of what would soon be unnecessary items I still wanted so badly to hang on to.

As the boxes of furnishings, dishes, and artwork were unloaded from the truck in Aspen, I felt a rush of familiarity. They would provide comfort for all of us during our transition from city to mountain town and from partnership to independence. The moving company unloaded the boxes in the living room of our rental house and left. There I was with a pile of boxes stacked over my head—again.

I thought after Mark and I separated, and I made a choice about where to go, life would be easier, or better, or something. I was excited and afraid. I was happy and sad at the same time.

Our divorce wasn't final yet, but my husband was living with another woman on a different continent, so I felt pretty darn single. Oddly enough, there was a sense of security in still being married—and yet independent at the same time.

My full-time job was taking care of the children and providing a loving environment for them in this strange new place. One thing that hadn't changed: I was a mother of three amazing children, and for that I was truly grateful. They were—and still are—my North Star.

I made friends easily in Aspen—mostly because of the children—but it was a challenging time for all of us. They often went to bed—especially the boys—tearfully missing their father and the only life they had ever known. But even through those difficult first years, living in the mountains made me happy, and I knew I had made a good choice for all of us.

When a forty-year-old woman moves to Aspen—and has time to go out—she gets a lot of freebies around town. The local population takes care of their kind, and I was, all of a sudden, "a local." In the beginning, there were free drinks and reduced bills from bartenders, among other perks. It was quite nice, and I enjoyed being taken care of.

Aspen has a reputation as being for the rich and famous, and while there are some wealthy people who live there full time, most of the big money comes from second homeowners who stay in Aspen only a few months out of the year. It didn't take long for people to notice I was clearly wealthier than the average sports junkie living year-round in Aspen. When some of the locals began to figure out I had some financial resources, the free stuff came less and less frequently.

Most people assumed I had received a large settlement after divorcing a Goldman Sachs partner. Never mind the fact that our divorce wasn't final. I couldn't really blame them for thinking that way, but I hated that people assumed everything I had was from Mark. I still hear it today occasionally over twenty years later. I didn't want to be known as a wealthy divorcee.

When we first moved to Aspen, I received temporary monthly child support from Mark on top of the money I received from the trust. But after the final dissolution of the trust in 2001 (more on this later), one year after moving to Aspen, I finally had some money of my own—and this money was *not* from Mark.

Once I got the money from the trust, I started shopping for a permanent home for myself and the children. After buying what would be our home for more than the next twenty years, the children and I lived off the money that was left over after buying the house, combined with the monthly payment from Mark.

After living in town for a couple of years, a girlfriend and I were out at a local Italian restaurant. We knew the bartender, Matt, quite well. It was off-season, so the bar menu items were at a special discounted price. The most expensive dish was about twelve dollars, and as per usual, the bartender kept filling our glass with wine during dinner.

We came to the end of the meal, and the check arrived. It was close to three hundred dollars.

I turned to my friend and said, "How could we possibly have rung up a bill like that? We barely ate anything."

When Matt returned to pick up my credit card, I questioned the amount of our tab.

Matt responded: "Well, you *were* drinking thirty-seven-dollar glasses of wine, and you had four," he said, laughing.

"Four? Really—thirty-seven-dollar glasses of wine? That's ridiculous!" I said to him in a very questioning tone. "There's no way we had four glasses of wine each in two hours, and besides, you weren't *asking* if we wanted more; you were just pouring."

"Suz, that's how many you had, and that is what is on the bill," Matt said.

The message was clear. I don't know for sure, but it felt like Matt had figured out I was wealthier than our other friends, and he was going to milk it for all it was worth. It was disappointing, and I never forgot that feeling.

I would still get a bartender or waiter who would treat me to something, but that was clearly the beginning of the end of most freebies. I felt different—and not in a good way.

And I know there is a difference. My daughter, who is now thirty-two and lives in town, gets free drinks and discounted dinners occasionally because she is considered one of "them." I'm not sure why I wanted to be one of "them." They were busy wanting to be me.

They wanted to be richer, so they could have more money to buy more things, or go on more vacations, or whatever their fantasy was. I wanted to be poorer, so I could be "part of the gang."

They wanted wealth, and I wanted to be included.

We always think the grass is greener on the other side of the fence.

But is it really?

The way I saw it, the locals who run the bars and restaurants had a pretty sweet life. People bought them stuff all the time. They sometimes got treated to vacations. They are usually amazing skiers and athletes. And they didn't have all of the responsibilities or challenges of being wealthy.

I was busy peeking over the fence, coveting their grass (without knowing the challenges they faced), while they were peeking over my fence, coveting mine (without knowing the challenges I faced).

Why were we all looking at each other's grass, wondering why it looks greener—rather than watering and tending to our own?

If you're divorced, you want to be married—and vice versa. Result: resentment.

If you're poor, you want to be rich—and vice versa. Result: resentment.

If you don't have kids, you wish you did—and vice versa. Result: resentment.

I was confronted by a man at a party—whom I had just met that evening—who flat out told me he 100 percent knew I had 40 million dollars in my bank account.

"How can you be so sure of that?" I asked him quizzically.

"Because everyone knows. You can't deny it," he responded.

I can promise you my bank statement didn't reflect a net worth of 40 million dollars—not even close—but somehow he knew for sure.

Everyone—including Bob, who owned a local shop—had opinions about my life. One day I mentioned at the register that I had to go home and work.

"Why would you ever have to work? You're rich. You don't need to work," Bob said to me, laughing.

I got so sick of hearing this type of comment. Word on the street was I was wealthy and *certainly* didn't have to work and *never* had any problems—or at least shouldn't have any problems.

The truth was the monthly payments from Mark kept dropping—without intervention from the attorneys—and eventually went down to zero long before they were supposed to end. He justified it with some reason or another, and I didn't have the guts to demand the payments. I didn't want to create waves.

I was also upset because he got some of my father's art. One piece of art I repaired and gifted to Mark for his birthday—never thinking I would lose it. I begged him to sell me the painting years later because of sentimental reasons, but he refused. It broke my heart.

And then there was the night he complained—for the third time—about me getting the wedding china. After hearing the same complaint numerous times, I wrote him a check so he could go out and buy his own—and *never* bring it up again. Now we have matching china.

But the biggest bone of contention in our divorce proceedings was my parents' life insurance policy. Both parents were still alive, and the life insurance policy—and its *possible* payoff—was sketchy at best.

Why was it sketchy? First of all, life insurance is extremely complicated, and payouts depend on interest rates and the age at death of the insured. Second, I knew it was sold to my parents by another crooked advisor. But if it did pay off, Mark's attorneys mentioned there was the possibility I might have to pay Mark money. I could end up with close to nothing. I think it was a scare tactic to get me to settle for less—and it worked.

Mark spent our ten years in New York City working for Goldman Sachs. In doing some research for this book, I realized Goldman Sachs went public on May 3, 1999—"coincidentally", just five days after my Black Thursday. Mark received a substantial amount of stock from Goldman's IPO. According to Mark and his attorneys, I was entitled to none of it.

The Goldman Sachs money was deemed to be a bonus for "future" earnings rather than for his earnings over the previous ten years. In my eyes, this was unfair, and yet Mark's attorneys argued Mark didn't have to give me anything. On top of that, they argued I was going to be "rich" someday—when my parents' second-to-die life insurance policy came due—so they saw no reason I was entitled to *his* money.

That was the moment when a prenuptial agreement was looking like something I should have definitely had in place. As far as I knew, what you come into the marriage with—or receive during the marriage from an outside source, like a life insurance policy with you as the beneficiary—has no bearing on how your joint assets are split through divorce. That's not how Mark—or his attorneys—saw it.

Because I feared the cost and time it would take, we never went to court. I didn't want to upset the apple cart. I don't honestly know how a court divorce would have gone, but I still wish I would have found out. Instead, I settled for what I got.

My divorce was finalized on April 28, 2003, exactly four years after my Black Thursday. We had sold our country house, so I got half the proceeds, and a portion of the money in our savings account. I was far from broke, but I was resentful then—and still am occasionally—toward my ex-husband about finances and our final settlement. I think he probably is as well.

An attorney friend said to me one day, "Suzanne, you gotta understand that if both parties think they are getting screwed, the settlement agreement is a success." He said this with a huge grin.

I felt like I got screwed—and so did Mark.

During our final weeks of settlement, Mark said to me, "Suz, you don't *deserve* any of my earnings. You didn't earn it. All you did was stay home with the kids. *And* you had help."

Maybe he didn't truly mean it—and said it in haste—but the sad part is I thought he was right. But what about the $8,000 times

12 months per year I brought in tax-free, or the house I had sold to buy our country house? Those didn't seem to count, as I didn't "earn" them.

For me, the real issue was standing up for myself—but I didn't want to take that chance. I was scared of rocking the boat. I was scared to stand up for what I felt I deserved—and take action rather than just complain about it. I was even more scared of upsetting the children. I just wanted to be finished with my divorce after four agonizing years. I am sure Mark's version of our divorce is much different than mine, but this is my memoir and this is the story I remember.

Years after our divorce, I got my first life coach. I was still upset over Mark not paying his child support and randomly determining what he was willing to pay without consulting the attorneys. I didn't feel Mark was acting with integrity around his responsibility to the children—or me.

My life coach finally said to me one day, "Suzanne, if you don't want to collect the past money he owes you for child support, you need to sit down with Mark over coffee and request he terminate the agreement legally. If you don't do this, *you* are also acting out of integrity."

The next time Mark was in Aspen visiting the children, I called him and arranged a meeting at Peaches, the local coffee shop. I was petrified. I asked him to legally terminate the child support agreement, and I explained why. I was calm and rational. Part of dissolving our financial agreement was Mark had to go to court and rescind the arrangement.

Mark agreed but never followed through. The statute of limitations never ends regarding child support, so the issue is still potentially pending. It continues to bother me, and yet I do nothing to collect—or terminate—the existence of the settlement.

CHAPTER 7

Do As I Say, Not As I Do

The most precious inheritance that parents can give
their children is their own happiness.

–THICH NHAT HANH

To catch you up on the full story: As my marriage was deteriorating that decade, so were my parents. It all began in 1992 when the Board of Circle Freight International discovered a complicated tax issue they felt could potentially negatively influence the price of the company stock. They unanimously decided it was best for my father to take the fall, and asked him to step down from his position as chairman.

During the annual shareholders meeting in May 1992, the Board announced my father's retirement. Whether he was responsible for the problem or not (which still remains a mystery to me), he complied for the good of the company—the company he had built and dedicated his life to. He never wavered in his devotion to the business, even in the end.

My father believed wholeheartedly he would live to be 120, and he made sure *everyone* knew it. He commented frequently that retirement meant the "end" and believed that hard work ensured a long, healthy life. No longer employed at Circle Freight, my father struck out to find something else to do.

Mark and I had been living in New York for about two years when my father decided to move there part-time. My parents had bought an apartment in New York City years before, so it was an easy move for him. My mother came and went, but as she was already having her own health issues, she came less and less frequently, letting my father fend for himself in the Big Apple.

Honestly, I think he was following me. Although our relationship was often strained, somehow I provided a sense of comfort to him amidst all the insanity. He called me daily for years—mostly to yell at me, but he called me, nevertheless.

For the next six years, my father found work—and more importantly, an office space to go to—finally settling on a venture capital firm that was happy to take him in. He personally invested in a variety of ventures with partners who wore cheap suits and clearly did not have his best interest in mind. Business with John Robinson was an opportunity for free money, and everyone knew it.

My father often slammed his hand on his desk and said, "I can get six million dollars tomorrow without any security, any day of the week."

Not necessarily a great thing to say when you were doing business with crooks.

There was the powdered ice cream business investment, where you just added water to some powder, and voilà: instant soft-serve ice cream. It was going to be sold on every street corner in China; 1.3 billion Chinese were going to be enjoying lukewarm ice cream. I never figured out why he thought it would be a success, but he did—110 percent.

There was an art gallery (which he loved), pipelines, and disposable needles that were going to put Johnson & Johnson out of business.

There were penny stocks, a business deal with a crooked Nigerian, and the list goes on and on.

The crooked Nigerian was both my favorite and my worst nightmare. At the time, there was a lot of talk about "Nigerians" trying to scam Westerners out of their hard-earned money. It was all over the news. Everyone knew about it—except, apparently, my father.

He gave $1.8 million to a man named James—as his Nigerian friend called himself—who would arrive to the United States with a suitcase full of unmarked bills totaling $36 million in return for my father's $1.8 million investment into James's business. I wondered, *How many suitcases does it take to transport 36 million dollars?* I had no idea.

As money kept flowing out of my father's bank account and into James's, I, along with a few others, tried to talk him out of the crazy notion that this scheme was going to pay off.

He would have nothing to do with these conversations and insisted the deal was legitimate. The exchange between my father and James went on for months. James was on his final attempt to deliver the money to my father in the United States at the end of December.

Mark, the children, and I were in Ross for Christmas (years before we divorced). The chaotic opening of gifts by young children had just ended. We were all in the kitchen I grew up in preparing breakfast when the push button wall phone rang.

It was James.

After exchanging Christmas cheer with my father, James said, "John, I have some bad news."

My father, very concerned, responded: "What happened? Are you okay?"

"I was shot this morning," James told my father in his heavy Nigerian accent.

"I'm okay, but I am in the hospital in Lagos, and I'm sorry to say I won't be able to deliver the money as promised this week."

"Oh James, I'm so sorry," my father said with a sympathetic tone, fully believing his "good friend" and supposed business associate.

My mother, brother, and I looked at each other, not shocked that James was not coming—and knowing James was *never* going to come with his suitcases full of cash.

My father's next phone call was to the hospital in Lagos. He so believed James really had been shot that he sent him flowers. I just shook my head, wondering how far down the road this delusional mentality was going to go before my hard-working father lost everything he had spent his life working for.

Mark and I both agreed my father was falling off the deep end. Besides the Nigerian fiasco, there were many signs his mental health was slipping, but there was not a lot anyone could do about it.

Toward the end of 1997, my father was diagnosed with Alzheimer's. He was forced to move back to California as the disease progressed, but he still did *not* want to retire.

His last venture capital investment was with a company in Modesto, California. They built modular school rooms that were to be sold to the government in Southern California to reduce class size in public schools.

Honestly, this seemed to be the best investment of them all, but my father's disease was becoming more and more severe and affecting his ability to think clearly and even take care of himself. He was failing fast. My mother was no longer able to take care of him and was forced to put my father in a home for Alzheimer's patients. Both physically and mentally, he was very ill.

Several years after my father moved to the Alzheimer's care facility, the modular schoolroom company declared bankruptcy. After an incomplete psychological evaluation from the court on my father's mental status, the CEO of the company held my father responsible for the huge debt—and eventual bankruptcy—of the business.

The CEO was another crook and took the company into financial ruin. My dad had personally secured the funds for the investment, just as he said he would, and the bank came after *him* for the money.

Somewhere during this process, some of my father's sketchy business partners decided that disbanding the trust that belonged to my brother and me was the only way to pay off the debt. I didn't want to see the financial ruin of my father, but I was angry about the entire deal. How could anyone have advised him to invest with no guarantee of a return or a proper safety net? What I also knew to be true about my father after all these years was even if they had advised him, he probably wouldn't have listened.

I wanted a share of the money in the trust, so I cut my father—and his crooked advisors—a deal. We agreed to dissolve the trust to use the money to pay my father's debt (which was large), give my mother a portion (which she was demanding), make the final payment on the life insurance policy, and my brother and I would split the remainder.

My last phone conversation with my father, as I was driving home from Long Island one day, was about how we were going to dissolve the trust and pay off his debt.

We had a very heated conversation. It was the first time I ever really stood up to my father, and I demanded I get some of what was in the trust. He didn't have any money left to cover the debt, so he had to agree to my plan, and I knew it. He reluctantly did, but after our conversation, I was told he just lay there on his twin bed in the care facility with a blank look on his face, unable to speak from that day forward. After all his success in life, his utter financial failure at his final business attempt broke him.

As his disease progressed, he needed to be moved to a new care facility. By that time, I was living in Aspen. I went to help my mother and visited with my father on many occasions over the years. On one visit, I flew out from Aspen with a boyfriend who, once again, I thought was the "one."

"Dad, this is Dan," I said to my father, holding his hand as he lay motionless in his bed, staring blankly. "I am going to marry him, and I wanted to introduce him to you."

Much to both my mother's and my surprise, my father, who had not spoken in over a year, sat up in bed, grabbed Dan's hand, shook it vigorously, and said, "Nice to meet you. Take good care of my daughter."

Then he laid back down in a comatose position, like nothing had ever happened.

I started to cry, realizing how important I was to him even though he had such a tough time showing it to me for all those years.

He died on November 13, 2003, only months after my divorce from Mark.

All in all, over the course of our forty-three years together, I was proud of him. I still am. I am in awe of the great work he did during his life. He had severe dyslexia and attention deficit disorder, but he still managed to persevere and achieve his goals. Despite his flaws, he will always be an inspiration to me.

Upon reflection, I understand why he did what he did, but many of the things he did and said hurt me—and left a lasting imprint, just the same. I often questioned my love for my parents. I sometimes hated my father when he was alive. I felt guilty about that, and guilt was the main reason I kept going back for more over and over again—until he was gone.

When my father died, my mother, brother, and I became responsible for trying to clean up and sort out the messes he made in the last few years of his life. We identified eighty-two financial issues in his estate when he died, and they were far from simple—or lucrative.

To this day, I am still dealing with some of the messes he created due to his obsession with being successful and not wanting to retire (and therefore feeling useless). When people assume I have nothing to do, as they often do, I invite them to come to my house and see what nothing really looks like.

During these years, my mother had also become quite ill. She wasn't able to enjoy life like she thought she would after years of taking care of her husband—and by the time he died, she was barely able to take care of herself. She spent most of her time in her beautiful bedroom—with her closets full of clothes—overlooking her beautiful Japanese garden.

It was difficult for me to watch her waste away, so I spent as much time with her as I could. I can't tell you how many times I helped weed through the endless collection of outfits in her closet. It became one of the things we did together. We called it "fanning," our endearing term for reducing the clutter.

My mother never minded giving me her clothes. I think she enjoyed it so much because she could both generously give me things and, at the same time, quiet her anxiety over her wildly unnecessary purchases. I was a bit bigger than her, so her pants were too short and her shoes too small—but everything else was fair game.

After we agreed on what I should take, we would prepare bags for the local Goodwill store. Many of those trash bags were full of clothes with the price tags still intact.

Time after time after time—bag after bag after bag.

My mother had a positive attitude all the way to the bitter end. She was convinced she was going to get better and wear one of her many fur coats to Paris and walk along the banks of the Seine one more time.

There were no trips to Paris or anywhere else. She did manage in her last months to publish a small book based on the teachings from the Course in Miracles. Like my father and his company, she stayed committed to her work with Jerry Jampolsky and the Center for Attitudinal Healing until she took her last breath.

She had many health scares and I jumped on a plane numerous times to see her, anticipating the end of her life. On December 30, 2006, I received a call from one of her hospice nurses, letting me know she was close to death. I immediately made a plane reservation, but just before going to the airport, her caretaker—and my longtime friend Christina—convinced me she was *not* dying and there was no need to come.

There was some real concern by my brother that Christina was going to "permanently borrow" some of the valuables in the house. My brother insisted that Christina, who was acting as my mother's caregiver on top of hospice—and oddly enough, my brother's ex-fiancée—did not want me or my brother to be anywhere nearby when my mother passed.

On the morning of December 31, my brother was ready to call the police and have Christina removed from my mother's house. The upset was escalating. My mother was too sick to know or care about what was going on, but for me the situation was shrouded in a familiar mess around money, and I felt helpless. I didn't know what to do. I only wanted her to be at peace.

I called her from the base of Aspen Mountain. I was just getting ready to ski, and I had one ski boot on and one off, pacing the locker room.

"Mom," I said with distress in my voice, "What do you want me to do? Please tell me how to resolve the upset over Christina and my brother. The situation is escalating, and I don't know how to handle this."

After noticeably gasping for air, my mother said, "I love you. You will know the right answer."

Still feeling helpless, I called Jerry Jampolsky and asked him to go to my mother's house and make sure everything was okay. I got on the next plane out of town, but due to weather delays, I missed her passing by a few hours. I was somewhere high in the sky over Northern California when she died on the evening of December 31, 2006, with Jerry and his wife Diane by her side.

I always say goodheartedly, "Of course, the party girl would go on New Year's Eve. It's perfect. Just the way she would have wanted it."

Jerry and Diane kept her body tucked in her bed with her arms crossed over her heart until I arrived around 2 a.m. I loved my mother and her faith in the good of all—even with the trauma at the end. Many others felt the same way. Her memorial service was overly crowded, and many testified to her loving nature and generosity that day.

Christina did not attend the funeral. Her bags were gone when I arrived that night. My brother and I went to mediation with Christina to settle what she would receive after my mother's death, but we met in separate rooms, so we never saw each other. Eventually, we came to an agreement no one was happy with, so it was probably fair.

The only time I ever laid eyes on Christina again was randomly sitting at a traffic light in Aspen years later, and there she was, walking across the street. I was at a loss for words, so I chose not to say anything to her. I know she loved my mother, and she and I had been good friends for years. It was heartbreaking to be a part of what happened in the end.

Although my mother didn't always appear to be a Woman on Top to me (I was her daughter, after all), she was in her own way. She held true to her beliefs and never wavered from her convictions. She made life happen through times of turmoil. She always saw the rosy side of just about everything and invited others to join her. She was generous with her time and money—and gracefully gave love to all.

In retrospect, I realized both my mother and my father spoke their final words on earth to me. I felt quite honored. My mother's final words, "I love you. You will know the right answer," remain with me to this day.

Seven years after I had moved to Aspen, with the death of my second parent (my mother), my life took another major turn. Not only was I an orphan at forty-seven, there was still the question of whether my parents' second-to-die life insurance policy would be paid out. But with the final payment to the policy I made after disbanding the trust—and months of pestering the life insurance company—I finally received two checks in June 2007. The first two checks they had sent somehow "got lost in the mail," but after even more pestering, they issued another two, and they arrived.

I was dumbfounded. I never truly believed the money would come.

My father had done one thing correctly.

And so it was. The true guarantee I could support my children—and myself—for the rest of my life (if I chose wisely and didn't fly around on private jets). I was very grateful and overwhelmed, but just like most things, financial freedom came with a price tag.

Looking back, it was like I had won the lottery. I hadn't spent years working for the money, at least not in the typical way.. It all came at once. It wasn't 40 million dollars like the man at the party insisted I had, but I now had wealth I couldn't possibly have imagined. And like many lottery winners, I was not prepared.

When I was in graduate school, I met the daughter of a family who had won the lottery fifteen years earlier, who shared with me that the money had destroyed her family and in the long run left them poorer than they started.

I found this quote in an article one day:

"Some winners can't handle this enormous change in financial worth. Some wish they had never won and suffer tremendous heartache and regret over winning. Some take their own lives."

I no longer remember the source of this quote, but it seems pretty darn accurate. I could certainly relate.

Being able to pay the bills and live a comfortable life is an incredible gift, but for many lottery winners, it can turn into a curse. Uncontrolled spending, new financial obligations (such as what to do with the money, how to budget, and tax issues), and the nature of relationships with friends and family are among common challenges many winners experience.

In the beginning I did what a typical lottery winner does and spent money like the well was never going to dry up. I finished the remodel of my house (doing dumb things like paying $22,000 for a light fixture), gave freely to charities, planned vacations, and bought a new car.

I made a series of bad loans to friends—mostly men. Why? I look back on those loans now and believe it was a way to attach myself to someone I liked. Sometimes it genuinely was to help a bad situation. Sometimes it was out of a sheer sense of guilt that I seemed to be luckier than those around me and therefore I had a responsibility to help them.

Public service announcement: Never make loans. Either give someone money and expect nothing in return, or don't give it at all. Some of these debts are still outstanding today. And several of the loans I made didn't help the person I loaned the money to in the long run. It just postponed the inevitable—none of them ended up any better off than where they started.

I had no grasp on who I was with wealth or how to handle it. Inheriting money is like child-rearing. Any idiot can get pregnant. You don't have to have a license or a degree, just some sperm and an egg. I had no clue what I was doing.

CHAPTER 8

Money Is the Root of All Evil

Everything that irritates us about others can lead us to an understanding of ourselves.

–CARL GUSTAV JUNG

On October 6, 2007, I was on my third date with another man when I first laid eyes on Greg. I was discussing with my date, Jim, why we should not go out and how we should just be friends. I got up to go to the bathroom to regroup from our conversation. Greg told me later he checked me out as I walked across the room.

As we were all leaving the restaurant, Greg came over to talk to Jim. The two had been acquaintances for years and knew each other from ski racing. While I was in the bathroom, Jim had told Greg about our future—or lack thereof.

Although we had never met, I had known of him for a long time and I blurted out: "Oh, so *you're* Greg. I've heard so much about you and can't believe we are finally meeting."

He was handsome and funny with an adorable smile—*and* he was a professional ski racer to boot. I was tongue-tied, all the while trying not to fall all over him. The three of us had a casual conversation with some talk of getting together again in the future.

The next morning my phone rang. It was Jim. He said casually, "Greg wants your phone number, and I just wanted to know if you want me to give it to him."

Greg had phoned Jim earlier that morning and asked about me.

After a brief conversation with Jim, Greg said, "Well, as long as she isn't gonna hang out with you, can I have her number?"

I was confused by Jim's call, but I said with a cocky tone to my voice: "Yeah sure, go ahead and give it to him."

The idea of going out with Greg sounded like fun, but I agreed to give him my number in a way to impress Jim.

Greg called later that day. We chatted for a while and agreed to meet a few nights later. I immediately called my friend Tracy and told her about the date. I laughed and asked her: "Where do you think he's going to take me, L'Hostaria?"

That was our standard joke. L'Hostaria is a wonderful restaurant, but back then it was a bit quieter than my normal haunts. I would go there if I didn't want anyone to see who I was with.

Turns out he took me to Rustique—also a wonderful restaurant—but even quieter than L'Hostaria. When I phoned Tracy to tell her he had chosen Rustique, we laughed even harder.

On the evening of our date, I was surprised at how excited I was. I changed my outfit ten times, wanting to look good but not too sexy, interesting but not too outlandish.

Greg picked me up, so there was no hiding my wealth. He said nothing about my home or financial situation that first evening. And I certainly had no clue about where he lived—or *his* financial situation. I just thought he was cute.

We had a lovely evening.

Did I mention he paid for dinner?

On our third date, however, Greg shared his concerns over my wealth as compared to his. He was a ski racer—an excellent one at that—but his income was limited. On top of that, I was twelve years older: I was forty-seven and he was thirty-five—though on our first date he claimed to be thirty-seven. He admitted later he pretended to be older to make our difference in age not seem so important.

I was flattered, but should I be concerned? I didn't want to see any red flags because he was a dream come true and exactly my type— handsome, charismatic, *and* a professional athlete.

I fell for him instantly. He fell for me as well—but had some strong reservations about getting involved. He told me he was not yet divorced (which was why he was taking me to Rustique and keeping me on the down low) from a woman who was also older and came from money.

Their relationship had financial challenges—she was wealthy, he was not—and although my situation was different, he was nervous about climbing that mountain again. Ironically, as I was paying for lunch, I insisted money was *not* going to be an issue for us. With my new windfall of wealth, I thought I was invincible.

During our lunch date, I explained to Greg, "I don't have a problem paying for you. "Do you realize how highly unlikely it is for me to date a man I'm *not* going to have to pay for? That is, if I want to continue living the lifestyle I'm accustomed to?"

I honestly had no idea what I was talking about. I had only inherited the money a few months before.

Not long after that lunch (and my comment about being totally okay with paying), Greg mentioned casually, "I need to sell my Jeep. I'm going to put an ad in the paper and hopefully I get $20,000 for it."

Greg had two cars he had won in different ski events. He didn't need two cars, but I could see by the look in his eyes he didn't want to sell the car. I felt bad for him.

I rationalized for a minute in my mind and thought, *Come on, Suz, you have the money. It isn't going to hurt you to help him out. Just give him the money.*

I got my checkbook and handed him a check for $20,000. In return, Greg promised to give the car to my son Carson three years later when he turned sixteen.

With the promise of the car for Carson, I felt good about my decision. I never asked Greg for the title or any proof he would give the car to my son. I didn't feel it was necessary. I hated to see him struggle, so I rescued him.

Shortly before I met Greg, after seven years in London, Mark moved to Aspen to be closer to the children. The soulmate had not worked out, and after years away from the children, Mark retired at the young age of 45 from his trading position in London, packed up, and moved to Aspen with a woman who would become his second wife.

During the seven years he was in London, I resented him for not helping more with the children, but once he moved to "my" town, I had a whole new set of problems. I often resented him and his girlfriend for being there and becoming friends with my friends. It sometimes felt invasive and cruel. And I didn't enjoy having another parent there to share in the children's upbringing, but he was their father, and therefore I learned to adapt to this new dynamic.

Lesson learned: Watch what you wish for.

The good news was that because Mark was in town and took the children every other week, Greg and I not only had time with them, we also had time on our own. We spent most nights together, which quickly turned into all nights, except when Greg left home to ski race.

When we were in Aspen, we stayed mostly at my house, but when the children were with Mark, we stayed at his house. Greg rented a room from a friend a few miles outside of town. We had many great nights there, but it was a totally different experience than living in my big house in town.

Six months into our relationship, during a life coaching weekend we were attending, Greg admitted to being unfaithful during his time away.

I was crushed. But I was strong enough in that moment to say, "I am so sorry, but I can't do this. It's way too painful."

I'm not sure I really meant it, but I was as prepared as I could be to split with him. After a long discussion, Greg and I agreed to a monogamous relationship willingly—and I felt it was from the heart, so we continued dating.

In October, one year after we met, Greg moved in with me and the children. I happily cleaned out half my closet to welcome him—and make him feel like my home was his home. I teased him for years telling him I had *tricked* him into moving in, suggesting that moving in meant he could save money on rent. He came back every time saying he had actually tricked *me,* knowing that I wanted him to move in.

In truth, we both wanted to live together.

Why couldn't I just say I loved him and I wanted him to move in?

Why didn't he just say he loved me and offer to contribute to our living expenses?

Actually, he did offer to contribute, but I turned him down. His rent had been $1,200 a month, and I felt ashamed to ask for what seemed like such a small sum of money in comparison to my monthly household bills. After all, the whole point of him moving in presumably was for *him* to save money.

When we agreed he should move in, I suggested we revisit our living arrangement six months later, on April 1 the following year, when his racing season was over. I was proud of myself for being brave enough to put an end date out there—just in case it didn't work.

Six months flew by, and all of a sudden, it was April Fool's Day. I was scared, but I had committed to reassess—and so I did. We were lying in bed when I brought the subject up. I wanted to get it over with before I lost my nerve.

The discussion lasted all of two minutes. It was clear to me I didn't want him to go—nor did he want to leave. Our lives had become intertwined. We decided Greg was going to stay right where he was—with me.

I loved him so much and I *never* wanted him to leave.

We spent the next two ski seasons together, traveling the world. He was competitively skiing for the United States, and I had a blast going with him. Much of my life today is shaped by those years with him. He introduced me to many people in the ski world, and it was great fun hanging out with them.

Greg's expenses were paid for by the ski team, and I paid my own way. During those trips, we had moments of financial equality. He was in charge and I followed. We were on equal footing. My relationship with Greg became easy and fun, especially when we were on the road together.

There were times when we did *not* see eye to eye. I specifically remember one of his ski trips home from Europe. He was supposed to be back in the early evening, and he had landed in Washington, D.C., hours before he was expected home in Aspen. I called and called, but he never answered. Finally, I gave up and went to a friend's house for dinner.

When Greg did arrive home hours later, he told me he was trying to "surprise" me.

My answer: "Surprise? Surprise is when you show up *before* you are supposed to arrive and *not* seven hours late."

This was one of the rare occasions when he genuinely seemed concerned over possibly losing me, and I felt I had some power. He knew he was in trouble.

From the beginning of our relationship—and particularly after the 2010 Olympics, when Greg finished ski racing—I honestly didn't know how to support him in making a good career choice. I'm not sure I wanted him to *have* a career. I liked having him by my side and being able to travel whenever we wanted to.

How would it work if I was free to travel and Greg had to work a full-time job? I didn't want to travel *without* him, but I wasn't prepared to give up traveling either. My children were growing up and leaving the house, and I wanted to take advantage of my new freedom.

He blamed me for not letting him be successful, trying to control him with money, always having hurt feelings, not appreciating him, nagging—and *often* talking about problems with money. The truth is I did a lot of these things. I had no idea how to handle being wealthier than him.

I wanted him to genuinely appreciate who I was and what I was doing for him. I wanted him to listen to my messages when I called and call back, to show up on time, to pick me up when I needed a ride, to admit to others openly that I was paying *our* way, and to never *surprise* me again.

But despite our occasional upsets, we were still in love. We bowled, we danced, we cooked, we skied. We helped raise each other's children.

At the beginning of 2011, after skinning up Buttermilk Mountain in Aspen, Greg asked me to marry him. It was 1/11/11. Greg knew I had a thing for the number 11. The number 11 reminds me of angels— and so I was extra excited to have him ask me on that day. I honestly wasn't expecting a proposal. We had an argument just days before over his concern about my controlling behavior—and I was under the impression he was *not* going to ask.

He did.

I accepted instantly—once again, just like I had done with Mark. We would be married on 11/11/11.

After we came down off the mountain, I was so excited I wanted to shout, *Greg and I are going to be married!*

But that feeling was shrouded in fear. I was unsure as to whether he had really meant it. He was reluctant to tell anyone about our plans, and that familiar feeling of not being good enough was simmering beneath the surface.

Shortly after he proposed, we were visiting Carson at his boarding school and had brought one of his daughters with us for a weekend getaway. As we were strolling through downtown Ojai, California, Greg bought me a gigantic fake three-dollar diamond ring from the toy store. His nine-year-old daughter helped pick it out. I was thrilled, but we still hadn't discussed any marriage plans.

In May, I was in Mexico with my daughter on a yoga trip. During one of our free times, we went to look at a possible wedding venue. When I got home, Greg showed little enthusiasm over where our marriage would take place. 11/11/11 was rapidly approaching and we still hadn't discussed our wedding plans. It's hard to get married without a plan—and only a three-dollar ring from a toy store.

The closer we got to November, the more agitated I became. I saw our lack of communication around a wedding plan as an enormous red flag and a turning point. I went from wanting to make the relationship work at any cost to questioning whether I should be in it at all.

In truth, red flags had been there from the very beginning. The first one appeared shortly after we met, when I gave Greg the $20,000 for his Jeep. I so desperately loved him I blindly accepted *nothing* for the money. Over four years had passed since then. Carson had turned sixteen a year ago, and Greg hadn't said one word about giving him the car, but I still couldn't fully admit to myself I gave him the money to keep him around.

Second, I continued to pay all the household bills after he moved in. When we did discuss bills, his opinion was I would have paid them anyway—so he didn't see the need to chip in. I was okay with the arrangement on the surface, but over time I harbored some resentment—resentment I was not discussing openly.

Greg did some things to help out. He enjoyed cooking, so when we were home, he cooked most of the time. I diligently worked as his *sous-chef* to make sure I did my part.

He occasionally remembered to take out the trash and pick up after himself, but I did most of the dishes and the laundry, gathering the stray clothes from around the house. I paid the bills and made sure *my* house was taken care of.

We often fought over taking care of the house. He rarely offered to help with miscellaneous household repairs, telling me I wouldn't "let him help"—and that I was "always" calling someone to help *before* he could get around to fixing whatever was broken. In his defense, I wasn't good at asking for anything I didn't pay someone to do. I was afraid Greg would say no to my requests—and he did many times. I hated it.

After a year or so of living together, I firmly asked him to take the trash out every Wednesday. He agreed, but over two-plus years, he rarely remembered. I would end up doing it myself and feeling resentful as hell. I was doing most of the work, paying the bills—and taking the trash out. All of it began to feel unfair, but I was still *not* communicating my feelings to Greg.

In reality, he was damned if he did and damned if he didn't. I'm not sure if he *had* paid me the $1,200 a month—*and* remembered to take out the trash—I still wouldn't have felt like he was doing enough.

There was no way our financial situation was ever going to be equal. I was always going to have more, and he was always going to have less.

In effect, I was trying to create a *quid pro quo* for Greg around money. I began the relationship saying: "I got this. I will pay for everything, and I will take care of you."

Now I was upset that he didn't take out the trash.

I don't remember which child said it, but I do remember the words: "All he does is sit on the couch, eat cereal, and watch the Golf Channel."

In the end I would nag, "Set your alarm on your phone. I mean *come on*. Trash day has been *every* Wednesday since you have been living here."

These discussions didn't usually end in anyone feeling the love.

I kept trying to fix our issues about money with more money. Two years after we started dating, I wrote him an extremely large check on his birthday. For his next birthday, I wrote him another large check— gifts with no strings attached.

Or were there?

The first check I handed to him lovingly, but when I gave him the second check, I had mixed feelings. I could feel the resistance as I handed it to him. My fingers were stuck to the check.

My thought at the time was to provide him with some assets so he could feel good about himself—and good about dating me. I justified all those gifts as sharing what I had with the man I loved, but over time I felt trapped and a responsibility to take care of him rather than giving out of the kindness of my heart.

Strings were attached.

I remember saying to myself, *Self, are you really doing and giving because this feels good, or are you doing and giving because you think it is expected?*

The truth was I thought it was expected. I gave him the money because I wanted to create a sense of monetary equality, which I thought was required to make a relationship work. But we would never have full monetary equality unless we split *all* the money equally. Instead, what I did was make him a little less poor—and made me feel a little more used. 11/11/11 needed to bring a miracle.

From the beginning, I embraced his two daughters, whom I loved (and still do). They were two and four when we met. From birth, his younger daughter has suffered from an unusual breathing disorder and lived on oxygen 24/7. Greg couldn't afford to have a nurse at home with us when they visited—a prerequisite by his ex-wife—so it became difficult for them to spend time with him.

I did everything I could to ensure he would be with his daughters. Not only did I create space for them when they were with us, I went so far as to become an EMT—another request of his ex-wife—although neither Greg nor his ex-wife ever completed the course.

I paid for the nurse during his daughter's time with us. I bought a generator for $16,000 to ensure his daughter could have a place to plug in her breathing device—another prerequisite by her mother—in case there was an extended loss of power. I was happy to do it. I did what it took to create a space for us to be together with all our children forever.

The list of things I did for him financially went on and on. I made a significant donation to an association where Greg had a leadership role. I paid for his other car to be rebuilt after he fell asleep at the wheel one June afternoon and crashed it. I didn't really want to spend the $18,000 for the repair, but I did.

As for the money I gave him, he spent a great deal of it on us. He now had the resources to pay for some dinners and buy me an occasional present. Still to this day, I own a beautiful bubble gum pink Vespa he bought for me for my 50th birthday. I loved it then, and I love it now.

Somewhere along the line, I accidentally uncovered Greg had put $40,000 into college funds for his daughters and made his ex-wife the "account owner" responsible for the distribution of the funds in the event of his death. I was impressed by his willingness to pay for his daughter's future education (albeit with the money I had given him) but incensed he had not given me that title.

A 529 can be liquidated by the account owner at *any* time, and I had this nagging nightmare of his ex using the money for herself—an unfounded accusation at best. I was mad as hell and disappointed he didn't trust me with his daughter's educational needs after what I had done to help them—and love them. Boy, was my ego out of control.

One day, Greg brought up the idea of selling my home in Aspen and buying a new house together. He said he didn't feel at *home* in my house and wanted to create something together that was ours. Greg's idea was to use the funds from the sale of my house to buy something in both of our names. I would put in the money, and he would do the work to fix it up.

Given the fact that he couldn't remember to take out the trash, I was leery of his plan. I did understand and acknowledge his feeling that my house wasn't technically *ours* together, but I had barely finished remodeling my dream home.

I found it difficult to hear that many of my close friends felt Greg was just there for the money. One of my friends said she was ready to "hurl herself in front of the altar to stop the wedding." Comments like hers and so many others always made me feel inadequate, as if I couldn't attract someone great into my life without the money.

The phrase, *Was I not enough?* constantly ran through my head.

If I was truly honest with myself, my friends were right—some of the "gifts" were out of love, for sure—but most of them were to keep Greg close.

I flip-flopped between being the sweet, loving girlfriend who didn't have a care in the world, and the not-so-sweet, controlling girlfriend who continually questioned whether Greg was the right man for me.

Greg did his part to a certain extent—otherwise I wouldn't have been with him—but he was an actor in *my* movie. The one about the woman who has too much [fill in the blank] and doesn't know how to handle it.

I was constantly questioning *my* self-worth— and *his* net worth.

One night we got into an argument, and for some reason, this one threw me over the edge. I was so filled with anger that my energy needed somewhere to go. I wanted to hurt him without hurting him. I grabbed a 12-by-14, professionally framed picture of him celebrating a ski racing victory off the wall and smashed it onto the floor, glass shards flying everywhere.

To be honest, he didn't do anything wrong that night. I had done such a poor job of setting appropriate boundaries I blew my stack. Now I was in so deep—and so unhappily—that I was smashing a picture to the ground. Later, I felt bad and got the picture repaired. Of course. But the damage had already been done.

We had another bad fight after he came to Lake Tahoe in August 2011 to spend a week with the children and me. This time our fight was *not* about money but about my upset over his apparent disregard for my children's integrity.

I had asked Greg to bring a vaccination for our new puppy from the vet that we had accidentally left behind in Aspen. Rather than putting the shot in his checked luggage, he had carried it with him. The needle alarmed the TSA, and they questioned him about why he was carrying it on the plane.

When Greg arrived in Tahoe, he accused Carson (or that's what I heard), who had packed the vaccination, of putting illegal drugs in it— making Greg the mule. The entire notion was ridiculous, and I should have just laughed it off—but instead I took offense.

Greg had been standing in the kitchen in Aspen as my son packed the shot in a box and put it in the refrigerator to keep it cold. I was disappointed Greg would show such disregard for one of the kids whom he was helping to raise.

That was the end of our relationship right there.

By the time I returned to Aspen at the end of August, Greg had moved out. His half of the closet was now empty. I felt sick. I was upset like nothing I had ever experienced, not even at the end of my marriage.

We obviously never made it to 11/11/11.

Greg had told me when we first started dating, I was supposed to be a one-to-two-week fling—a notch in the ol' belt, as he put it—and then he was moving on to the next conquest. As it happened, I was a four-year notch. I had made an offer he couldn't refuse.

I had tried to even out our financial situation as much as I could—or, more accurately, with as much as I was willing to part with. I tried so many ways to make it all okay. But I still felt Greg wasn't contributing—and he felt I was controlling him with money. The truth lay somewhere down the middle, and our relationship paid the price.

At the beginning of September, Greg came back to pick up a few items he had left behind.

Before he left, he asked me, "Why do you hang out with people who have so little money?"

I felt sad because he was at least partially correct. Aspen is home to many wealthy people. Why was I always choosing to spend time with people who were broke?

I didn't have an answer.

Was it really that I wanted to control them?

Was I still rebelling against my father, who had told me repeatedly, "Never date a man worth less than five million dollars"?

I remember declaring to Greg as he was leaving my house for the last time, "I am going to write a book called *A Woman with Means*."

As Greg slammed the door on his way out, he shouted: "You can't do that. You have no idea how to handle *anything* to do with money."

They (whoever "they" are) say everyone has one book in them, but I wasn't one of those people. I hadn't taken a single English course in college. I knew what I had just said represented a light bulb moment—and possibly a chance to deal with my issue of money and relationships.

Not only had Greg moved out, but for the first time since Alexandra was born, all my children were gone. I mean really gone—not at Mark's house for a week. Alexandra had returned to college in North Carolina, Carson was in California finishing his last year at boarding school, and I had just dropped Derek off for his freshman year at a school in Connecticut. After all those years of single-parenting my children, I was an empty nester.

It was September 8, 2011. It was my first night at home alone.

As I stood by myself in my empty house, I looked from side to side and said out loud, "Self, we're going to have to find something to do."

It was a moment of reckoning for me. I had not only ended my relationship with the man I was going to live happily ever after with—I had ended it because of money. I had it all on paper—three beautiful children, my health, financial security—but even with all of that, my life had taken another unexpected turn.

I have everything I need, I thought to myself calmly. In reality, I was terrified.

We tried again during the middle of November. Greg had called me on the phone and told me he loved and missed me. I readily agreed to another shot at happiness. Over two months had gone by without him, and I missed him.

We dove in right where we left off. Everything was going great until the weekend of my birthday. Greg was headed to Vail for a ski event and didn't want to take me for fear of my jealousy issues rearing their ugly head.

I gave in and came to peace with Greg going to Vail on his own. I made plans for the evening of my birthday with a group of friends so

I wouldn't feel lonely. I was okay with him going *until* the day before my birthday. I hadn't heard one word from Greg about *any* plans to celebrate. I was devastated. Even coffee would have been nice. The night before he was leaving, I came unglued. I accused him of being insensitive with thoughts only of his own well-being.

His response was: "Well, if you would've waited, you would have realized I was planning on coming back for your birthday to surprise you."

I had heard that *surprise* thing before and I didn't really like it— nor did I believe he had made any plans to return. Greg went to Vail, and I had a birthday party in Aspen with my friends. He did *not* come home to surprise me.

Seven days after my birthday, on December 9, 2011—with a little liquid courage in me—I called him twenty times in one night. In each call, I flipped-flopped between telling him how much I loved him— and how I thought he was selfish, greedy, and unkind.

Lesson one: no phone calls at night to your ex.

Greg and I met for lunch shortly afterward, and he told me he was in love with another woman.

I found out days later after the twenty phone calls, Greg was listening to my messages—with the new girlfriend, who owned a soup business—laughing over how crazy I was. That was the last time Greg and I spoke more than three words to each other for years. I didn't have to dig very deep into my core to realize how I contributed to the demise of our relationship.

The first few months post-Greg were challenging. There was no room for going back—or calling him late at night crying and telling him how much I missed him. He had moved on into a serious relationship.

After the breakup, for right or wrong, I wanted my money back. The last place I wanted *my* money was *in the soup*.

When I realized I was never going to get any money back, I told him I at least wanted the twelve shirts I had bought him. Even though they were a very small portion of what I gave Greg over the course of four years, those shirts became a major source of upset for me. I didn't want him to keep *anything,* and I especially didn't want him looking good in those shirts.

I never got the shirts back.

In the end, I was thankful for having been smart enough *not* to sell my house and make him an equal partner in a home we would build together. A $338,000 loss plus a generator and a donation began to look cheap compared to what I could have lost in a divorce settlement.

After our breakup, that $16,000 generator stared me in the face for months until I could finally unload it for next-to-no money. I wanted it out of my sight for good. The memories of the oxygen machine–which conjured up our dysfunction with money–made me feel like I couldn't breathe.

CHAPTER 9

The Gods Must Be Crazy

When there's a big disappointment, we don't know
if that's the end of the story. It may just be the
beginning of a great adventure.

–PEMA CHÖDRÖN

I asked myself again and again, What could Greg and I have done differently?

Where did it all go so wrong?

After our breakup, I dated many men, and although they were not as serious—or long-term as Greg—all of them had a similar ending. I couldn't seem to make a relationship work with a man who had fewer financial resources. Honestly, I couldn't seem to make a relationship work with *any* man.

Then I began to ask, *What is wrong with me?*

I did pick cute ones—mostly men who were successful athletically—but I seemed to be consistently drawn to men who were less than successful financially. I wanted to unravel this mess, or I would live with it forever.

The questions kept coming:

Do I like the control I have when I am holding the purse strings?

Who pays if a woman has more than a man?

Will someone stick around if I stop paying?

Can I ask for what I really need without the fear of rejection?

Am I capable of setting healthy boundaries around money?

I was determined to find a new way to ensure I did *not* end up in the same boat again.

I asked one man on our third date if he owned a car—and had somewhere to live. He told me yes, he had a car and lived in a tent.

He was serious.

I was horrified.

I can't tell you how many times the answer was closer to no than yes.

I had one man tell me how upset he was that I had dared to inquire about his financial status. In his case, I knew he owned a car—and a beautiful house—but I wanted to know what I was getting into. My delivery on this one may not have been so polished, but why shouldn't I ask? We had been on several dates and I felt it was time to broach the subject of finances.

This approach didn't work either.

Two weeks after those final twenty calls to Greg, the children and I headed to Lake Tahoe for Christmas. My love affair with Tahoe was still strong, and getting out of town seemed like a good idea. I had no interest in running into Greg and his new girlfriend over the holidays.

It was December 27. Christmas was behind us, but the thought of New Year's—and who I might kiss—was approaching rapidly. I was afraid of spending not only New Year's on my own—but what seemed like the rest of my life alone. I was lying on my bed in the late afternoon overlooking Lake Tahoe, thinking about life and wondering what my future without Greg was going to look like, when the phone rang.

"Is this Suzanne Leydecker?"

I had no idea who this person was, but I responded, "Yes, it is. Can I help you?" (Translation: "Who the heck is this and why are you calling me?")

Luckily, for once I kept my inside voice inside.

"My name is Christie. I know you don't know me, but we have some mutual friends, and I wanted to talk to you about something. Do you have a few minutes?"

"Sure, no problem," I said reluctantly, wondering what she was trying to sell me.

It turned out she was calling to ask if I might be interested in going to Africa with her and a group of women in January. (Translation: In just four weeks.)

Christie told me one of the women in the group had become ill and couldn't make the trip at the last minute, and someone had suggested to someone I might want to take her place. I knew two of the women out of the fourteen—kind of.

Their trip had been planned for over a year, but here I was deciding on whether I should go to Africa with only four weeks' notice. I had none of the required shots, nor did I have the necessary visa, but for some unknown reason, I decided to go. After I got off the phone with Christie, I had a friend go to my house in Aspen that afternoon to locate my passport—which, thank God, was current—and overnighted it to Christie.

I was still deeply in the throes of Heartbreak City, and I wasn't a girl's girl. The thought of traveling with all those women—and no men—for two weeks frankly sounded kind of boring, but I rationalized a trip with some new faces would *somehow* make me feel better.

I was Africa bound. What did I have to lose?

After returning to Aspen, I again stood by myself in my living room, looked from side to side, and said—this time with a grin on my face—"Self, we just found something to do."

I was excited until I arrived at the airport. Just before I was scheduled to board the plane out of Aspen, I called my ex-husband Mark of all people, crying. "What am I doing?" I sobbed. "This is insane."

Mark chuckled and said, "Suz, get on the plane."

I did. It was a harrowing journey. My plane from Aspen to Chicago was delayed due to weather, causing me to miss my next plane. I had the next two long flights and twenty-four hours to worry about how I was going to meet up with the group—and what would happen once I did. (Remember, this was before cell phone coverage in Africa and I had no way to contact anyone.)

After landing in Africa, there I was in the Nairobi airport, feeling nervous at best. Somehow, someone found me. I arrived at the hotel and was greeted by thirteen unfamiliar women and a South African man named Shawn who turned out to be our guide.

Apparently, I was less than friendly to Shawn when we first met. He mentioned this several days after our initial introduction, but to be fair, I was tired and still somewhat terrified upon arrival. Unexpectedly, Shawn and I bonded within days. We spent evenings together enjoying the fire after the other women had retired for the night, discussing our lives—specifically my breakup with Greg and Shawn's stressful marriage.

Being a guide and living in the bush most of the year wasn't doing much for his family unity, and Shawn's wife was less than thrilled with his lack of time spent at home with her and their two children. We both went on and on about our lives as we sat around the roaring fire. As the nights went on, I fell for Shawn.

Here he was. The one who was going to save me.

That wasn't so hard, I thought to myself.

I had butterflies every time I saw him. I couldn't wait for everyone to go to sleep at night so I could have Shawn all to myself.

With one charming male guide and fourteen female guests vying for his attention, some of the women began to notice we were spending evenings together and got a little jealous of our growing relationship. During the daytime it felt like Shawn was purposely paying attention to the other women, which he told me later he was intentionally doing for fear of us being found out.

Found out about what? I asked myself. Nothing had happened between us, although I wanted it to.

I enjoyed feeling special, but Shawn was the guide. By day, he treated me like everyone else (barely), but by nightfall I was sucked back into thinking he was going to be the one—at least temporarily.

I'm not the first woman to fall for a ranger. There's actually a name for it—*khaki fever*—and I was desperately looking for someone to fill the void Greg left behind. Over the course of our time together, I decided to book Shawn as a private guide for another trip so that I could share Africa with the children for two weeks the following summer.

Somewhere in my mind, I knew that by offering to secure Shawn as our guide, I would ensure an ongoing relationship. Although I truly did want to share Africa with my children, deep down I knew I was also trying to buy Shawn's attention. Again, I was going to pay a man to spend time with me. But at least it would be without thirteen other women.

At the time, none of that seemed to matter. I had fallen in love with Africa, fallen in love with many of the women, and fallen for yet another man—on another continent, no less.

For the following six months, Shawn and I kept in touch. We talked mostly via email. Our initial emails were filled with romantic notions—on both our parts—but as time wore on and he knew I was committed to the trip in June, his correspondence was all business. I knew the chance of us having a long-lasting relationship was slim, but my heart was yearning to see him again.

June arrived, and off the four of us went to Africa. When I first laid eyes on Shawn, I knew in a second my fantasies were not going to be realized. That didn't stop me from trying, but romance was clearly not part of the arrangement. Thankfully, our trip was amazing, Shawn was a wonderful guide, and the children loved him—and Africa. It was a trip of a lifetime, even without the romance.

With no promise of another commitment to hire him, Shawn's attention and our email love affair waned. Again my feelings were hurt, my ego bruised, and my pocketbook lighter. I saw Shawn on many other trips over the next few years with the same group of women I had first traveled with, but the attention I so yearned for to fill the hole left by Greg was never returned again.

When I arrived home in June, I was faced with the same life I had when I left in January—and the same questions.

Ever since those fateful words "I'm going to write a book called *A Woman with Means*" came out of my mouth, I continued to try to figure out *how* to be a woman with means—or, alternatively, more like everyone else.

I went so far as to consider giving the money away and getting a job at the local sporting goods store for $22 an hour. Rather than *pretending* to be poor, as I had done so many times before, I *would* be poor.

But would that really help?

Just like when I lived in Lake Tahoe after college, I felt if I had a regular nine-to-five job, I would be more like my peers, toiling away, and I would quiet the mouths of others. But giving all the money away didn't seem to be a great plan either. People would *still* have their opinions. I would just be seen as a rich girl doing a job for fun—or whatever twist someone wanted to put on it.

Then one day, I thought to myself, *I live in Aspen, Colorado. I know tons of women in my shoes. Maybe I should find out what they know about being wealthy and dating men.*

If I didn't have the answer, certainly someone did. I started asking some of my single friends how they dealt with having more wealth than their potential suitors. At the time, I believed I was the *only* woman on the planet who didn't know how to negotiate this situation. I genuinely wanted to know how other women in similar circumstances were making an intimate relationship work with a man.

After several lunch dates, I discovered few women knew much more than I did. Most of the women I knew personally were wealthy because they had been successful in business, or they had divorced from a wealthy husband, and/or they had inherited money like me. Many were lonely and unable to figure out how to have a successful, satisfying relationship, even though they desperately wanted a partner.

Some of them said to me, "Definitely date rich. Don't be an idiot. Then you won't have to worry about it."

I heard what they were saying, but I didn't want to judge people based on their net worth. Maybe I was still rebelling against my father's expectations.

———

Shortly after returning from Africa, a friend suggested I see a healer named Ray. According to what I understood, Ray was a transformation energy worker who did hands-on work to help people clear old patterns, experiences, and beliefs that release pain, disease, and addiction in the physical body. I didn't really know what that meant, but I figured, *Why not? What did I have to lose?* Ray's work was far from traditional and right up my alley.

I enjoyed Ray as a person during our first meeting and was intrigued by his work. Ray worked down the street from my home in Aspen so it was convenient—and I was curious—so I arranged to meet with him once a week.

As he was waving his hands over my body on my fourth visit, he looked me square in the eyes and said: "The gods have something to say."

I wasn't shocked by his comment. I had a mother and father who started the Center for Attitudinal Healing. I was interested in what would follow.

I looked up at him and said in a rather amused voice: "What gods?"

"Oh, well," he said with a smile on his face. "The gods talk to me all the time when I'm with clients,"

"Usually," he continued, "they tell me to keep the information to myself. But in your case," he paused, "they insisted I tell you what they have to say."

"Well, lay it on me then," I said with a slightly skeptical look on my face. "What do they have to say?"

"The gods told me you need to be on your own *without* an intimate relationship for at least two years."

"Two years?" I said shaking my head. "Are they crazy? Are *you* crazy?"

"Hey, take it easy," Ray said. "I'm just the messenger."

I looked at him and said, "Well, tell the gods thanks for the advice."

I left his office, chuckling to myself. Ray's message from the gods wasn't telling me to date rich men rather than poor men. They were telling me not to date *anyone*—at least not for two years.

How can I possibly be on my own for two years? I asked myself out loud.

I tried to take what the gods said seriously, but deep inside I was dying to meet my next love so I could mend my broken heart.

CHAPTER 10

Rinse and Repeat

Awareness is the greatest agent for change.

−ECKHART TOLLE

Seven months after my breakup with Greg, as I was putting some condiments on my burger at a Fourth of July picnic, a man came up to me and commented sarcastically on my excessive use of ketchup. He was very handsome. He told me he was partially deaf—which was obvious by the way he spoke. He was wearing a walking boot on his foot.

I asked him equally sarcastically and somewhat flirtatiously, "What, did you fall off a curb?"

He looked at me with a funny grin. "No, actually, I fell sixty feet down a crevice in Alaska skiing in the spring, and now I have twelve metal plates and sixteen screws in my ankle."

I stared at him with a smile on my face. As usual for me, a handsome man with an adventuresome, athletic background caught my attention immediately. That afternoon we talked for a while, and I discovered his name was Harry. To my delight, Harry asked me to have a drink with him at a local bar after the picnic had finished. As we sipped our Moscow Mules, he told me he was twenty-six. I was fifty-two at the time—exactly twice his age. I almost choked on my drink.

"You need to stay on that side of the imaginary line," I said laughing. "You're way too young. It's such a shame because you're so cute."

Harry disappeared after that day. He never called, and I had no way of contacting him. I was disappointed, but there was nothing I could do. Three months went by, and out of the blue I got a text from him. I was elated—and anxious to reconnect despite our difference in age.

Within a short period of time, I was madly in love again. Here was my chance to try *not* to repeat the mistakes I had made with Greg. Harry was awesome, and I adored him.

I wanted him around, and just as I did with Greg, shortly after we started hanging out, I made Harry an offer he couldn't refuse. I paid for everything.

Harry always paid our dinner bills—usually with *my* credit card. Finally, he asked me one day if I could get *him* a credit card. As long as I was going to continue to pay, he thought it would be better if the card were in his name. I called Visa that afternoon and had a card sent to me.

We went out all the time to restaurants, clubs, and events. We traveled the U.S. and even went to Australia. I did *not* write him big checks, but I did take care of him. We were always doing something fun. I checked my credit card statement each month to make sure he wasn't using my card on his own without me knowing. He never did.

And just like Greg, after less than a year, Harry moved in.

This time, we had a five-minute discussion. I didn't ask if he wanted to move in, and he didn't really ask if he could. He just moved in.

I spent every night with Harry—mostly at my house—but as I did with Greg, I spent many nights in his rented room in a rundown house across town. My justification for him moving in—just like with Greg—was it made financial sense for him. But did it make sense for me? I wasn't sure I had learned my lesson, but I was in love again, so I ignored my hesitation.

Harry was a great boyfriend. Because his hearing was impaired, he wore hearing aids that he would remove at night. I could get up in the middle of the night, snore, talk in my sleep, or do whatever I pleased. He couldn't hear me.

Occasionally, when I was talking to him, questioning the logistics of our relationship, he would look at me with a big grin and say, "Suz, I can't hear you," while tapping on his ear. "What did you say?"

This was his way of deflecting the conversation and keeping things light. Many times it worked, and I was able to let go of my concerns and enjoy our time together.

My friends continued to remind me that both Greg *and* Harry were obviously with me—the rich older woman (a.k.a. cougar)—for the money. My friends liked them both. It was hard *not* to like either of them, but the general consensus among everyone was they were both just using me for money.

I hated every single one of those conversations. I didn't want to believe my friends, but because I heard it so often, I constantly questioned Harry's love. Did I not have *any* value other than money?

At the same time, Harry was busy questioning what he was doing with *me*—not so much because of the money but because of our significant age difference. He wasn't the only one. When my daughter, Alexandra, realized I was seriously dating a man just a few years older than she was, she was livid. She didn't speak to me for months, but eventually even she succumbed to his charm, and my relationship with her got back on track.

Mostly, I didn't mind paying—especially in the beginning—but as the days, weeks, and months went on, I became more and more concerned. I constantly brought up issues related to money, age, and my fear around his intentions.

Why wouldn't I? Someone reminded me of it every day.

In October of 2013—one year after I started dating Harry—I began meeting with a life coach. Twice, Sam had been introduced to me as someone I may enjoy working with. I had been coached before years earlier, after attending several of the Landmark Forum courses, so I was familiar with the process. I wasn't looking for a coach, and the decision to make a year-long contract with Sam was difficult for me. He was expensive, and I was unclear of the value he was going to provide. I went back and forth—mostly adamant about how I was not going to hire Sam.

As it turned out, I did hire him, but there was still a part of me that questioned my motivation. Was I unable to say no to Sam for fear of him not liking me if I turned down his coaching? Was I just trying to take care of a man—even in a professional relationship? Or was hiring him really in my best interest and something that was genuinely good for me? I didn't have a definitive answer. I hired him anyway.

Our first order of business was my relationship with Harry. I vented a lot about our age and money differences. Sam patiently listened. He offered me some tools and then waited for me to come to my own conclusions rather than offering solutions. He did *not* tell me either Greg or Harry were there just for the money. His goal was my empowerment—however that was going to unfold.

Harry and I—despite my concerns—were for the most part still having a good time together. I had now been dating Harry for about a year and a half, and we were still living together. He didn't buy into my worries and assured me many times he loved me. We loved our adventures, and we traveled a lot. I wanted to continue traveling—and I wanted him to come with me.

I had to pay.

I didn't see I had much of a choice.

Just like with Greg, I didn't want to give up my lifestyle because of *his* lack of funds.

And then one night, out of the blue, Harry came home and told me he was moving out. He had met a woman his age, and he knew she was the one for him.

I was sad, but I knew in my heart it was the right thing to let him go gracefully. She's a wonderful woman, and I was genuinely happy for them. Unlike the end of my relationship with Greg, everyone accepted the situation, and I am blessed to have a friendly relationship with Harry and his now wife.

At least I had learned something—and my supportive life coach was right there with me. In my heart, I believe both Greg and Harry loved me. I definitely loved them, but doubt is a tough pill to swallow—for a woman or a man—when you question why your partner is around.

The way I saw it, those two experiences were a wake-up call for me to STOP IT. For those of you who have watched the Bob Newhart YouTube video *Stop It* (and if you haven't, I highly suggest you do), you know what I am talking about. Specifically, it was a wake-up call to stop the insanity. To reference the famous quote attributed to Albert Einstein, which I apparently was not heeding: "The definition of insanity is doing the same thing over and over again and expecting different results."

I knew I wanted to find a different way of having an intimate relationship. I wanted to take responsibility for my actions, for my net worth, *and* for my self-worth. I also cut myself some slack for not knowing what I was doing. Given my past—and lack of any wealthy female role models in my life—how was I to know how to handle wealth? How was I to know how to be a confident, empowered woman?

I didn't believe it was wrong for me to pay, but I wanted to take responsibility for when I chose to pay—and what I *expected* in return.

After all, there was a guaranteed chance I would again date someone without as much as me.

After my breakup with Harry, I wanted to seriously straighten up my life. My work with Sam now focused on cleaning up the piles of paper scattered all over my office floor. My rationale for the piles of papers on my floor was if the projects were visible—and I didn't stuff them in a drawer—I couldn't avoid them.

I consider myself to be organized, and I think I am one of the few people on the planet who does *not* have a junk drawer. I tried—but the drawer upset me too much and I had to clean it up. Yet even with this strong personality trait, I felt overwhelmed with the sea of paperwork cluttering up my life. Just like a lot of other people, I didn't think I had enough time to do all the things on my list.

I've always been a hard worker, taking responsibility in all areas of my life, but I, like many others, fell victim to the P word: procrastination. For quite some time, I had been overwhelmed with kids, work, and challenges from my parents' deaths seven years earlier, and I felt like I was barely hanging on. But with Sam's guidance, the sinking ship of my life started floating—or at least was beginning to stabilize.

After years of denying I needed help—and being reluctant to pay for that help—I finally hired a computer tech and an assistant to help me. Within two months of them coming to my house once a week, I made back in lost revenue and back bills their fees for the entire year. And the clutter began to clear. Projects were getting started—and occasionally completed. I began to see the fruits of my labor. The floor of my office became partially visible.

My tech guy, who was a godsend, commented one day, "Well, your office floor is still kind of a mess, but at least there are different piles on it every time I come."

We all have our own long laundry list of to-dos that are constantly interrupted by our busy lives and all the emergencies we don't expect to happen, like sick children, flooded basements, or our transmission suddenly dying. That being said, something strange started happening as I went about my daily life: I began to feel like I was actually accomplishing something.

In truth, I went up and down with my progress, but there was more forward movement than I had experienced in the past. (The shift was probably at least partially the result of *not* having a relationship and having more time to spend on my own goals.) The process was slower than I anticipated and took longer than I budgeted for. Fears such as *there isn't enough time, I'm not smart enough to handle all of this,* and *everything is too overwhelming* often worked their way into my thoughts.

One day, as I was going through all the things I had to do with Sam, he said, "I have an idea. How about you add one more thing to your list of to-dos?

"What?" I said. "Are you nuts? I'm trying *not* to add anything to my plate. It's full enough."

"Why don't you write that book you've been talking about?" Sam said in a nonchalant tone.

I had told Sam about my breakup with Greg and how I had blurted out on the eve of his departure from my life that I was going to write a book called *A Woman with Means*. I had been journaling on the topic for a couple of years off and on, but otherwise hadn't made much progress. Sam thought writing a book was a great idea. I wasn't so sure, but he had so much enthusiasm it was contagious.

Why shouldn't I? I thought.

Some women go to therapy after a breakup.

I would write a book.

The only problem was, I didn't have a clue about how to write a book. In high school I was more interested in sports and boys than

English class, and as I said before, I'm the only person I know who managed to make it through college without taking an English course. Nevertheless, I agreed during that coaching session to commit to write every day for the next thirty days.

Sam suggested I come up with a consequence for myself that was so severe I wouldn't want to break my commitment. He shared with me that one of his other clients had agreed to get a tattoo—something she abhorred—as her consequence for not following through on her word.

A tattoo seemed easy. After some thought, I chose the consequence of *not* going out for thirty days. I was going out seven nights a week, so not going out seemed like the most severe punishment I could imagine. I had just broken up with Harry, so going out—as not to face my fears of being alone—seemed critical to my survival.

I easily reported after two weeks that I was on track with writing each day, but somewhere in the two weeks that followed, I missed two days. I didn't think anything of it. I had written for twenty-eight days out of thirty. I considered that a huge success. Apparently, Sam did not and he called me out on it.

"Suzanne," he said, "You committed to writing thirty out of thirty days, *not* twenty-eight days out of thirty."

I stared at him with a quizzical look on my face. I thought he was kidding.

"But I wrote twenty-eight days out of thirty. That is a huge win for me."

"It's a huge win, *and* it's not what you agreed to," Sam said.

I know most life coaches are big on integrity and the value of keeping your word as sacred, but this was ridiculous. Ridiculous to me—and dead serious to him.

"That is not what you agreed to," Sam said with a daunting voice of authority.

Thoughts like, *Aren't I paying him?* and *he's not supposed to treat me like this* ran through my head.

And yet, I knew at a gut level this *was* part of what I was paying him for.

"And the consequence you came up with for not following through with what you said was if you do not write for thirty days out of thirty, you will not go out for thirty nights."

I cringed.

"When would you like to start?" Sam said in a parental tone.

N*ever*, I thought to myself.

I was devastated. I was angry. I couldn't *not* go out for thirty days.

"I will get back to you," I said reluctantly.

I left his office in a state of panic. What was I going to do at home alone for thirty nights in a row? I couldn't stay home two nights in a row. I had, in fact, chosen a consequence that seemed too severe to handle.

The next day, I called Sam and offered an alternative consequence of not drinking while I was out, rationalizing to him that not drinking was more serious than not going out. In reality, I was trying to come up with something I could live with.

He finally agreed to let me alter my consequence to going out and not drinking, but as soon as we got off the phone, even that seemed harsh. I associated drinking with having fun, and not having fun seemed like an idea as painful as the first.

I walked into his office two weeks later, and before he could ask, I said, "I didn't do it. I did pretty good in the beginning, but I can't tell you honestly I never had a glass of wine."

The discussion ended shortly thereafter. I refused to talk about it. I mean really, was I now going to get a consequence for not doing my consequence? How serious could the consequences become? Was I to chop off my arm because I didn't stay home for thirty nights? I was the client and the one paying his bill.

The conversation ended; however, the one thing I can say with a great deal of clarity is I learned a deeply valuable lesson about commitment. Never again would I make a commitment I would not do, or not clear up if I was unable to follow through.

I kept writing. Along the way, I created a SurveyMonkey survey. I developed strategies for interviewing first graders to hear their thoughts on how they saw their parents handling money and finances. There was idea after idea, most of which did not come to fruition, but my mind was working overtime to gather material to write about. I read books written about bread-earning women like *When She Makes More* by Farnoosh Tarabi and *Lean In* by Sheryl Sandberg. Each author enlightened me a bit more, and I kept writing and talking to people.

Then a whole new set of fears emerged.

What would I ever have to say that might help others?

How was I remotely qualified to address these issues?

Don't I need to be in a successful relationship if I'm going to help other women?

I was afraid people—and especially men—were going to think I was silly for talking about problems rich women have. In the beginning, there was more than once during some conversation or another where I took something personally and felt shame about wanting to write a book, or became upset about how someone was misunderstanding—or not getting the importance of—what I was saying.

I was invited to a charity event for our local suicide prevention treatment center one beautiful, sunny September afternoon in Aspen. During the cocktail portion of the event, I was talking to a couple. I had met Carolyn once before but not her husband, Chris. Carolyn was friendly, and the three of us struck up a conversation.

After the usual pleasantries, Chris asked me what I did.

"I've been a stay-at-home mom for my three children, who are now grown up and in college and boarding school," I told Chris. "Now that I have more time, I'm working on writing a book."

Whenever I mentioned I was writing a book, almost everyone's next question was, "What's your book about?"

Over time I had developed a short answer summing up my topic, depending on what level of interest someone seemed to have. Both Carolyn and Chris seemed interested.

"Well, it's about the shift currently taking place around the globe with women, money, and how the dynamics of breadwinning women affect a couple's relationship."

We talked about the rise of women as primary breadwinners and how we are encouraging women—especially our daughters—to embrace the success of women in the workplace. I explained I was writing about the challenges for both men and women when a woman has more money, whether she made it working, acquired it through a divorce, or inherited it.

I openly shared with them my parents had died a few years before and I had inherited some money. I strive to be as transparent as possible around my wealth and where it came from—even though I often felt embarrassed to admit I inherited it.

Carolyn, Chris, and I continued to talk for quite a while. Chris began to explain to me—in a genuine way—how he felt about women having more money.

"Well, if a woman *earns* the money herself that is one thing, but if she got it from a divorce settlement, an inheritance, or a trust fund, that's quite a different thing."

"What do you mean by that?" I asked Chris politely. "How do you see the two as being different?"

Chris began to explain his viewpoint that women who do *not* earn their own money shouldn't have any right to call the shots in a relationship.

"After all," Chris said, "They were just lucky. They don't know what it's like to make their own money like the rest of us."

I was feeling a bit uncomfortable with the conversation. I was sure I never said that when women earn the money they should call the shots, and I was wondering how I was going to remind Chris that I *was* one of those trust funders, when Chris suddenly turned to me mid-sentence, bright red with embarrassment.

"I'm so sorry," he said awkwardly. "I forgot you inherited your money."

I explained to Chris that it was okay, and he didn't need to feel bad. But I left the party shortly after, not feeling so great about my life.

There was a part of me that said, *No one understands. I'm always going to look like a rich, entitled woman who didn't leave home at eighteen to make my way in the world and build a successful company.*

Post mid-2007, I *was* a trust funder. I had inherited second-generation wealth. "Making it on your own" is an attribute many people reference with pride. Creating your own success commands respect from others—or at least it seems to make people feel good about themselves no matter what they accomplish after that. The younger a person is when they leave home to fend for themselves financially, the prouder an individual seems to feel.

On the other hand, we've all heard that "trust funders are lazy, spoiled, and entitled." I realize some trust funders *are* lazy, spoiled, and entitled. This was not the first time I had heard comments like Chris's. My dad reminded me of it regularly when I was growing up, and I've seen it myself. The reputation of trust funders didn't come out of thin air.

That wasn't the way I viewed myself. My father was successful, and he died. I inherited the money. I didn't consciously choose who my parents were—or where I was born. Everyone has opinions about how much I have, what I do with my time, and how lucky I am. It's a hard label to wear.

As far as I can tell, nothing in life that is worthwhile ever comes for free.

As I was washing dishes in my kitchen, digesting some of the things I had learned from my recent conversations, Rachel walked through the mudroom door. Rachel had been my children's babysitter for years. She is sixteen years younger than me and in a different demographic. I no longer needed a babysitter, as all the children had flown the coop, but Rachel remained a friend long after years of devoted service.

"Hey Suz, what are you up to?" Rachel said as she walked through the door with Oliver, our golden retriever she had been looking after.

"Not much. Just thinking about this book and whether I can really write it. I'm not sure whether anyone is going to want to read a book for women who outearn their partners," I said to her, vigorously drying a plate.

Rachel was working at the St. Regis Hotel in Aspen at the time and doing quite well, but she had two young children, and I knew she and her husband were struggling financially.

She looked at me with a grimace, head tilted, and said, "Actually, I have the same problem."

I looked at her, confused.

"Things at home haven't been going very well recently."

She paused. "I make $38.50 per hour at work, which is a good hourly wage—and I love my job."

I listened intently, wondering what she was going to share next—acutely aware her financial situation was different than most of the women I had spoken with previously.

"As you know, my husband has been working as a ski instructor. He's making $36.50 per hour," Rachel said, shaking her head.

"He is beside himself that I make $2 an hour *more* than he does. He is actually quite angry about it. It's $2 an hour, for God's sake. It's ridiculous. The other day he actually said, 'I can't believe you really make $2 more an hour than I do. How does anyone think you are worth more than me on an hourly basis? You're a woman. I deserve to make more.'"

Rachel told me on the outside she was chuckling at his absurd comment, but on the inside she knew it wasn't a good situation, and it was going to fester.

Within months of our conversation, Rachel inherited a bit of money from her family. Together, she and her husband bought a house outside of town in a place *she* could afford. Their deal was she would buy the house and he would do the work to fix it up.

Disagreements around money continued over the next few years, and in the end, Rachel was forced to give up control of the money and her investment in the house. Years later, she lost most of what was left in their divorce. Both of us could have probably anticipated the outcome of their marriage when we spoke that day.

This conversation was a turning point for me. I now knew with no uncertainty it wasn't just me—or my wealthy friends.

CHAPTER 11

Things Will Never Change

Change the story and you change perception; change
perception and you change the world.

–JEAN HOUSTON

After breaking up with Harry, I had to admit to myself I wasn't doing
what the gods had in mind. According to Ray, they had asked me not
to date anyone for two years. I assumed it was so I could embrace my
independence and practice self-love rather than relying on love from a
man. In all honesty, I was still out there looking for The One.

Take Philip, for example. I met Philip on the golf course with a
friend of mine one October afternoon. He was thirty-eight and I was
fifty-five. That day he showed zero interest in me; he seemed much
more attracted to my girlfriend who was twenty-eight, hot, and a semi-
professional golfer.

Months after our golf game, however, I got a Facebook message
from Philip asking me out to dinner. I wasn't sure why he was asking
me out, but…why not? I willingly accepted.

Philip and I had a lovely evening. He paid, and I thanked him for his generosity.

Is a man supposed to pay on the first date? I considered a man paying to be a chivalrous gesture, so I didn't think too much about letting Philip pay. Many women I knew expected men to pay not only on the first date but on *every* date.

We had several more dates over the next couple months. I wasn't deeply in love with Philip like I had been with Greg or Harry, but we had feelings for each other, and we were having fun.

By our fifth date, thoughts of what I should do when the bill came were swirling around in my head. By this time, I knew I had about a thousand times more money than Philip, and I was having the familiar feeling I needed to start paying.

I picked up the check on our fifth date—not because Philip asked me to, but because it was what I felt I should do. During our next dinner, I decided it was time to have a conversation about money—for my sake more than his.

I was nervous. Should I bring up the subject before or after we ordered? Should I wait until the bill came? Or should I pay the bill and discuss it later? Philip knew I had more money, so I doubted the conversation would be that shocking.

I decided to bring it up before the bill came. Our conversation went something like this:

"Philip, you know some of my history with men and money, and I am beginning to feel uncomfortable about when I should be paying and when I should let you pay," I said awkwardly.

"I know I have more money, and I want to find some way to work this out. It makes me feel sick to my stomach to bring it up, but I'm doing it anyway."

I mentioned to Philip how I had, in the recent past, gone so far as to ask a date if they owned their own car and had a roof over their head. Tents didn't count. Neither did sleeping in your car, or living in your RV.

"Suz, I live in a house, and I own a car, so you have those covered," Philip said with a big smile.

"As far as paying, it's no big deal. Don't worry about it, but the truth is I do hate always having to pay for women. Why don't *women* ever pay? You all just expect *the guy* to pick up the tab, and it's so unfair."

Great, I thought to myself. I wanted to be different from all those *other* women and not be a burden to any man, so I often picked up the tab. In truth, I was secretly hoping my date would insist on paying the bill.

Even though an attempt at equality was coming out of my mouth, I still believed I was *supposed* to be paying because I had more. But at least I was trying something different.

This wasn't the first time I had had this type of conversation with a man—and it wouldn't be the last. Some men even tried to convince me if *I* paid their way, then they would be the *perfect* man for me. I have had men offer to adore me (whatever that means), carry *my* luggage when *we* go away (something I believed they should be doing anyway), get me coffee every morning, or some other vague commitment related to taking care of me.

Coincidentally or not, after this conversation with Philip about who should pay, our dating came to a halt. It just petered out. There was no further discussion. There didn't seem to be a need for one.

As I was sharing my question about who should pay with my friend Michael, he suggested I adopt a policy of going Dutch with everyone—men and women—and particularly men I was dating. He also suggested, if I were going to date someone who had less, I should choose to do things that didn't cost money or were inexpensive. That concept, though valuable, made me feel like I would be giving in. Call me spoiled, but at least I'm honest.

The child in me said, *Why should I always have to sacrifice things I love to do and places I want to go to accommodate my date?*

Michael's suggestion was a good one and presented another option, but it was foreign enough to scare me.

Months later, out of the blue, Philip called me and asked if I wanted to meet for a drink. I chose a local, inexpensive place on purpose. We each had one drink. When the bill came, I suggested we go Dutch, figuring I had nothing to lose by experimenting on Philip.

He looked at me quizzically. "Okay, whatever you want."

Philip had been prepared to pay for both of us, but I stuck with my plan. I left feeling different but not particularly empowered. The whole thing felt weird. The only thing I can honestly say is I was proud of myself for taking a risk.

During a coaching session with Sam in October 2015, about a year and a half after Harry and I went our separate ways on February 6, 2014, I finally shared the story of the gods. I hadn't mentioned it to him before, I suppose, because I hadn't taken it that seriously. As I laughingly told him the gods' advice, Sam had a strange look in his eyes, much like when he suggested I add writing a book to my laundry list of things to do. I knew his wheels were turning.

Sam leaned in and said, "I have an idea."

"What this time?" I asked, slightly reluctantly.

"Well, I was thinking, since you have gone nineteen months without really dating anyone, why don't you go another five months and finish your two years that the gods were talking about and see what happens?"

"Hmmm," I replied. "That's not a bad idea. I like it. Five months is nothing. I can do that."

This time I was clear on what I was committing to. What did I have to lose? Nothing else seemed to be working. Maybe I would be pleasantly surprised by the outcome.

"I'm in," I told Sam. "We start today."

Over those remaining five months, I finally took what the gods were saying seriously. I did go out with men, but if the possibility of dating came up, I told them I wasn't available. Of course, that just made them want me more.

I may have failed the godly two-year challenge according to its original design, but I did the best I could at the time. On February 14, 2016, two years since my breakup with Harry (and an extra seven days thrown in for good measure), I waited for an earth-shattering experience.

This is it, I thought. I was ready for something to happen. The first day of the rest of my life would be Valentine's Day.

Nothing happened—except for the realization it was apparently going to be up to me to change.

I met Brad in Alaska on a ski trip that spring. Brad and I had a brief romantic encounter but nothing more than a passing kiss. He was flirtatious in a boyish kind of way. Brad was thirty-nine, I was now fifty-six. Greg, Harry, Philip, and now Brad. This was becoming a pattern. I did like younger men, but they were chasing me just as much as I was chasing them, and sometimes more in the beginning.

That summer, Brad came to Lake Tahoe during our annual family vacation. Brad and I had an amazing romantic few days in Tahoe hiking, biking, golfing, and waterskiing. He was cute and fun, and I loved being with him.

As usual, from the time I realized I liked him, I was already mentally plotting out how we could spend more time together. While he was still in Tahoe, I asked Brad if he wanted to come with me to Dana Point, California. I had won a golf weekend earlier in the year, and I wanted him to join me.

His response:

"Suzanne, I really like you, but I want to find someone to marry, have babies with, and build a life. I need to find someone my own age."

Although I had only spent a little bit of time with Brad, my heart was broken. I cried for days. I liked him, and I didn't want him to say those things to me.

After the tears dried up, I let go of my hurt feelings and moved on. *No big deal; men are a dime a dozen*, I thought to myself.

A year later, I still had no one to go with me to Dana Point.

How hard can it be to find someone to join me on a free golf vacation? Yet I didn't want to go with just anybody.

I only had one room, which meant sharing the room—and the bed.

Just before the deal expired, I was telling my son, Derek, about the trip, and he adamantly said, "Mom, I would love to go with you. That sounds amazing."

I was so excited. Derek and I get along really well—especially when golf is involved. It was set. Derek would come with me. It was going to be great.

Once again, "coincidentally," after I had committed to my son, Brad texted me. We had had limited communication since the summer, but this text felt different. It felt more connected. He seemed to have come around.

I mentioned casually that I was going to Dana Point.

"Oh," he stammered, "I thought you had probably already gone."

"No, I couldn't find anyone to go with me," I said.

I baited him for sure. I wanted to see what he would say. I didn't tell him I was taking Derek.

"Well, I told you," Brad said, "I would go with you. I just figured you had found someone else."

My recollection was that he had turned me down quite clearly in Lake Tahoe. I didn't believe he had really forgotten he had turned me down, but I didn't care. I was excited because it seemed like he wanted to go. I felt like I had won a prize. My son graciously backed out, and I decided to take Brad, even though my inner voice was shouting at me to take my son.

Red Flag #1.

I finally got up the nerve to phone Brad a week before our trip and tell him I was feeling uncomfortable. We went back and forth, neither of us really telling the truth, and in the end we decided to go together— me knowing it was the wrong decision in my gut. The good news was at least I had an inner voice—which I almost listened to.

The Friday I left Aspen to fly to Southern California, my plane was late. I didn't know if I was going to make my connection. I called Brad and told him the situation. He wasn't concerned and told me he would pick me up whenever I arrived, which I thought was an appropriate gesture, considering I was treating him. As my departure time continued to get pushed back, I realized I was probably not going to make it that evening. I called Brad again and told him.

"Hi," I said in a friendly tone. "It's not looking very good for me getting there tonight."

"No worries," Brad said. "Do you think it's okay if I stay in the room without you?"

"Of course. Let me call the front desk and arrange it."

I called him back and told him it was all set. He would have to put down a credit card to get into the room for incidentals, but I would put mine down when I got there. He agreed to put down his credit card but was a bit taken aback by the suggestion.

Red Flag #2.

In the end, I sprinted for the plane in Denver and somehow made my flight. I texted and called Brad with yet another change of plans. When I did finally get a hold of him, he told me he had made other plans and he would meet me after his dinner. I was hoping he would volunteer to give up his plans and pick me up—or invite me to join him wherever he was going—but I'd told him I wasn't coming, so I felt like the whole thing was my fault. I was crushed, but instead of being honest, I told him it was okay.

In other words, I lied.

In the end, the night went fine. He pulled through and showed up, and we had a lovely evening at the hotel bar. I was feeling good again, and we headed out for a fun day on the course early the next morning.

The room was free, but the golf was not. I never told Brad golf was not included. I was going to pick up the tab—without saying anything—just like I had done so many times before. I wanted him to come and was afraid he wouldn't if he thought he had to pay. I knew he didn't have a lot of money. I also knew he often relied on others to pay his way.

In other words, I was buying his affection with a trip. Of course, Brad didn't know any of this, and as far as he knew, it was a free weekend for him.

Oh Lord, I thought, *I've done it again*.

During the course of the weekend, we wined and dined. Everything went on the room charge—food, drinks, golf balls, gloves, and golf carts on top of the green fees. Brad took me out to dinner one night, but at the end of the weekend, I was stuck with an enormous bill. What did I expect? I never asked him to pitch in.

Had I learned *nothing* from all my previous mistakes?

I went home disappointed—with a big credit card bill to remind me of my behavior.

Brad and I never really spoke again.

More tears flowed.

When were the tears going to stop?

How many lessons did I need to learn?

How many times would I *expect* something in return?

I was so sad about Brad. I swore to myself this would never happen again. *Never!*

I was on a ten-day trip to Europe. I had some work to do during the week, but my weekend was free, and I accepted an invitation to the men's Alpine World Cup in Wengen, Switzerland.

The evening I arrived at my hotel, my friend, who was a ski coach for the Canadian team, was nowhere to be found. Someone told me they thought he was sick, so with nothing else to do, I headed to the hotel bar.

I was sitting by myself having a glass of wine when a man looked at me from across the bar and said: "Trouble, is that you?"

I recognized him immediately. I had met Christian skiing in Chile the summer before, and we had hit it off. Over the course of that week together, he had given me the nickname Trouble. At the time, he was a coach for the Austrian ski team, and I honestly never thought I would see him again, but he was now coaching for the Canadian team, so he was also staying at the team hotel.

Christian is a rugged, conservative, fifty-year-old Austrian male. His colleagues and team sometimes viewed him as crabby, but I enjoyed his truthful, snappy attitude.

After some pleasant banter, Christian asked me in his thick Austrian accent, "So, are you still writing that book of yours?"

"Yes, of course I am," I replied, smiling. "And I am even going to finish it one of these days."

We began talking about my book and the roles of women and men in the workplace—and ski coaches in particular. Christian had told me his opinion in Chile and reminded me of it again that night. He saw no reason for any of us to try to fix what he did not consider broken. He 100 percent believed the roles of men and women will *never* change.

"We have our roles for a reason, and women—and men—should just accept reality," he said bluntly.

"In the world of ski coaching, at the top level, there are few women coaches—not even for the women racers," he added, apparently believing this made his point.

I try not to argue or disagree with anyone regarding women, men, relationships, money or work. I know what I think. I want to know what others think.

My question to Christian that night was, "Why? Why are there so few women coaches? There are definitely women out there just as capable as their male counterparts," I said. "Maybe they don't apply?"

"Maybe they don't exist," replied Christian, jokingly.

At first I dismissed Christian's perspective, as a traditional male with outdated beliefs, but then I began to wonder why we want to change things so much.

What if things never change?

I didn't have an answer as to whether society would ever change, but even if everything stayed the same, I still felt *I* wanted to continue to work on myself so *I* could feel good. Not for anyone else's sake, but for my own.

CHAPTER 12

She Who Makes the Gold Doesn't Always Make the Rules

Why not go out on a limb?
Isn't that where the fruit is?

—FRANK SCULLY

Some authors believe it is best not to talk about your book until you have at least a first draft, but in line with my overly outgoing personality, I took completely the opposite approach.

As soon as someone asked me what I was up to—wherever I was in the world, I boldly told them, "I'm researching the topic of women, money, relationships, and sex." I threw in sex to get their attention—then I just sat back and listened. Almost everyone had a story to tell.

In July 2014, my friend Beth, who worked at the Aspen Institute, suggested I attend the Aspen Action Forum later that month.

I learned from Beth that the Action Forum was a three-day, invitation-only event for 350 people from around the world who come together annually to discuss social issues and ideas on how to improve some of our major global challenges.

"I think you should go," she said.

I didn't hesitate for a second and accepted her generous offer.

I was quickly aware after the first morning's event that I was in the company of some extremely smart individuals. I was excited to be there but intimidated by my colleague's collective accomplishments. All the people invited to the Forum were dedicated, disciplined agents of global change.

What could I possibly contribute? Feeding a million school children in a year or creating a distribution plan for delivering medical supplies to populations dying from dysentery around the world seemed more pressing than unraveling the issues of female breadwinners—or so I thought at the time.

Out of the fifty or so sessions offered that year, only two seemed to address the issue of women and money.

The following year I returned to the Action Forum. I was still nervous about discussing my topic openly. I felt I would be judged as a rich girl with rich-girl problems. Nevertheless, during one hour-long session, I got the courage to share my experience with the group. After the session was over, I was shocked at the feedback I started getting from others. Out of twenty people in the room, a line of ten women from all over the world formed in front of me, including Pat, a Black woman from Canada who is highly successful in her career.

Pat looked at me with sadness in her eyes and said, "I have so many friends who are in this situation—including myself—and we don't know how to handle it. Many of us are the breadwinners, and we don't have the skills or information to know how to make our marriages work.

"Myself, and many of my friends, really need some guidance on how to talk to our husbands about finances. Please finish your book."

During my third year at the Action Forum, I attended a session called Network Interviewing. I didn't really know what network interviewing was going to teach me, but the title caught my attention. The facilitator informed us that the goal of the session was to spend two minutes introducing ourselves to a partner, and after two minutes our partner would give us feedback on what we said. We would each get a chance to spend four minutes total with all thirty people in the session. It was speed dating for business—an elevator pitch of sorts.

Halfway through the session, I sat across from Nigel. Nigel was a schoolteacher in Nigeria committed to making a difference in young people's lives. He was a large, kind man with a big heart. When it came time for my two-minute pitch, I told him about my topic and how I was interested in exploring issues women face when they are wealthier financially than their partner.

During my two minutes of feedback, Nigel looked at me and said sadly, "That is the reason my parents divorced when I was three.

"My mother came from a wealthier class, and my father was a scholar. My father was very smart, but he was *not* from a wealthy class. At least not wealthy enough, I suppose.

"My parents fell in love and married," he continued. "My mother's parents were extremely upset with her choice to marry my father. She did it anyway. She truly loved him, but the pressure from their families was over time too much for them to bear, and she eventually left him."

"I never saw my father again," Nigel said, now with tears in his eyes.

Nigel was a forty-year-old Ugandan male who was still carrying the pain of his parents' separation due to money. Because his mother was born into a higher class and had more money, it was not okay for her to love a poor scholar.

At that moment, Nigel's experience convinced me again I had to keep sharing my story. I wish he knew he is now a part of it.

My babysitter Rachel's story had shown me that the complex relationship between love and money wasn't just an issue for wealthy women. Now Nigel's story showed me this struggle wasn't just a problem for the Western world. It crossed global borders as well.

I was continuing to visit Africa, sometimes more than twice a year. I have traveled to Africa eighteen times in ten years, and I have visited seventeen of the fifty-four countries. Africa is the second largest land mass in the world with over 1.2 billion people. Clearly, I have only scratched the surface of this vast continent, but I have had many different experiences from rural villages to large cities, which allowed me to engage with a wide variety of people.

On one particular trip, I was on my way to Uganda via France to do some volunteer work. I arranged for a car to take me to the airport in France. My French is passable but not fluent by any means, but as I got in the car with my French female driver, I struck up a conversation. After some pleasantries, I shared with Julie that I was researching female breadwinners and their challenges in intimate relationships.

Even though I couldn't see Julie's face except in the rearview mirror, I could see her head nodding. She understood what I was saying perfectly. She too made a good living and found herself in a relationship where she was outearning her partner. She shared with me that she kept finding herself choosing men who were not financially successful. She was frustrated and expressed her unhappiness with herself for not knowing how to make a relationship with a man work.

What I heard during our forty-minute car ride was that her struggles were the same as mine and the same as so many women I had spoken to in the United States. When we arrived at the airport, I hugged Julie goodbye. We exchanged information and I promised to keep in touch. It was an auspicious beginning to my five-week journey through Africa.

I went to Uganda to attend a music concert with the Global Livingston Institute (GLI), a not-for-profit organization based out of Denver, CO. The iKnow concert series was designed to promote awareness of HIV and encourage Ugandans to know their status. Uganda has a population of 47 million people living in a country smaller than the state of Oregon. Seventy-five percent of those 47 million are under the age of twenty-five and sexually active, so knowing your HIV status is extremely important.

On our way to one of our concert stops, fifty of us—men and women—were packed like sardines in a bus designed to hold twenty-five.

As we got on the bus, a beautiful Ugandan woman named Penny said to me, "Suzanne, will you come sit with me? I would like your company."

Penny was one of the artists performing at our five-concert series that year. Despite having just met Penny days before and not knowing much about her, I responded, "Of course. I would love to sit with you."

Penny and I had plenty of time to get to know each other. We were traveling in the back of the crowded bus for the next seven hours on a bumpy ride to Northern Uganda.

Penny was twenty-four then, and a well-known performer. She was, and still is, a beautiful, talented model, singer, and songwriter. It didn't take me long to see Penny was not only talented, she was also genuinely kind.

After an hour or so of getting to know each other, Penny shared with me her desire to make a difference in the lives of young women in Uganda through her music. Through her phone, we listened to the new song she had written and performed. It was about fighting for what you want in a gentle but determined manner, no matter what it took.

"Wow, what a beautiful song," I told her. "You are amazing."

"May I share some things with you?" Penny asked hesitantly.

"Of course."

"I look like I have it all together," Penny said. "Everyone wants to be a rock star, but they don't realize how hard it is."

She turned toward me. "I am lonely, Suzanne. I cannot find a man to be with. Money and fame create problems in a relationship. I am a successful artist, and I can't find anyone who doesn't want to take advantage of me. I want someone to be here unconditionally."

I was moved by her honesty, and although I completely understood and could relate to what she was sharing, I was shocked to hear someone of her talent expressing the same concerns I often felt.

Penny and I were about as different as we could be. She was a young, famous, Black Ugandan singer/model, and I was a fifty-six-year-old white woman from Aspen, Colorado. On paper we didn't have a lot in common, but here we were, in the back of the crowded bus, sharing our most intimate secrets about how we wanted to feel loved for who we were and not what we had.

Penny lived a life most would envy. She sang to thousands of fans. People wanted her autograph. She had what appeared to be a glamorous life. But Penny had troubles just like everyone else.

Throughout my travels in Africa, I heard story after story of the struggles and occasional successes both women and men were having living in a world where the rules about breadwinners were changing.

Although women in Africa have safety challenges many of us in the Western world do not face, I realized our core issues are the same.

From Africa to France to North America and beyond, we share similar fears of standing up for ourselves, taking precious time to take care of ourselves, and ultimately standing in our authentic power.

After seeing how widespread this issue was globally, I couldn't help but wonder if the younger generation was any better than my generation at negotiating this dynamic of women outearning men. While visiting my son Carson who was studying abroad in Cuba, I had the opportunity to spend some quality time with some of the twenty-plus girls in the program. Ninety percent of them were from Brown University. Needless to say, they were smart, accomplished, young women fluent in Spanish and studying subjects like astrophysics at the University of Havana.

As young people studying together in a foreign country, they were a tight-knit group. Carson had told the girls a bit about my book subject before my visit. When I arrived in Cuba, several of these young women approached me to share their thoughts on the subject of women's empowerment. We had several lively group discussions, and I had the opportunity to explore with them both the pros—and cons—of being smart, successful, empowered young women.

I left Cuba with several impressions. First, these young women's parents had clearly encouraged them to be the best they could be. This did not surprise me. I have heard many parents—especially fathers—sing the praises of their daughter's accomplishments, future goals, and possible lofty financial success. Second, the young women appreciated their parents' praise and support.

Third—and most significant for me—the real concern these girls had was not about their success in the workplace, but their success in relationships with young men.

"We don't know how to be successful and have boyfriends at the same time. It's complicated, and we are just as confused as you are," one of the girls said to me.

Another said, "My boyfriend says, 'I think it would be great if you make all the money, babe. That means I get to sit at home and hang out.'"

It wasn't the first time I had heard this from a young man.

I don't blame them for thinking like this. Until you are in a committed, long-term relationship or marriage, it is difficult to understand the challenges. It would be like me telling you I know everything about being a professional athlete. How could I? I have known many professional athletes, but I haven't been one—at least not yet.

Here was my question: what will that girl's father think when she is making six figures and brings home a man who announces he is going to be a stay-at-home dad? I don't think most fathers—or mothers— have considered how this news would impact them, even though that choice is a fine one. As admirable as it is for us as parents to encourage our daughters to be successful in the workplace, few of us have been taught how to negotiate a marriage based on *traditional* roles, much less how to navigate the new direction our global society is taking, and what it means when roles are reversed.

We assume they will figure out how to balance their careers and future relationships, but how can we assume that when we're just learning how to ourselves?

One evening, at an event for the U.S. Ski and Snowboard Team, I was talking with a woman in her mid-twenties named Emma. Emma was an excellent ski racer and one of the up-and-coming females on the U.S. team. I was sharing with her my research topic and ended up telling her the story of purposely losing the tennis match with Dave because I was afraid of being better than him.

She looked at me and said with a knowing grin, "I can relate to that one. What do you think it is like to be a better ski racer than your boyfriend?"

She added seriously, "It's not easy when I outperform him. "He sometimes doesn't take it so well."

Shortly afterwards, I shared Emma's story with my friend Aimee.

"Oh, *that* sounds familiar," Aimee chimed in. "What do you think it is like to be *smarter* than your husband? He is bright, but we often argue because he thinks he's not as smart and he doesn't like it. It's hard for me to pretend I'm not smarter, but I have to, so he feels good about himself.

"Neither of us like this dynamic. We have a hard time, and we fight a lot about all kinds of issues."

Keep in mind these stories were told to me *without* both partners present, so they are possibly slanted, but these women arguably are capable and exemplify the struggles women have with success. In order to have a successful relationship, many women—including myself—feel like we have to dumb ourselves down, defend ourselves, or leave.

I sat next to Anne one night at dinner. Anne's job was choosing topics for TED Talks. I knew this and took the opportunity to express that I would like to do a TED Talk. I enthusiastically explained why my writings and discoveries about women, money, and relationships would make an ideal TED topic.

Anne looked at me. "Well, I get approached every day by people who want to do a TED Talk, but you have to have a solution to even begin to get my attention."

And even though at the time she was right, that didn't stop me. I tried a few more times with no better luck, so I went back to the dinner conversation *not* giving up but temporarily putting the idea on hold. Oddly enough, Anne kept bringing the subject back up. She seemed to be probing me for information.

I was confused by her interrogating manner until our final moments at the table.

"I'm going through a divorce," Anne finally said.

"I'm not in love with my husband anymore. He is a writer and doesn't seem to be writing anything." Her tone expressed disappointment, anger, and sadness.

"He hasn't written a book in years. He is lazy and doesn't contribute financially to our relationship. I am the breadwinner, and I'm sick of it."

I went home that night realizing that even though I didn't ultimately know where my journey was going to lead me, I did know I had something to say. And that those who openly resisted the topic, like Anne, might be experiencing it firsthand.

At another charity event in Aspen, I was talking with a woman I barely knew about my book topic of women, money, and relationships. She immediately introduced me to Ross and suggested the two of us find some time during the evening to speak. I was flattered and curious about the introduction.

Ross was a banker in Denver, and since the bank he worked for was the title sponsor of the event, he was in town to participate in the weekend-long activities as a representative. Ross's job—I found out quickly—was private wealth management. As we were speaking, Ross seemed quite interested in what I was working on and immediately asked me for my business card.

"Many of my clients are wealthy women," Ross said to me. "I think they might be *very* interested in a book like yours."

"I have one client in particular who could benefit from reading your book. She *really* needs it."

I was intrigued by his comment. As we continued to speak, he shared he had dated this woman prior to her being a client and that he knew how much she struggled with finances and dating. He also made it clear he was no longer dating her.

I asked him gently, "Did your breakup have anything to do with money?"

"Well," he said with a big smile, "she is quite a bit wealthier than I am, but money had *nothing* to do with our breakup. I'm just concerned with her welfare and know it would be a helpful book for her to read."

I was honored Ross felt—after our twenty-minute conversation at a cocktail party—what I was writing about would be helpful to his ex-girlfriend and current client. Intuitively, I thought there was more to the story.

As I probed a bit deeper, I found out (as I often do) that their breakup was, in fact, a result of money. Throughout their one-and-a-half-year relationship, Barbara was, as so many of us are, a giver. Because she liked Ross, she wanted to do things with him. Barbara took care of him financially so they could enjoy their time together and live the lifestyle *she* was accustomed to.

So she paid his way.

This went well for a time until Barbara started to feel resentful. Over time, Barbara had more and more difficulty accepting she had to pay and was angry at Ross for not contributing more. In the end, this dynamic is what broke them up.

Toward the end of our conversation, I saw Ross's wheels turning. He said to me, "I never quite thought about it this way. I thought it was strange. I didn't understand what was happening."

Personally—after living through several similar situations—I didn't think it was strange at all.

I found myself in an isolated community at the top of the Simien Mountains in Ethiopia with another not-for-profit organization, Empowers Africa. We were there to help a school get funding for books and computers for their students.

As it is about a three-hour bumpy car ride from anywhere over potholed roads, we stayed a few nights in the only small local hotel. After a long day, guests gathered around the outdoor fireplace in the middle of our rustic accommodations.

Andreas and Camilla were from Norway and traveling in this remote part of Ethiopia doing some work for their charity. As my group was also there doing charity work, we had a lot to talk about. Eventually the fact that I was writing a book came up, and they were clearly excited to share their story with me.

Andreas had left his job two years earlier to start a foundation to support young girls in Northern Ethiopia. His new life included building their foundation and staying home full-time with their two young children.

"My career is blossoming. Two years ago, I was climbing the corporate ladder and my salary was much higher than Andreas's," Camilla said with Andreas by her side.

"Together, we made a choice that it would be in our best interest for Andreas to stay home and for me to earn the money."

"We feel quite sure of our decision," Andreas chimed in. "We love each other very much and both think this is the best choice for our family. We want our children to have a parent at home, and because Camilla's income is so much higher than mine, I am all for her working and me staying home."

"And," he continued, "because I stay at home, I have time to work on building our foundation while our girls are in school."

I was impressed with them both and delighted to hear of their success. They were genuinely pleased with their choice. Both Andreas and Camilla accepted and respected their own role in the family—and each other's. They found this new style of family to be a perfect fit for their lifestyle.

And then came the challenge. Society.

"Our problem is not our choice to live differently than most of our friends," Camilla said. "Our problem is what people think of our choice."

She continued, "My challenge is at my job. I am doing so well at work. I find myself in a position just below the CEO and vice-president of the company. I am happy with my success, but I want to be the CEO," she stated with determination.

Camilla recounted her CEO's comment to her after she shared her goal with him one day.

"I know you want to continue to rise in your career, but don't you think you should be happy with your current level of success?" he said to her, laughing, as he patted her on the shoulder in a friendly but condescending way.

"Why, as a woman, would you ever want to be in any position higher than you are right now?"

Camilla was dumbfounded. Why would she *not* want to continue to reach for the top?

"How do you think it feels to be excluded from the mommies in the park because you are not one of them?" Andreas added. "I try to fit in, but they won't talk to me. They wonder why I am not working."

His comment took me back to when I was raising my children in New York City and spending many days in the park while Mark was working. On the few occasions I would see a father in the park with his children on a weekday, I would silently wonder what was wrong with him.

Unless it is Mother's Day, and he's giving his wife a break so she can take a nap, get her nails done, or just have some free time, what kind of a man would be in the park on a weekday?

Doesn't he have a job?

I'm sure I was not the only person having this silent conversation.

I wondered what happened when someone like Camilla takes Andreas to the company Christmas party. Was their choice to live outside of the bell curve really accepted by others?

Andreas and Camilla—although bothered by what others thought of them—were brave. They didn't want to live by what society thought they *should* be doing. They were doing what worked best for them and didn't buckle under the pressure of society.

But at what cost?

Overall, I discovered this problem with love and money crossed more lines than I would have guessed. It wasn't just an Aspen problem, a wealthy woman's problem, a Western problem, an older woman's problem, or even a money problem. Relationships tend to suffer whenever a woman is visibly outperforming a man. Whenever women are on top.

The question becomes: *now what?*

When I talked to men about my book topic and they didn't understand why I was writing a book for women, instead of feeling nervous and uncomfortable, I would tell them this story.

"Do you remember when you first met your girlfriend or wife?" I would say. "She was a woman who knew who she was and what she wanted. That's why you liked her.

"And then you fell in love, and she moved in, and life got more comfortable. She would rest her head on your shoulder as you lay on the couch together and say, 'What do you want to do tomorrow? Where do you want to go?' with those ogling eyes staring at you like she had no opinion anymore, only wanting to please you.

"All of a sudden, you were the center of her world. She sat around waiting, longing for your call—and God forbid you didn't call her."

By this time, I have their attention and I know they can relate to what I am saying. Even if this dynamic was *not* true in their current relationship, nearly every man I have met finds this experience familiar.

I go on. "She would pick up your underwear off the bathroom floor every day without a word, or always agree to go for a hike (or whatever you wanted to do) whenever you asked. She just did it—and of course you let her—because she didn't seem to mind. Or maybe you even thought she liked picking up your underwear or going hiking."

"Then one day, she screams, 'Ryan (I would typically insert the name of the man I was talking to), I just don't understand, why don't you ever pick up your underwear?' Or 'Why do we always have to go hiking? Why can't we ever play tennis? You know I love playing tennis.' And she storms out of the room, leaving you dumbfounded."

"You chase after her and say stuttering, 'But Sarah, I, I, I didn't know it bothered you that I didn't pick up my underwear. I would've if you had asked. I thought you didn't mind.'

"Or 'Rebecca, I thought you liked hiking. Why didn't you ever ask if we can play tennis? I mean we both have tennis rackets and there is a court down the street.'"

"Your girlfriend or wife turns to you with anger, tears, or both, and says, 'If you really loved me, you would know these things. I can't believe you don't know I don't love hiking all the time. I like to play tennis, but I was waiting for you to ask me. It doesn't count when I have to ask you!' she says, choking back the tears."

Not all men can relate, but the majority have experienced a scenario similar to this one. They usually chuckle and nod their head.

Then I say to these men, "If I can encourage your woman to say what she *really* means and wants from the beginning, it's going to make your life a lot easier. If she can learn to do what men do naturally—speak their mind, nap when they feel like it, or eat when they are hungry—couples will be able to build a more solid foundation created on mutual respect and admiration rather than on smoke and mirrors.

"Wouldn't it be easier for everyone if we women told you how we felt right from the beginning, rather than do what we often do—give, give, give and then shout 'fuck you' when we get sick of giving too much, and expecting something you are not even clear on in return?

"This is why I am writing my story."

CHAPTER 13

Old Dogs Can Learn New Tricks

As long as the candle burns, there
is time to make repairs.

—RABBI SALANTER

Although I found few women who had mastered this problem of having more money than their male partners, I did have several acquaintances in Aspen who seemed to have the inner peace I was yearning for. I admired their calmness, kindness, and integrity. Somehow, one day I figured out they were all graduates of a program I had never heard of called Spiritual Psychology at the University of Santa Monica (USM) in Southern California.

As it turns out, my coach Sam was also a graduate. I had been meeting with him bi-monthly for almost two years, and I had only now realized it. I had no idea what spiritual psychology really meant, but I intuitively knew this program was my next step. Just like in the movie *When Harry Met Sally*, I wanted what they had.

I hadn't been looking for a graduate program to attend—especially not one in Santa Monica, California, but this time I did not procrastinate. I completed the comprehensive application within two days.

Just weeks after I submitted my application, the University suddenly announced they no longer wanted to continue to comply with the State of California's licensing requirements. USM decided the state requirements no longer allowed the University to offer a program in a way they felt was most valuable to their students, and so they chose to give up their status as an accredited university.

I was devastated.

I'm not going to attend a three-year graduate program and only receive a certificate of completion, I thought.

I already had my master's degree pulled out from under me almost twenty-five years earlier when I moved to New York City, and it felt like the same kind of thing was happening again.

I had to honestly ask myself, *Was it the experience I wanted, or the degree?*

As I considered this question, I began to see my life as guided by a higher source. How did I happen to have Jerry Jampolsky as my family psychiatrist when I was twelve? And why did I eventually follow in my mother's footsteps and become so involved with the Center for Attitudinal Healing? Because of those experiences, I had left my career in Landscape Architecture to get a master's degree in Marriage and Family Counseling.

After we moved to New York, and I couldn't use my degree, I often wondered what had been the point of earning my first master's? Apparently, it was so I could enter USM and not worry about receiving a traditional degree. I already had one.

After much thought, I realized I wanted the experience even without the degree.

Little did I know, this decision would change my life forever in ways I could never have dreamed possible. Many students attend USM to become coaches for others, but for me, the journey became intensely personal.

My first year of the program started a few months later in Santa Monica, with over two hundred students learning as a group for one intensive three-day weekend a month. We began by learning basic skills: "soul-centered skills," as the University called them—like how to be heart-felt listeners, how to see the loving essence in others, and how to ask open-ended questions. We practiced using tools for co-creating our life with our intuitive, wise Self to find new freedoms and joys in life.

The days were long and packed full of information. During our monthly three-day weekends, we would break into groups of three several times each day and then come back together as a big group to share our learnings.

Ron and Mary Hulnick, co-directors of the University, provided wisdom and knowledge from their over forty years of teaching at the University and many years before earning their PhDs, maintaining private practices, and co-authoring two books. They were teachers I could only have fantasized about working with before I came to the University.

I went to school with two goals in mind. First, I was going to listen more and talk less. If you ask my kids—or anyone else in my life—they will tell you I talk way too much, so this was a big goal for me. As my daughter Alexandra often tells me with a big smile, "Two ears, one mouth. Listen twice as much as you talk. Take note, Mom."

Second, I was *never* going to cry. I didn't mean crying after a sad event; or a tear-jerking movie. I meant crying intentionally to protect myself. I had used tears so many times to protect myself from others' anger (including my father's), or to condemn myself before others could, that I made a commitment *not* to cry in these situations so I could experience feeling vulnerable.

Both were solid goals—and I met neither of them.

Each month, we received a suggested reading list. From our first list, the book I chose to read was *The Life-Changing Magic of Tidying Up* by Marie Kondo. I have always been what I refer to as someone who likes to clean and putter, and I had already made some headway in clearing clutter with Sam, but Marie Kondo took organizing to a whole new level.

I began to look at why I created the busyness and clutter in the first place. Best as I can figure, it allowed me to hide from my thoughts, emotions, and feelings. Clearing my outer clutter helped me clear my inner clutter. I began to get rid of all those things I thought I would need someday—like the twin bed sheets, even though we didn't have twin beds anymore; the coat with the broken zipper that I was *definitely* going to get fixed someday; and all those gifts from loved ones I was never going to use. Who really needs an indoor s'more maker? I finally decided I did not. It is the thought that counts, *not* the gift itself.

Within months of discovering *The Life-Changing Magic of Tidying Up*, I started renting my house on a short-term basis to put my assets to work and make some money—which turned out to be another important step toward my empowerment. I cleaned out every drawer in our house in preparation for my first rental. It took me weeks.

My youngest son, Derek, asked me one day as I was tidying up the linen closet, "Mom, if we have all these drawers, why aren't we allowed to put anything in them?"

"You can put whatever you want in them," I said, turning to Derek, "as long as what you keep sparks joy."

"Sparks joy?" he said quizzically.

"Yes, sparks joy."

He wandered out of the room shaking his head, surely thinking his mother had lost her mind.

Since that time in October 2015, I have been working on becoming a minimalist. I have cleared more clutter than you can possibly imagine. Marie Kondo applies the concept of "spark joy" to clothes, books, gizmos, papers—and the most challenging for many of us—photos. I applied it to every aspect of my life as time went on (except the photos, which still seem to be on my "to-do list"). I not only cleaned out things, I cleaned out (and up) situations, events, people, thoughts, and attitudes—anything and everything that did not spark joy or restricted me in some way.

I also discovered that clearing clutter is a lifelong journey. You don't just unclutter once. I am positive I will be tidying up until I am six feet under, and then maybe there as well.

Over time and through the process, I was showing up in a new way. People—friends and strangers— started treating me differently. I felt different. I felt more empowered. I had a smile on my face more often. I focused less on what wasn't going right and more on what I wanted to accomplish. I felt more inspired than in the past. I still had things I didn't feel like doing, but I saw a glimpse of light at the end of the tunnel.

———————————————

When I began my studies at USM, I believed what most of us were taught: Our beliefs and behaviors take years and possibly generations to change.

I have often said, mostly to men, "We [women] act the way we do not because of the *jeans* we are wearing but because of our *genes*.

"And guess what, you can't live with us, you can't live without us, and you can't shoot us."

I would say this in a joking manner typically to explain women's habits of thinking too much, overreacting, and taking things personally. I believed we tended to share these habits due to our genetic makeup coupled with our observations of other women—until I read *You Are the Placebo: Making Your Mind Matter* by Dr. Joe Dispenza from our second month's reading list. According to Dispenza, we can shift our thoughts at any time, change our behavior, and even modify our DNA much more quickly than we used to believe.

Dr. Dispenza's research shows that as we use our brains, they grow and change, thanks to *neuroplasticity*—the brain's ability to adapt and change when we learn new information.

Neuroplasticity is an idea that has been around for years, but it didn't become popular until the early 1950s (depending on what research site you use) and wasn't widely accepted as plausible until more recently.

Neuroplasticity suggests old dogs can learn new tricks. Just because something is in our DNA and/or how we were raised no longer means we have to stay that way.

This was new information for me and honestly gave me hope that, with practice, I could find new ways of behaving in my relationships. I no longer felt trapped by my jeans *or* my genes. According to Joe Dispenza and the study of neuroplasticity, we can rewire our brains, and as a result make more conscious choices. In fact, we can begin to rewire our brain by doing simple things such as brushing our teeth with the hand we don't normally brush with or putting the opposite pant leg on first.

Now I had some scientific proof that what Christian said that night in the hotel bar in Switzerland wasn't necessarily true.

Things *can* change. It just takes work.

For me, the idea of rewiring the brain successfully required an understanding of how our brain was wired in the first place, from both our genetic makeup and what we learn from our families, peers, communities, and more recently the media. I realized that before I could make a lasting change, I had to first understand my own wiring and my own beliefs—what I wanted to keep *and* what I wanted to discard.

As I looked at my own upbringing, I realized I mirrored what I saw in my parents—the good and the bad. The apple hadn't fallen far from the tree—but I was also *a chip off the old block*, an idiom typically used to describe children who exhibited the positive attributes of their parents. So, I took a good look at my apple tree (or my block, as the case may be).

On one hand, I was definitely like my parents in some ways. I grew up with a father who had a strong work ethic and a mother who was generous with her money. I have a strong work ethic and am also generous with others. Also, like my father and my mother, it was a challenge for me to separate love and money, and I had trouble managing intimate relationships and monetary success.

On the other hand, I was also trying to roll as far away from my apple tree as I could. Once again, I heard my father's voice in my head saying not to marry a man with less than five million dollars in his bank account. I often jokingly say I must have misunderstood him and thought he said, *Don't marry a man with anything more than $500 in his bank account.* The truth is, I knew exactly what my father was saying. My rebellion was in reaction to my apple tree.

The question was, did my 180-degree behavior serve me anymore? Did I truly want to date men who had $500 or less in their bank account, or was I still reacting out of rebellion?

Neuroplasticity proved to me I had a choice and no longer *had* to act in response to—or rebel against—the messages I received from my parents regarding money, relationships, or any other area of my life. This new information began to set me free and allowed me to take more responsibility for myself and my beliefs.

At the same time, sometimes we choose *not* to change because we feel more comfortable doing what is familiar—whether it still works for us or not.

A practical example is the way we celebrate holidays. Many of us celebrate the way our families did. We safeguard traditions and teach them to our children. We serve creamed onions on Thanksgiving—or some other favorite food made from the family recipe box—because we grew up having creamed onions *every* Thanksgiving. We serve them long after we move out of the house due to our sentimental attachment to our family tradition.

But sometimes our tastes change. Maybe we don't like creamed onions anymore, even though we have been eating and serving them every year as far back as we can remember. My suggestion is if we like them, keep them; but if they no longer spark joy, we can consider serving a different kind of onion—or maybe really go out on a limb and serve a different kind of vegetable. Not in a rebellious, 180-degree kind of way, but because we have put thought into what works for us and what doesn't. Thanks to neuroplasticity, I was beginning to see how this was possible.

In addition to *The Life-Changing Magic of Tidying Up* and *You Are the Placebo*, I also loved reading Louise Hay's book, *You Can Heal Your Life*. She writes about the power of affirmations, how to heal your body and your mind, and become more aware of how we talk to ourselves—and the world. I learned I could make enormous mental shifts by watching what I say.

Rather than saying, "I'm never going to find the man of my dreams," I could change my language to "I'm working toward becoming my best self and attracting the right partner." This simple change in wording dramatically altered how I saw the world, and how the world saw me.

In addition to learning from the books on our reading lists, I also learned many different daily practices, such as meditation, prayer, and free-form writing, where I would write whatever came to me. I would fill up a lined 8x10-inch piece of paper on both sides, and when I was finished, I ripped up the paper into tiny pieces and threw it away. The original instruction was to burn the paper to let all my thoughts go, but after setting off smoke alarms in several hotel rooms, I opted for the garbage can.

Some areas of my life were changing for the better, but many were not. I fully participated in my monthly classes at USM and then went home and back to my life as I knew it. I was still going out every night and/or traveling around the world and keeping myself way too busy.

I didn't want to sit quietly with myself.

The idea of sitting quietly scared me.

Loneliness scared me.

It's not to say that spiritual transformation and personal growth *require* one to sit still, but sitting quietly was so foreign to me. Keeping busy felt familiar. I still believed that if I didn't keep busy, something terrible might happen.

Even though I was attending school and participating in the program, I was *not* fully finding that inner peace I professed to want so badly.

CHAPTER 14

Hire Slowly, Fire Quickly

Busyness is not a reason for not getting other things
done. It is an excuse for not claiming your true priorities.

–ALAN COHEN

I completed my third year with Sam just before entering USM, and at
that point I knew it was time to move on. My plan was to take a break
from coaching, but toward the end of 2016, I met my next angel. Sam
had helped me clean up some projects and move forward with my life,
and I wouldn't have been ready for Catherine without working with
Sam. Catherine was a life and relationship coach. As soon as we met, I
knew I was where I was supposed to be.

After just two weeks into our coaching, Catherine and I took a trip
to Hawaii to begin working on my relationship issues one by one, like
peeling an onion.

As we were standing at the front desk to check into our hotel,
Catherine pleasantly said to the man checking us in, "Can you send
room service to my room immediately? I would like six bottles of water,

and can you have them open two of the bottles completely and the other four slightly so I can get into them easily, please?

"Sometimes I have a hard time opening them," she explained, laughing a bit.

"And can you also have someone take off the top sheet on the bed and remake it? The top sheet gets in my way when I am sleeping."

"Of course, ma'am, I will send someone right away."

I didn't say anything.

I occasionally asked for some kind of help, but I had never seen anything like this. Needless to say, it was far from how I operated in life. I didn't know Catherine very well, and I wasn't yet sure whether I liked that she was genuinely asking for things that made her happy, or if I despised her arrogant, self-centered behavior. Either way, I was impressed with her determination to get what she wanted.

We spent one of our first days on Maui in a beautiful flower garden. After walking the grounds, Catherine asked me to choose a flower that could be a healing symbol for me.

After looking around carefully, I announced, "I found my flower."

I pointed to a large cactus in the middle of the garden.

"I choose the cactus. I love her because she is powerful and tall and has thorns and a tough outside to protect herself. She requires little water, so she can sustain herself with very little need from outside help."

Catherine looked at me with a compassionate smile. "Oh honey, I appreciate your honesty, but why do you feel you have to choose a flower symbol that is so tough?"

This made me sad. As I thought about it, the last thing I wanted to be was thorny and alone.

After a few minutes I responded softly, "I'm tough on the outside. That's what everyone tells me, anyway. "I'm just so not tough on the inside. I get my feelings hurt a lot."

"I know you do, lovely one. We are going to make some changes so that won't happen anymore."

In the end, I chose the lotus flower. Often the lotus is revered because of its ability to grow in the dirtiest of water and still produce a resilient, beautiful flower for the world to see. I realized this is how I wanted to see myself. Assured, yet loving—and I wanted to grow with other flowers in the garden rather than survive on my own as a lone cactus.

After our inspiring visit to the garden, with a greater understanding of myself and how I wanted to be, our work turned toward self-care.

I learned self-care was about pampering myself and luxuriating in all the beauty that surrounded me. I also learned that self-care didn't work unless you practiced it.

Over our five days together, we explored Maui and took in the beauty of the island. We also began working on what Catherine referred to as my love print. Our goal was to identify my beliefs about love, sex, and relationships and replace them (where needed) with a new set of beliefs.

I discovered some of my old relationship beliefs included ideas such as:

- When looking for a partner, athletics are more important than financial success.
- Age-appropriate men are boring and unattractive.
- If you don't have sex pretty soon after you meet, you're not a good match.
- I don't deserve to have someone take care of me.
- The only way to be in a loving relationship is if we spend a lot of time together.

Once I uncovered these old beliefs and brought them to consciousness, I could, from that vantage point, begin to develop a new love print more in line with what I wanted in a partner.

Understanding how my current love print was working and where I might need to make some belief shifts reminded me of my apple tree and neuroplasticity. It was right up my alley.

When we returned from Hawaii, the first thing Catherine suggested to me was that I slow down and get off the hamster wheel I still continually found myself on.

"Suzanne, as your coach, I really think we need to *slow down*," Catherine told me enthusiastically.

"Breathe."

I took a deep breath.

"Just breathe," she said again.

"That feels so good." I took in three more deep breaths. "I think I forget to breathe all the time."

The breathing did feel good, but I was acutely aware of the overwhelm I felt with life and all my commitments. I had list after list written in very teeny writing on sticky notes in varying colors spread all over my desk. Weekly, I would take all those notes and combine them into one long list until more appeared. The process felt never-ending.

As a single mother, my children witnessed many meltdowns as I barely hung in there, burdened by chores, events, holidays, bills, laundry, and all. As my children flew the coop, I continued keeping busy. Sam had helped me with so many projects, but more kept appearing. I started my own property rental business. I was going to graduate school, attempting to write a book, and traveling the world trying to save the planet, among all the other normal tasks of life.

I was also aware I chose all these commitments. Looking back, I didn't know how to stop the chaos. It all felt so familiar and safe.

When thinking about how busy life was and why, I realized I had decided at the young age of seventeen, during my first year in college when I was feeling lonely and bored, that I was going to make sure I would *never* have those feelings again. Then I realized I could go back even further: I remembered the long summer days as a young child when all my friends were busy, and I was home with nothing to do and no one to play with. Both these times stood out as pure misery. I made a decision to *never* let loneliness or boredom enter my reality again.

The decision I made at ten and then again at seventeen kept me from slowing down, living more peacefully, accepting what I could reasonably get done during a single day, and most importantly, taking precious time to love myself and others.

I felt comfortable on my hamster wheel, justifying my behavior to complete just *one* more thing before I would slow down and make my life easier.

I'm sure part of this need to stay busy was to impress my father—even after he was dead. I was a doer just like him. I was a bulldog charging ahead, feeling like I had to achieve and could never let anything slip through the cracks. As time went on, I took on more and more projects, berating myself when anything was left undone, which happened often.

Now, years later, I was far from bored, but I was always overwhelmed—which didn't exactly bring the inner peace I was looking for.

In one of our early sessions, Catherine said to me, "What would it be like to take a break from *all* the busyness?"

"I can't. There's just too much to do, and it all has to get done," I said, resigned to my sad fate. It wasn't like I could stop managing my parents' estate, spending time with my children, doing the laundry, or paying the bills.

"Well, what would it be like if you took a break from the added pressure of writing a book? That seems to me like something you could let go of. At least for the time being."

This made my stomach hurt. Yes, I could stop writing, but what would people think after I told so many of them I was writing a book and now I've decided not to finish? What would my children think?

Alexandra's voice rang in my ear: "Mom, you have to finish. Look at all the time and energy you have put into writing."

Alexandra's intention was based in love and meant for my own good, but every time I heard these words echo in my head, I felt ashamed. I heard, *You are frivolous and silly, and you have to finish.* The mother turned into the child.

One voice in my head would say, *Of course, I must finish. It wouldn't be fair to my children or me if I didn't finish after I spent so much time and money on it.*

Another voice would chime in, *Screw that, this is my money and my time, and I can do with it exactly as I please. Who cares what it costs? Maybe writing this book is just for my own healing. Some people buy clothes, I'm writing a book.*

This was cognitive dissonance at its finest—two beliefs working against each other. I wanted to finish, but I also felt I had to finish to be okay in everyone else's eyes. I wasn't thrilled with this realization.

I began to consider what Catherine was suggesting. The more I thought about it, the more I realized writing was adding to my self-imposed torture.

I decided to trust and let go. I decided to stop being a hamster and start being a guinea pig—and try some new things.

I stopped writing, and I have to say it was glorious.

Then Catherine introduced a concept she referred to as "Hire Slowly, Fire Quickly."

She helped me apply this simple concept to all aspects of my life. My past had already taught me it was easier to get into a relationship than to get out. It was easier to get married than divorced. Once you have children, there's no going back. And buying something was easier than trying to sell that house, or stock, or whatever. There are exceptions to this rule, but for me Catherine's motto hit a home run.

With the exception of my computer man, every other attempt at finding help—including the financial assistant who initially was so helpful—had failed. I had paid every one of my own bills until I was 58. I hated paying bills, but I was so attached to *how* everything was being handled, I couldn't allow anyone else to do it for me. It always felt like it took more time to train someone—and clean up after the things they didn't do well—than to just do everything myself. And there was always the inevitable conversation of letting them go that I abhorred.

I felt the same way with men. I would get involved too quickly, and then realize I did not want to be in a relationship with them. Not wanting to hurt their feelings, I would claw my way out by making excuses—or resorting to my fallback "tears" plan so *they* would not feel unloved. I was good at getting into things but not great at getting out gracefully. I decided to take a chance and do what Catherine was asking me to do.

I began talking with people who worked for and with me and rearranged many existing contracts. I was terrified at each phone call I had to make. I was fearful they weren't going to like me—or be upset, angry, or disappointed—and trust me, some of them were.

One by one, I let go of situations and relationships that were no longer working. I lit a candle and called in the light for each phone call and informed people I was taking a break from my commitments to reassess my life. It was like clearing more clutter. I no longer wanted anything—or anyone—in my life that did not spark joy.

What was new and different for me was I made no excuses for my decisions. I cleaned up many financial arrangements in ways I felt were fair to both the person I was dealing with and myself, *rather* than buying my way out of an arrangement, lying, or crying. I even stood up for myself on occasion and didn't pay for future contracts.

Hire Slowly, Fire Quickly.

I was putting the expression to work. I quickly discovered there were a lot fewer chances for mishaps when communication upfront was clear. And yet, this was life, so when things did go awry, I reopened lines of communication, looked at what I initially wanted to achieve, and figured out how to make it happen.

During my time at USM, Ron Hulnick, co-director of the University, invited me to join him in his office for an hour one afternoon between classes to discuss my book. Ron made it clear he was not charging me for his time, which I was grateful for. I took him up on his offer.

I'm not going to lie. I was nervous and intimidated. Ron is a powerful man and a leader in the world of transformation, and I didn't know what to say so that I would sound smart and actually learn something at the same time.

As it went, we had a beautiful meeting. I believe wholeheartedly in the work the University is doing, so I offered to make a donation to their foundation for Ron's time. Admittedly, I am not great at receiving something for nothing, and maybe I was buying his time, but I felt good about my offer.

"Suzanne, I appreciate your donation. If you would like to meet again sometime, just let me know and I will make time for you free of charge," Ron told me graciously.

"Thank you so much, Ron. I appreciate your time and wisdom."

I left his office feeling proud of myself and excited I'd been invited back.

Some time passed, and I requested another meeting a couple of months later. I was under the impression we would spend an hour together and was surprised the meeting lasted a full two hours. I was aware of the time but felt uncomfortable about pointing it out.

At the end of the meeting, Ron said with a smile, "That will be $1,000. I charge $500 per hour, and after all, I have to make a living somehow."

Oh boy, I thought to myself.

How many times had I been in a similar extremely uncomfortable situation involving money?

I *could* let him know he had agreed to spend time with me at no charge, but I was terrified. I didn't know what to do. This type of confrontation might not be a problem for anyone else, but it was a problem for me. That ever-so-familiar feeling I hated so much was here again.

I said to myself as I had a hundred times before: *Just this one last time. I will do it this one last time, and next time things will be different. I will be clearer and remind Ron* (or whoever) *of what our agreement was.*

Things were *never* different. It wasn't just the money—although a thousand dollars is a thousand dollars. And I was ready to take the licking of losing that thousand dollars, but I also didn't feel appreciated for the donation I had made during our last meeting. I felt unloved and undervalued. But the real licking was that I was repeating the same behavior of *not* standing up for myself yet again.

I wrote Ron a check and handed it to him, leaving his office angry about why I could never stand up for myself. As I walked out the main door of the University, I promised myself I would never request another meeting.

I shared my experience with Catherine the next time we spoke.

"What an incredible opportunity to stand up for yourself," she said excitedly.

"This is so great. I suggest you write him an email explaining what happened and how you didn't think you were paying him for his time as you and he agreed to that before the meeting."

I cringed.

Maybe hiring Catherine wasn't such a good idea.

To make a long story short, with much trepidation I wrote a brief email to Ron—with just the facts—and waited for his response with bated breath. Much to my immense relief, he wrote back, apologizing he had simply forgotten, and returned my check.

It was a hugely powerful experience for me.

I had spoken up for myself, and much to my surprise, it worked. It wasn't even close to being as scary as I had imagined. I had taken an important step toward breaking a recurring pattern of giving in and not standing up for myself.

Around the same time as my experience with Ron, I was looking for a much-needed new loan on my house. I had a variable loan in place and was running out of time before the payments on that loan were going to increase substantially, and I wasn't going to be able to meet the new financial obligation.

I was desperate. I had already contacted my long-time financial advisors and got an unexpected runaround with no hope of a loan. Catherine suggested I meet with a firm run by her husband, Jack, in Los Angeles. Since I was going to the LA area once a month, I took her suggestion. Two weeks after our initial meeting, that firm offered me the opportunity to get a loan that met my criteria.

I was elated, but there was a catch.

"I thought you understood I secured the loan for you in anticipation that you would move your portfolio over to our firm," Jack said during our follow-up phone call. "We're not in the business of making loans to people unless they are our clients."

I didn't know what to say. An agreement to move all my assets wasn't made clear to me during our initial meeting—or at least I didn't think so—otherwise, I would have told Jack I didn't want to change firms. I thought a loan with them was enough, and I wasn't prepared to make that kind of drastic change.

I liked Jack, and Catherine was my coach—and Jack was her husband. I felt a strange obligation to work with him, but intuitively it didn't feel like a good fit. Once I discovered this expectation, my nice, "don't want to upset anyone little girl" jumped in the driver's seat. I was back in a familiar predicament, feeling like I was going to disappoint Catherine, Jack, or both if I didn't move my assets and take the loan. But if I didn't get some kind of a loan, I'd have to possibly sell my house—and that was scary.

I didn't know what to do.

When Catherine and I met again, I wanted to talk to her about my latest predicament, but not only was I terrified of dealing with Jack, I was extra terrified of bringing up a misunderstanding between me and her husband. Then I figured, if I had hired a life coach, I might as well tell the truth even if it's messy, so I decided to talk to her about it. I was paying her, after all.

Just like with Ron, Catherine encouraged me—for my growth and to break the pattern—to have a frank conversation with Jack and reassured me there was no reason I had to feel obligated to move my assets—loan or no loan—if it didn't feel right.

Having two honest conversations—first with Catherine, and later with Jack—was challenging, but frankly not as bad as I had envisioned. I was proud of myself for doing what I needed to do with no excuses, hurt feelings, or sense of obligation to do something that didn't feel right.

I survived both scary challenges. I will *never* forget these confidence-building situations. Even today they are a source of strength.

Hire Slowly, Fire Quickly.

Always!

CHAPTER 15

It Takes Two to Tango

We cannot advance without new experiments in
living, but no wise man tries every day what he has
proved wrong the day before.

–JAMES TRUSLOW ADAMS

In the fall of 2017, Catherine and I went on a second retreat, this time
to Ojai, California. We spent three days continuing to work on self-
care and creating a new, improved way of relating to love and intimate
relationships. The retreat was just as spectacular as Hawaii.

On our final early dinner on the balcony of the Ojai Valley Inn,
overlooking the rolling hills of Southern California as the sun was about
to set, I said to Catherine: "I'm headed to Bays Head next week for a
weekend date after I see my son in Charleston."

"Tell me all about it."

I gave Catherine the backstory. When this man named Peter first
started texting me, I thought he was someone I had met on my travels
somewhere. I meet so many people, and I often forget where or when I

met them. After communicating back and forth with him for a month or so, I finally got up the nerve to ask how we knew each other.

"We don't," he said. "I saw your profile on Facebook, and I liked what I saw and read about you. So, I contacted you."

I was a little shocked that Peter reached out to someone he didn't know, but the more I learned about him, the more he intrigued me.

Peter owned and ran a successful company that makes hats, socks, and other paraphernalia for big events and professional athletes in the motocross racing and skateboarding world. Not my realm of professional athletes, but still interesting, and he was a talented, passionate athlete himself.

Peter lived about an hour and a half from Charleston, where my youngest son was in college. I was headed to Charleston to see Derek, so I had asked Peter if he would like to have dinner in Charleston one night.

"Sure, I'd love to," Peter said. "I'm actually traveling north on Thursday to deliver some product, and I can stop in for dinner and then head out."

"Perfect. That sounds great."

Thursday would be the first time Peter and I would meet. I chose one of my favorite restaurants in Charleston. We had a nice meal (he paid), kissed a bit outside the restaurant, and said our good-byes.

We kept in touch over the next month or so.

One day I called, and after exchanging some pleasantries, I said, "I am coming back to Charleston for Derek's 21st birthday in three weeks. Can we get together for another dinner?"

"Well, I'm not sure I can do that, but would you like to come to visit me in Bays Head and spend a couple of days before you head back to Aspen?"

The dinner had gone well, so I said, "Sure, I'd love that."

My plan was to go a couple weeks after my retreat with Catherine.

"Peter invited me to visit him for three days," I said to Catherine. "We had one date and it went pretty well, so I told him I would come." I hesitated.

"The only problem is, I'm not sure I really want to go now. But I said I would, so as usual I feel obligated to do what I said I would do."

I was afraid to just say *I'm not coming*, but on the other hand, I was unclear about what intimacy the weekend might hold, who was going to pay, and how I should handle myself. My lack of clarity made me nervous.

I let Peter know that even though he had invited me to stay at his three-bedroom house, I was going to get a hotel room I would pay for. I didn't know his financial situation, and as usual I felt it was my duty to take care of myself.

Here we go again, I thought.

"So," Catherine said, "This looks like a perfect opportunity for you to practice some of what we've been working on. You can do what you always have done, probably getting the same results, or you can choose to do something differently."

I didn't like where this conversation was going. That familiar knot in my stomach was getting more twisted by the minute.

"Why don't you just call him and tell him you can't make it?"

"That sounds like a terrible idea," I said with obvious fear in my voice.

Catherine knew she had touched on something uncomfortable. There was no doubt in my mind I was going to end up having to do *something* different—and I knew her intention was sincerely for my healing and growth.

"Why don't we call this the Bays Head Experiment?" she said excitedly.

"It's an experiment, all right," I said reluctantly. "One I'm not sure I'm going to enjoy."

Just like asking for six bottles of water and getting the housekeepers to redo her bedding, Catherine was asking me to do things that were comfortable and natural to her, but not at all comfortable for me.

"If I'm hearing you correctly and you're not going to phone and tell him you won't be making it, what are you going to do if you go? I think you should be very clear upfront that you are *not* going to sleep with him. Part of our love print work is to teach you to take your time and slow down with men—and sex—and this is the perfect opportunity to practice."

"I can't *not* go," I said, shaking my head. "But even though it feels weird, I can agree to no sex while I'm there."

I am a carefree, go-with-the-flow type of person, and I didn't really want to be locked into having to do things a certain way. But I agreed anyway.

"The other thing I suggest is that you do *not*, for any reason, pull out your credit card until he pulls his out first."

Catherine knew my conflict around money and intimacy.

She seemed to be enjoying this.

It felt like hell to me, but it was an experiment, right?

I had already practiced going Dutch with Philip, and that went okay, so I agreed.

"After he takes out his card—and then only if you want, you can offer to pay *your* half," she continued.

"I can do that," I said, relatively confidently.

Even though I had pulled out my card so many times in the past, not pulling it out first seemed like the least of my problems.

I was a bit nervous when I arrived in Bays Head around dinner time, but kind of excited to see where this would go. Peter picked me up, and we went to a Spanish restaurant. His taste was completely different than mine, but I ate what came anyway, somewhat reluctantly.

I didn't eat a lot, and Peter offered to pay for the meal. I graciously accepted.

After dinner we took a walk on the beach. So far, there had been no intimacy short of a kiss in a parking lot in Charleston, but one passionate kiss on the beach led to sex the first evening.

Damn it, I thought to myself. *I've already blown it. Now what? At least I made it through dinner without offering to pay.*

The next day came.

"Can we go to Starbucks or somewhere this morning and grab a coffee?" I asked Peter the following morning.

"I don't drink coffee. But we can go."

That wasn't what I expected, but instead of pretending I didn't want coffee, we went to Starbucks. I saw this as a win in the area of self-care. I wanted the Bays Head experiment to be successful so I could go back and report my triumphs to Catherine, knowing I had already broken one of my commitments.

After coffee, we went paddleboarding through the tidal marshes, sheltered from the big waves of the Atlantic. We returned to Peter's house, and he made me lunch. It was a beautiful day, and we had a nice connection.

I sat on his veranda as he cleared the dishes and thought to myself, *This is going pretty well. Piece of cake. Maybe it's not so bad I slept with him last night.*

I returned to my hotel to siesta and shower before Peter picked me up for dinner. We went to one of his favorite restaurants owned by one of his close friends. When he asked me where I wanted to sit, I suggested the bar (which is my favorite place always). I got what I wanted, but after a drink at the bar, Peter wanted to sit at a table. So I went with the flow.

Peter doesn't drink liquor—or coffee—but I ordered a glass of wine. The food was exceptional, and I enjoyed the ambiance of his favorite restaurant—even though we were at a table. We finished dinner, and I knew the bill was coming soon. I also knew my portion would be more expensive than his because of the wine.

I wanted to pull out my card so badly.

After all, I thought, *he bought me dinner last night and took me to Starbucks this morning—and made me lunch.*

I didn't.

I kept my hands folded opposite of the way I normally would, thinking of Joe Dispenza and rewiring. I waited and waited and waited. It seemed like it took an eternity for the bill to arrive. And then it came. Peter went for his wallet and pulled out his credit card.

I turned to him and nervously said, "Would you like to split the bill?"

He looked at me and said, "No, I got it, but thank you for offering."

Success.

I had done something differently than what I always did, and it felt like a win. Although it might seem like a small change to some, for me it was a big achievement and something I would remember with pride.

I still had to fess up to Catherine. I didn't want to admit to sleeping with Peter. It wasn't about disappointing Catherine. I had disappointed myself. I wanted to put that conversation off as long as possible, but I'm pretty sure I called her on my way home—probably to get it over with.

I would love to share with you exactly how Catherine responded to my call, but I really don't remember how she reacted—or what she said to me. All I do know is it was an experiment, just like Philip and Brad. It was another learning experience and part of the journey in exploring my love print.

Peter and I were still talking regularly, and a week or so later, I invited him to come to Aspen to ski over the Thanksgiving holiday. He accepted and was gracious and generous to me and my kids over the weekend, and even brought each of the children a pair of socks.

And although I appreciated his generosity, I knew things weren't going to work between us. I explained to him I didn't have romantic feelings for him, and I apologized for changing my mind *after* asking him to come see me.

I was so relieved when Peter got on a plane that afternoon and went back to Bays Head. I knew it was the right call, and although I felt guilty, I was proud I was able to speak my truth—even though I knew the truth would hurt his feelings. To this day, we keep in touch occasionally. I want him to be happy, and I want me to be happy.

Looking back, I know Catherine was right about not sleeping with Peter. But I—like so many women—thought I could share this precious part of myself without any ramifications. I knew when I was making the choice to sleep with someone I didn't know, it probably wasn't right. Sex rarely leads to love, and I was beginning to see that sex too soon often leads to upset—and/or heartache.

I now understood why the woman who wrote *How Not to Stay Single After 40* handed me a copy of her book years before and said to me, "Sweetheart, I think you need to read this."

The one thing I remember about the book was her advice to wait eight dates before you sleep with a man.

Eight dates? I thought at the time. *That is insanity.*

My personal number was between three and six, and six was pushing it. Although I thought her advice was crazy back then, I get it now.

After the Bays Head Experiment, I decided to put men on hold for a bit and focus on my own life journey.

CHAPTER 16

The Year of the Bear

Do whatever is put in front of you with all your heart and soul without regard for personal results. Do the work as though it were given to you by the universe itself—because it was.

–MICHAEL A. SINGER

For the four years leading up to 2017, my New Year's resolution had been to stay home and watch more TV. My friends thought I was nuts. Who has a New Year's resolution to watch more television?

The first year I never even turned the TV on. I didn't know how.

The next three were barely any better. I was always busy, especially at night. Sometimes I went out with people I didn't really like that much, or to events where I didn't have a lot of fun, just to fill the time.

Now that my children had left home, staying home and watching TV felt even more like a death sentence. But I wanted to stop avoiding feelings and emotions and to start feeling more comfortable with myself. I was tired of looking over my shoulder for the next possible man to have fun with—or who might make me feel good about myself.

So, on January 1, 2017, I didn't set a formal New Year's resolution (because resolutions clearly don't work). Instead, I started praying every night for the *willingness* to stay home. My commitment for the year was to slow down and spend more time by myself rather than my normal pattern of going out every night, or traveling constantly, or working obsessively when I was at home.

I told people of my intention, and occasionally I laughed out loud about it—and trust me, so did they.

"Right, Suz stay home?" I often heard. "That's a joke. You are always out."

But by summertime, I had actually managed to stay in for a few nights.

Well, this isn't so bad, I thought. *In fact, I kinda like it.*

That summer I also got back into course waterskiing. I have loved waterskiing for as long as I could remember. Whenever we were in Lake Tahoe (or anywhere else with a lake and a boat), I have been waking up my kids, friends, or anyone else I could possibly find, knocking softly on their bedroom door, greeting them with a smile and a hot cup of coffee shortly after the sun poked out its first rays of light, in hopes they would rise and shine *quickly* so we could get out on the lake for some flat water.

Most mornings I was met with grunts and pillows tossed in my general direction. I have figured out over the years there are only a few people out of the almost eight billion on the planet who think getting up at the crack of dawn, squeezing into a wetsuit, stuffing your feet into bindings mounted to a thin board (otherwise known as a waterski), and jumping into a cold body of water, only to be yanked out of the water by a boat with a big engine, is fun.

I have now determined that the passion for waterskiing must be part of one's genetic makeup. Most people just don't understand or have any interest in this strange sport—thus the grunts and pillows.

When I moved to Aspen in 2000 as a forty-year-old, I quickly discovered there was very little water nearby to free ski on. However, I did find a private lake with a course twenty-five minutes from Aspen. I knew very little about course skiing, but just being able to ski was motivation enough for me to become a member at Kodiak Ski Lake.

I skied at the lake three times a week for years, and I even ran the course on occasion. I enjoyed working on perfecting my skills, but over the next ten years (because of my lack of coaching, lack of ability, and old age creeping in), a lot of bad habits got worse, and my desire to ski a course began to wane.

I hadn't lost my love of being yanked around behind a boat, but trying to get around those six orange buoys that make up a course became frustrating over time. Eventually, I threw in the towel and gave up my time slots. Occasionally, I would get invited by a friend to go to the ski lake, and just for fun I would accept and try my luck again, without much success.

On one of these occasions, I happened to see Brett, the hot bartender from town, at the lake. I had been ogling him for the last six years, and even though I thought Brett was cute, he paid almost no attention to me. I barely knew him, and I assumed his specialty was serving drinks and hanging out with hot women.

I was confused when I saw him at the lake, but that day I got the chance to ride in the boat while he skied. I discovered he was a *very* skilled skier.

When we returned to the dock, I turned to Brett enthusiastically and said, "Wow. You are amazing. Can you teach me how to do that?"

"Well," Brett said, "I'm also a coach, so you can hire me to get some instructions on the water, if you want."

With the help of a coach, rather than being left to my own devices and never getting any better, I was inspired to get back out and try my luck on the course.

Brett turned out to be a great coach, and after working with him on a regular basis over the summer, my skiing improved, and I was loving course skiing once again.

Now I was ogling him for a completely different reason.

In October 2017, three-quarters through my year of being *willing* to stay home and watch TV, I entered my third and final year at USM. Unlike year one (and honestly year two), when I was not fully utilizing the teachings outside of our monthly onsite classes, I made a firm commitment to apply what I was learning to my day-to-day life and see what would unfold.

I got on my knees and prayed each morning, and although I still had not returned to writing my book, I recommitted to free-form writing each day and began pulling cards from Jamie Sams's *Medicine Cards: The Discovery of Power through the Ways of Animals*. I also started paying closer attention to my Inner Knowing, better known as our Sixth Sense or gut feeling.

We're all familiar with our five senses, and we are lucky if we have all five available to us. Even if we don't, we know what these five senses are, what their functions are, and how to use them. But what about the Sixth Sense?

A common example of the Sixth Sense is when you randomly think about someone and they call—or you run into them on the street unexpectedly. These seemingly random calls and meetings happened more and more frequently as I got in touch with my Inner Knowing.

After starting a dream journal, my Sixth Sense skyrocketed. I won't list all the incredible "accidental" synchronistic events I experienced—and still do—but I urge you to try listening and responding to your Inner Knowing for yourself. I joke that I no longer really need to call anyone. All I have to do is think about them and they appear.

A new theme that was arising in my life was *personal responsibility*. Applying what I was learning at USM was one way of taking personal responsibility for my life. Some of my new habits stuck and some didn't, but committing to them felt powerful.

Personal responsibility was also an obvious solution for my ongoing issue of paying for men I date. Building on my work with Catherine, I wanted to take personal responsibility for my own actions and keep practicing new behaviors to create new results—even if they were scary—instead of expecting the men in my life to change.

I purposely use the word "wanted" because taking personal responsibility is not something anyone *needs* to do. I recognized I didn't *need* to take personal responsibility, because "need" implies I have to do it. If there was one thing I was learning from my USM curriculum, it's that no one *has* to do anything. We always have a choice.

I just didn't know exactly *how* to do it—yet.

At the end of November, I decided to go on my first week-long waterski trip. Seven other women and I, along with my waterski coach Brett and his brother Matt (also a waterski coach), packed up our gear and headed south to a waterski resort in Mexico. I celebrated my fifty-eighth birthday that week, and I fell in love with the skiing, the warm water, and Mexico itself.

On day four of our weeklong trip—ignoring Brett's advice to take the day off and rest my body—I was out skiing and showing off for the hot coaches in the boat. Back then, I thought I was pretty good, and I wanted to impress Brett and Matt with my skills.

I was doing a simple lean drill when, to my surprise, I double-ejected out of the ski, flipped 180 degrees, and hit my kneecap on the ski. I knew something was wrong, but not wanting to give in to pain, I continued skiing.

When I got off the water, I could barely walk. I spent the next three days hobbling around. I was still loving this magical vacation, but that was the end of my waterskiing in Mexico.

I flew directly from Mexico to Los Angeles for my December USM weekend. My knee hurt so badly, I had to request a wheelchair to get through the Mexico City airport. In the past I would have been mortified to be in a wheelchair (after all, I was the party girl who could do anything), but at that point I couldn't have cared less what anyone thought, and I certainly wasn't looking over my shoulder for hot men.

I arrived in LA and dragged a suitcase and an enormous ski bag to a taxi and on to my hotel. I went to school the next morning after being up all night in immense pain. I lasted about two hours in class and finally told Catherine (who was also attending the class) I couldn't finish the weekend and needed to go back to Aspen.

"Oh, my sweet girl," Catherine said lovingly. "Why don't you go to the emergency room and have it x-rayed?"

With a pained look on my face, I said, "If there's no orthopedic doctor at the ER, there's really no point, and I'm pretty sure there won't be on a Saturday."

Catherine insisted I go to the ER anyway and recruited her mother, who was close by, to take me.

An ER visit is never fun. I waited forever. Four hours later, I finally got an x-ray, and as I had predicted, there was no ortho in the ER on a Saturday, but the nurse told me my knee looked fine, and I believed her. At least, I wanted to believe her. They gave me a brace and some pain medication and sent me on my way.

I returned to class but lasted only another two hours. I hobbled back to my hotel and immediately scheduled a flight back to Aspen. I was disappointed in myself for not staying in LA and knew I would need to make up my missing time, but I could no longer bear the pain.

After returning home to Aspen and resting in bed with my knee elevated, I developed a low-grade fever on top of my knee injury. After four days with a temperature, I went back to the ER—this time in Aspen.

I endured many tests—and several skeptical looks from the ER doctors, who were ready to send me home and were clearly indicating they thought I was a hypochondriac of some kind.

Just before I was supposed to be let go with no diagnosis, I asked one of the doctors if he had taken a urine sample. (My Inner Knowing helped me to ask the question.)

They had not.

"Could you take one, please?"

"Sure," one of the ER doctors said, sighing like I was taking up more of his precious time. But they did it anyway.

I will never forget when the doctor came back into the room.

"Wow, lady," he said, with eyes as big as saucers. "You are really sick. Your blood has turned septic."

"I told you I was sick," I responded emphatically. "Why would I come to the ER days before the end of the year when I have a huge deductible? If I wasn't really sick, I would surely have waited until after January first."

The doctors did allow me to go home rather than checking into the hospital, but only if I agreed to come back every morning for intravenous antibiotics until I got better.

For five days, Alexandra drove me to the hospital in the morning and picked me up well after it was dark. I slept on a cot in the ER all day while liquids and antibiotics were fed into my veins.

Finally, I turned a corner. They sent me home with more medication and told me to rest.

Christmas was around the corner, and all three children were home for two weeks. I struggled to get out of bed to be with them. As the x-ray in LA had shown my kneecap was not broken or fractured, I feebly attempted snow skiing and socializing with family and friends, but I knew things weren't right.

I had rented out our house at the last minute, so after the children went back to school, I lay in an uncomfortable bed in a rental home, still not feeling like myself.

It was two weeks post the sepsis diagnosis, well after I finished my course of antibiotics. *I feel so crummy,* I thought. *If there is nothing wrong with me, why do I feel like sleeping all the time? What is going on? Am I depressed?*

New Year's 2018 came and went. I still wasn't feeling well and was wondering what was wrong with me. I had a lot of quiet time on my hands to reflect on my life and continue practicing many of the things I had learned at school, when I could manage to lift my head off the pillow.

One day as I lay in bed, I realized that if you separate out the numbers of 2018 and add them together, 2+0+1+8 = 11. 2018 was numerologically an 11 year. I was still obsessed with the number 11. 11s appeared everywhere for me, and now it was an 11 year. I decided no matter what was going on, I was going to make the most of it.

On top of 2018 being an 11 year, I noticed I was pulling the same Medicine Card again and again: the Bear. Like bears hibernating in the winter to rejuvenate and prepare for the spring, the Bear card's message is about going within and taking time for oneself.

It became clear 2018 was the Year of the Bear for me, and I decided to honor that one and only card throughout the year. It was my time to go inside. Since hurting my knee and being sick from this kidney infection, I was staying home whether I wanted to or not. Life had made the decision for me.

Although I was feeling a bit better from the sepsis, my knee still didn't feel right. Three months after my fall in Mexico, I finally went to see an orthopedic doctor in Aspen. He did another x-ray and an MRI and quickly discovered my kneecap was in fact fractured. My Inner Knowing had been correct all along. I knew I had fractured my kneecap when I made that trip to the ER in Los Angeles. I also knew it wasn't smart to rely on a nurse who was not an expert at reading x-rays.

Three months earlier, six weeks in a brace would have allowed my knee to heal. Instead, it took a total of ten months to recover from the fractured kneecap. I had known not to go to the ER in LA that day, but I went anyway. Having faith in my Inner Knowing could have helped resolve my knee sooner.

At least I had the sense to listen to my Inner Knowing when I went to the ER in Aspen and they wanted to send me home without a diagnosis. I knew there was something wrong, and I wasn't leaving that hospital they figured out what was wrong. Untreated sepsis can quickly trigger septic shock, which can lead to organ failure and death.

Note to self: Follow my intuition. Always.

I also realized somewhere in the middle of my long recovery, my prayer for *wanting* to stay home had been answered. Life may have made my decision to stay home, but *having* to stay home eventually led to *wanting* to stay home. No more FOMO.

I then began to see a higher purpose in my physical issues. In *You Can Heal Your Life*, Louise Hay talks about how different body parts are associated with different emotions and experiences. Knees, for example, are associated with moving forward and humility. Some people believe this is the reason we get on our "knees" to pray. When we get on our knees, we humble ourselves to a greater power.

Kidneys are associated with cleansing.

Hmm . . .

Viewing my knee injury as an opportunity for humility—and sepsis as the cleansing of my old ways in order to embrace new ways—was an extremely powerful way of looking at my "accident."

There are no accidents.

As I spent more time at home, I was practicing self-love and self-care rather than looking for love from others. I remembered when my coach Sam had asked me to come up with a consequence for not meeting my writing commitment, and the worst thing I could think of was staying in for thirty nights.

Staying home was no longer a consequence I abhorred. It was a miracle.

Now, I'd have to get a tattoo.

I sat in my backyard listening to the Aspen trees quake—or curled up watching a miniseries in front of the fire. Occasionally, I even took a hot bath, complete with candles and music. When I did go out, I was no longer looking over my shoulder for someone—*anyone*—to fill me up.

Even though I had replaced my FOMO for JOMO (the "joy of missing out"), I was still a little uncomfortable with my new identity. I had to face the idea that I wasn't the "fun" party girl anymore in everyone's eyes—including my own.

How would people see me now?

My internal voice quickly answered: *As old and boring.*

I didn't want to be seen as old and boring.

And even with these unresolved feelings, I made a choice to live into the Year of the Bear—hibernation and all.

In May, I had the opportunity to attend an intensive five-day Enneagram training in Santa Monica, sponsored by USM.

Nearly a year and a half earlier, as part of our initial work together, Catherine had encouraged me to take a personality test based on something called the Enneagram. I had never heard of it, so she explained the Enneagram was a 2,500-year-old system of thought that identified nine personality types. To discover my Enneagram type, I needed to take a test consisting of 144 questions answered through a website. I agreed immediately and took the forty-minute test that day. The results popped up on my computer within minutes.

The test identified me as a type Two, known as the Helper, with type Eight, the Challenger, as my next highest number.

According to the test, Twos at their best are caring, empathetic, generous, appreciative, and affectionate. At their lowest, Twos are people-pleasers who put their needs behind everyone else in order to be loved by others.

Eights are strong, independent, assertive, inspiring, and action-oriented. At their lowest, Eights can be blunt, willful, and confrontational.

"Does this feel familiar to you?" Catherine asked me inquisitively.

"Yep. All of it feels pretty darn accurate," I said.

I signed up for the Enneagram training at USM so I could learn more about this ancient personality system and what these numbers really meant.

The five-day workshop was led by Robert Holden, a charming, funny British psychologist who has written many amazing books, including my two favorites, *Lovability* and *Holy Shift!*

Days prior to the training, I took the test again. Much to my dismay, type Two was once again by far my highest score. But rather than type Eight, this time type Seven came in second. I liked identifying as a Seven, which is, in short, an Enthusiast. Sevens are extroverted, optimistic, and playful. Sevens can also be over-extended, scattered, and undisciplined. And even though all of us have a bit of each Ennegram number, these characteristics resonated with me as well.

On the first morning of the workshop, Robert asked us, "Who doesn't like the number they received?"

Nearly 80 percent of the people in the room raised their hands.

"Let me tell you all something," Robert said to the class cheerfully in his very British accent. "If you are *not* happy with your number and you *don't* want to be whatever number you are [and some people are a combination of two or three types], you are more than likely that number."

I wasn't so sure. *Maybe the Enneagram isn't as widely used as some of the other personality tests because it isn't as accurate,* I thought.

We spent the first half of the day learning how the Enneagram was designed and the second half on each of the nine personality types. Robert explained each type in depth and shared examples of movies, songs, and people who exhibited the characteristics associated with each type. According to Robert, a person's primary Enneagram personality type remains the same throughout their life.

Now I was really confused. I had learned from Joe Dispenza that it's possible to rewire your brain and create new neural pathways at any time during your life. Why couldn't I go from a Two to some other number if I really set my mind to it?

Plus, I thought I resonated with Seven much more than Two.

I approached Robert over one of the breaks to share my insight. "I just figured something out."

He looked at me inquisitively and said, "Go on."

"I am happy to say I don't really think I am a Two. I have put a lot of thought into this, and I think I'm actually a Seven. I'm an enthusiast. I'm playful and optimistic. I am even an enthusiast about the things I *don't* like," I said, laughing. "I think I have been masquerading as a Two my whole life when I'm really a Seven."

Robert looked at me.

"Oh, really? Maybe you are."

That was pretty much the extent of our conversation.

I had a lot of time over the next few days to think about my type—and to witness how many of my fifty or so classmates continued to struggle with the dark side of their type as well.

Even though I didn't *want* to be a Two, I had to admit the characteristics of Twos sounded very familiar. Less healthy Twos do for others, expecting love in return. They overgive to compensate for their own misfortune and are not good at setting boundaries. They get walked on—and know it—but don't want to make waves for fear of someone not loving them.

I also learned healthy Twos at their best are truly here to serve others with genuine love in their hearts.

Maybe being a Two wasn't so bad after all.

I thought about my earlier question as to whether we could change our type. Maybe I was asking the wrong question. Maybe a better question was, "How can I become a healthier Two and appreciate my positive qualities?"

Before this realization, I wanted to rewire myself out of being a Two because I thought being a Two was bad. But now I understood the journey was to become a healthier version of my Enneagram type.

Toward the end of the workshop, and after a great deal of self-reflection, I went back to Robert on another break. "Okay, I am a Two, Two, Two, Two, Two."

Robert looked at me in a loving way and said, "I know."

I nearly cried.

"I am proud of you for recognizing your unique Twoness," Robert said. "From this vantage point, you can now begin to make some substantial changes in your life."

Thankfully, Robert cleared up my confusion over not being able to rewire my brain to change my personality. He said that although it's not possible to change your type, there is a scale within each type, and the goal is to go from an unhealthy state of expressing one's personality type to a healthy state. I could now understand how both Joe Dispenza and Robert Holden could be right. I could rewire my brain and use my Twoness in ways that better served myself and those around me.

The Enneagram may not be as widely used as the Myers-Briggs and other personality tests, but I began to see how valuable it was for not only understanding myself but also those whom I loved but sometimes acted in ways I didn't get.

After that eye-opening workshop—and additional reflection—I accepted that, as a Two, self-care was not my strong suit. I also saw how my tendency to please others negatively impacted my relationships with Greg, Harry, Philip, Brad, Peter, and all the other men I dated—serious or not.

Working on *not* trying to please others (especially when pleasing others hurt me) and self-care were two things I wanted to put high on my priority list in my Year of the Bear—and beyond.

As flight attendants announce on every flight around the globe, "Put on your own oxygen mask first, then help others."

Today, I tell everyone about the Enneagram test. It's an incredible tool for understanding ourselves and why we do what we do. If you are interested in exploring the test for yourself, you can visit www. enneagraminstitute.com.

From my New Year's resolution to slow down in 2017, to my firm commitment to my USM practices, being laid up with a fractured kneecap and sepsis, entering into the Year of the Bear, and now a new appreciation of being an Enneagram type Two, I could see how the past year and a half had been teaching me about the importance of self-care.

In August 2018, I graduated from my three-year program at USM. I was so proud of myself for all the work I had done to make this dream a reality. Shortly after graduating, I knew it was time to return to my book. I was still working with Catherine—and didn't want to disappoint her with my change of heart—but I was clear that although the year-and-a-half break had been good for me, it was time to complete what I had started.

Even though I hadn't been writing, I had still been talking to people. I knew for sure the problem was not just mine, but I was still scared. I felt if I told *my* truth, some of the people mentioned in this book would hate me. To take a page out of Susan Jeffers's book, I made a declaration to *Feel the Fear and Do It Anyway.*

The one thing I had going for me was my mother and father were dead, so they couldn't be upset—at least not in this lifetime.

I made a firm schedule and rehired my editor. I started by rereading what I had written. To my surprise, I recognized how much I had changed without realizing it. I knew the practices I had committed myself to were paying off. I could see it in print.

I decided to let go of my notion of perfection and replace it with the notion of excellence. I wanted to write an excellent book, one that would inspire conversation and connection in this new world.

I continued my education by reading many books on how to be an empowered woman, from *The Queen's Code* by Alison Armstrong and *Worthy: Boost Your Self-Worth to Grow Your Net Worth* by Nancy Levin to *Pussy: A Reclamation* by Regena Thomashauer. They all taught me a great deal, but the book that stood out the most was *Calling in the One: 7 Weeks to Attract the Love of Your Life* by Katherine Woodward Thomas.

I struggled to complete the entire book, but one thing stuck with me. Calling in the One had nothing to do with Prince Charming. The One was me. I had been focused on calling in the wrong one. We are born alone, and we die alone. That doesn't mean I shouldn't yearn for a relationship, but the honeymoon phase always fades after some period of time, and every time the one I am left with is myself.

Things were good that fall. I was living high on life, not dating anyone (and okay with it), renting out my house successfully, writing my book, and continuing my USM-inspired practices.

Then, in early November, the phone rang.

CHAPTER 17

The Year of the Butterfly

We delight in the beauty of the butterfly, but rarely admit
the changes it has gone through to achieve that beauty.

–MAYA ANGELOU

Caller ID is a magical thing. One can choose to answer or not depending on the name that appears. Plus, my phone ringer is off ninety percent of the time, so I tend to miss calls unless I notice the flash of Caller ID. This phone call I not only noticed, I definitely wanted to answer.

"Hey, hey," Brett said. "How are you doing?"

"I'm good. You?" I responded, curious as to why my waterski coach was phoning me out of the blue. I knew he had moved out of Aspen, but besides seeing him for a few days during the summer of 2018, we had had no contact.

"I have an idea. Why don't you come to Acapulco for two weeks? Come spend your birthday here like you did last year, and then stay for another week."

What? This is so random. Why is Brett inviting me to Mexico?

I hesitated for a minute and finally said, "I would love to, but I just can't. I'm going on a trip to Europe next week with my daughter and her boyfriend, and then we're celebrating Thanksgiving at her father's house in France. All three of my children are going to be there.

"After that," I continued, "I'm only home for three weeks, and then I leave to go on another family vacation with my ex-husband again and the children for Christmas."

I never miss an opportunity to be with my children no matter what, so there was no way I could squeeze in a two-week trip to Mexico. Nevertheless, after some creative thinking about how I could make it work—and a lot of encouragement from Brett—I decided I could go for a week. I had had such a great vacation the year before, I might as well throw an additional week of sun and waterskiing into my overly busy plans, right?

I arrived home from our Thanksgiving trip on a Monday, unpacked, repacked, and headed to Acapulco on Friday. For some reason—and to this day, I don't really know why—I bought a one-way plane ticket.

The trip to Mexico City was smooth, but when I arrived, my next flight was delayed. There are very few information boards telling you what gate you are leaving from in Mexico City, and my flight was nowhere to be found. When I finally located someone who worked for Aeromexico hours later, he told me they had lost the plane.

How do you lose a plane? I thought. *They're enormous.*

But it's Mexico City, and they seemed to have done it. My flight was meant to land in Acapulco at 11 p.m., but because of the missing plane, it didn't look like I was going to arrive until around 2 a.m. I felt bad keeping Brett up that late to pick me up—plus I had a cold, so I wasn't feeling so hot. We texted back and forth about my arrival, and I finally suggested he go home and I would catch a taxi to the hotel I was staying at for the night.

"No way," he said. "I will be there to pick you up. Don't worry."

I finally arrived, and there he was, waiting with a big smile and a huge hug. I was excited and oddly nervous at the same time. We headed to the hotel, checked in, and went to the bar where you can get a glass of wine any time of the day (or night). Afterward, we went upstairs and crawled into bed.

The next morning, we woke up late and had a beautiful lunch on the beach before heading to the villa where Brett now worked as a waterski coach and where we both would be staying. I had my own room, and he stayed downstairs in the coaches' room. I got settled and joined the six other guests that evening who were also at the resort for the week.

Having only been there once before with the group of women friends, I felt a little uncomfortable joining in with six strangers. They were all friends, and I felt like I was imposing on their vacation. I realized later there were a lot of single people who went to this amazing place and met new people for the first time, but for the first part of that week, everything felt awkward at best.

Bedtime came around, and I went to my room. Since arriving at the villa earlier that day, Brett and I had had no interaction with one another except as part of the group. I had no idea whether he would be staying with me or not.

God, I thought to myself. *I am really in deep shit again. What have I done?*

That night, Brett snuck into my room with a backpack filled with a few things.

I looked at him and said hesitantly, "What is going on here? What am I doing in Mexico? Why did you invite me?"

He looked at me from across the room and said, "I love you. I've always loved you."

I melted. I had dreamed about him saying those words to me many times.

I stayed in Mexico for eighteen days. I can't tell you Brett's actions during those eighteen days always matched his words that night. I vacillated between feeling comfortable and happy to be there and painfully uncomfortable.

During our second week together, the only guests at the villa were me and another guest coach, so the owners closed for the week. We were allowed to stay, but with no access to the kitchen, we had to go out for every meal. The three of us spent the next seven days together skiing, dining, and having fun.

Waterski coaches don't make a ton of money. Like most coaches in the world, it's the passion of the sport that drives their desire to be involved. I knew I had more money than both coaches put together—and then some. I was afraid to have a conversation with the two of them about money and the perennial question, "Who should pay?"

There I was again, feeling like I needed to pick up the bill for most of our meals—and any other activity we did. I was happy to do it at first, but as time went on, I was beginning to feel obligated—and resentful.

We had a good time that week, but that familiar thought of *He's only here for the money* swirled around my head again.

Sometimes I wondered if God was playing a trick on me. Here was another hot, young, poor, professional athlete dropped at my feet. The problem was I didn't know whether God (or my Higher Power) had called Brett in to teach me how to say no and move on, *or* whether Brett was there to give me another chance to do things differently: to learn how to be an empowered woman with money and build a successful relationship with someone who had less. Honestly, neither path seemed easy.

Brett was very present when we were by ourselves, but in public he wasn't very attentive, and most of the time I had that uncomfortable schoolgirl feeling of wondering whether he liked me.

"Can we just hold hands while we walk?" I asked one afternoon at the mall as we were doing some shopping. "There is no one around we know."

He looked at me, smiling. "No way, are you crazy? I don't do things like that. Get over it."

One night, Brett said casually, "Don't get too attached. I don't date women for more than eighteen months. Other than Courtney, who I was with for seven years, all of them end after a *maximum* of eighteen months. I've never been married and never will be. I get bored and have to go."

I didn't respond.

Was he serious?

After about ten minutes I turned to him and asked him, laughing nervously, "So, how are you counting the eighteen months, exactly? Does the eighteen months start the day I arrived in Mexico? And is it the total number of days we are together, or do days apart count as well?"

He looked me directly in the eyes and said, "Relax, it hasn't started yet."

I loved hearing that, but I wasn't sure it could last. Maybe I didn't mention this before: Brett was forty. I had turned fifty-nine shortly after I arrived in Mexico.

During those eighteen days in Mexico, I tried to break up with Brett about twenty-seven times. I was tainted by my past two relationships with Greg and Harry, with the same concerns over age and money.

Each time I would bring up some reason we shouldn't be together, he comforted me and assured me he loved me. That assurance quieted me down—until the next time. In order to protect my heart, I told him before I left Acapulco he could do or be with whoever he wanted—and so could I.

"This isn't a monogamous relationship," I told him. "Just please do me a favor and don't tell me about any other women."

At least, I thought I was trying to protect myself so I wouldn't get hurt. The truth was, I was hoping he would think I was cool and easygoing—and really fall in love.

I made it home from Mexico with only two days to unpack and repack again for the family Christmas trip. The family trip was wonderful, and I returned to Aspen on December 30, planning to stay home for a while.

That very day, I got a phone call from Brett. He was spending his two-week Christmas holiday at his cabin in Michigan, near where he grew up. He and his brother had bought the property together two years earlier.

"Hey, honey. How was your trip home?"

"It was fine," I said. "We had a good time, but I am happy to be home."

"What are you doing for New Year's Eve?" he asked.

"Nothing. I have no plans. Honestly, I really don't care. I am over New Year's."

I paused. "What are you doing?"

I had never been to his cabin and had no idea what he might be up to. I asked the question, but wasn't entirely sure I really wanted to know the answer. Sometimes FOMO still crept in. It did then.

"I have no plans either. Why don't you hop on a plane and come visit me?" he said.

I breathed a sigh of relief. His answer made me feel happy and secure. He wanted to spend New Year's with me.

"Well, as usual, I have a few things on my plate," I told him. "Derek is leaving for Australia on his semester abroad for five months on January second. Basically, I would have to fly tomorrow and come home January first. I really want to be here to send him off."

"That's great. Come for the night. Go buy a plane ticket."

I hesitated for a moment, but I already missed him, so I bought a ticket, packed an overnight bag, and headed to the airport twelve hours later. I arrived in Grand Rapids at 7 p.m. and was on a plane the next day at noon back to Aspen.

The plan was to go to his cabin, but we never made it that far. Instead, we spent the night celebrating at the bar at the Holiday Inn a half mile from the airport with some couple I will certainly never see again. It wasn't a fancy New Year's Eve by a long shot, but our short time together reminded me how much I liked him.

I got Derek off to Australia and finally had a moment to breathe and sit quietly by myself. Intuitively, I felt it was time to come out of my cave. I had chosen the Bear Card just after New Year's in 2018, and it was time to let it go. I began pulling cards again every morning. In the beginning, I pulled different cards each day out of the fifty-two possible cards. Then—just as I had pulled the Bear Card over and over—the Butterfly Card kept showing up. My Inner Knowing knew 2019 was the Year of the Butterfly.

A butterfly, as most of you already know, begins as a caterpillar, morphs into a chrysalis, and then transforms into a beautiful butterfly with color and wings. I knew it was time for transformation in my life, but I really had no clue what it would look like. I did know, after the Year of the Bear and my year of hibernation, I didn't want to go back to the restaurant and bar scene in Aspen full-time.

Brett and I kept in touch after he returned to coach at the villa in the beginning of January. Sometimes I wouldn't hear from him for days, and I would start freaking out. Just then, my phone would ring. He always seemed to know how far he could push before he needed to call. It was kind of eerie.

I went back to Mexico several times that winter, paying my way as a guest. My rationale was that the only way I was going to see Brett that winter was if I went to him. This wasn't difficult for me. I loved the waterskiing and everything that went along with it—including the resident coach.

Brett and I had a lot of fun, especially by ourselves. He still often ignored me during the day, blaming it on not wanting to take attention away from the other guests. I couldn't really argue with him on this one since he was very attentive when we did have time alone.

Since Brett was building a name for himself as a coach, he asked me on several occasions to help him purchase a variety of water-ski-related apparel. Every order had something in it for me, so I rationalized I could help him out. It started with twelve ski vests with his name on them—which were meant to be sold to guests—and waterski equipment for both of us.

One afternoon, as we were getting ready for dinner, I got the question I was hoping to avoid.

"Honey, can you please give me a credit card with my name on it?" Brett asked.

I had already given him a credit card with my name on it to use when we were together, but now he wanted his own. I had walked this path before—and it wasn't a path I really liked.

"I don't have a lot of expenses down here, but when I go home to Michigan in May, I'm going to need to buy gas and groceries, and I could really use the help."

I reluctantly said, "Sure," wondering why he needed *my* help. All I knew was he had been a bartender in Aspen and wore nice clothes and made what seemed like a lot of money in tips. Now that we were dating, I definitely knew what he made as a waterski coach. But I didn't question his finances for fear of being too nosy or making waves—and

I was all for his new, healthier job choice and wanted him to follow his passion.

On my next trip to see Brett, I handed him a credit card linked to my account—just as I had done with Harry—with *his* name on it. I knew I could always cut him off, but once again, love and money were intertwined. I was pretty sure if I ever took that card away, it would more than likely be the end of our relationship.

I was still trying to unravel what lesson I was meant to learn by him being in my life. I continued to practice daily exercises like meditation and free-form writing. I was still working on my book. But I wasn't feeling so successful around love and money. I didn't want to end my relationship with Brett before it had a chance to go anywhere, but it felt like the same thing all over again. I wasn't prepared to go through the upset I went through when I broke up with Greg until I was 100 percent sure of what I wanted.

Then I remembered the Butterfly Card. I made a choice to surrender to giving him the credit card, just like a caterpillar entering its chrysalis, and see what would unfold without me trying to control the outcome.

Men take care of women and give them a credit card with their name on it all the time, so why shouldn't a successful woman like me take care of a man if I love him? I thought.

During my final trip to Mexico that year in April, Brett and I decided to go to Europe together during the summer. We had thrown the idea around several times, and it sounded like fun. I had to go for business anyway, and Brett wanted to compete in two waterski tournaments, one in Spain and one in France.

I planned the trip with some help from him. I was used to traveling on my own, but the places we were going seemed to be a bit remote and challenging to get to. I wanted to travel with him.

I purchased two business-class tickets to fly over the pond. I have put in my time flying in the back of the plane, and in the last few years figured if I can't afford the cost of a nice seat, then I shouldn't be going overseas.

Did I want to purchase two business-class tickets? Not really, but I again felt guilty. What was I supposed to do: fly up front and put Brett in the back of the plane?

After all, if as a woman I want to gift my man a business-class ticket, why shouldn't I? I shouldn't have to hide what I spend or what I give. I should be able to do what I want to do and what feels best in the moment—and more importantly live with the consequences of my choices.

This is amazing. We will have a blast this summer together, I thought, barely containing my excitement. Our trip was two months away. In my mind, I had just secured at least another two months with him.

I was continuing to meet with my relationship coach, Catherine. Unsurprisingly, many of our coaching sessions centered around my relationship with Brett.

I often felt like Catherine was telling me if Brett couldn't take care of me financially, I shouldn't choose to stay with him. I resented her for saying that. I had heard the same thing so many times—since my mother died and I inherited the money—but I wanted this time to be different. I wanted to be an empowered, wealthy female who had figured out how to have a successful relationship when the woman held the purse strings.

I also realized since Catherine had never sat in my shoes, she couldn't really understand what it was like to be a woman with means. Catherine had a thriving coaching business and made her own money, but from what I understood, she grew up without a lot of financial resources and married an older, financially successful man. Her experience was quite different from mine. How could she really understand?

This was a familiar feeling. I didn't feel understood by many people—not even my life coach. I felt lonely and isolated and different from nearly everyone around me. I was constantly having to hide my feelings of inadequacy. After all, I was wealthy—I wasn't supposed to have a problem in the world.

My time with Catherine came to an end. At this juncture, I wanted time to integrate, digest, and practice all I had learned from my graduate work, readings, and coaches.

———————

In May 2019, I went to visit Brett after his season in Mexico had finished. This time we actually got past the airport Holiday Inn and went to his cabin. I walked through the front door, and my eyes were as wide as saucers.

I looked around at one of the messiest places I had ever seen. It hadn't been cleaned in forever, and stuff was everywhere. It was filled with dust, dirt, and dead flies.

It was more than my neat, clean, organized brain could handle.

When we went to bed that night, we climbed up a six-foot commercial ladder to a mattress on a platform above the bedroom they had turned into a closet. If you sat up in bed, there would be about a 12-inch clearance above your head.

The only other bed in the house was a king-sized mattress in the garage. I also slept there a couple of times. Sometimes I heard mice scurrying around me at night.

The kitchen sink didn't work when I first arrived. You had to do the dishes in the laundry tub in the garage.

That sink needed to be repaired. On this, Brett and I agreed.

We went to the local plumbing store to rent a snake to clean the drain. It turned out, we needed a very long snake because the well was a long way from the house. Brett fixed the sink, which brought me immense joy.

We were only six months into our relationship, so I didn't want to make a fuss over the mess. This was not my home. I bit my tongue, rolled up my sleeves, and quietly started cleaning. I reorganized the spice cabinet, combining several jars of the same spice into one. I tidied up on the sly, hoping Brett wasn't going to notice or be upset. But it was above and beyond anything I had ever lived in—or seen.

If I couldn't clean inside the way I wanted, at least I could clean up and tend to the outside. Together, we worked side by side to plant a rudimentary vegetable garden beside the house and enjoyed some peaceful time together in Michigan. Gardening took me back to my landscaping days, and I realized how much I missed having my hands in the soil.

After a couple of weeks in Michigan, we packed our things into Brett's truck and took to the road. We spent most of June traveling up and down the East Coast together from lake to lake where Brett coached some of his clients. Our last stop was Virginia, where we would stay for five days before heading on the trip we had planned to Europe for his two waterski tournaments.

The day we arrived in Virginia, Brett got word his father was sick and in need of a serious operation scheduled the day we were leaving for Europe. Teary-eyed, Brett got in his truck—leaving me in Virginia with a friend and client of his—and headed back to Michigan to be with his dad.

I stayed in Virginia, waiting for what seemed like an eternity to hear news about what was going to happen with Brett's father and our plans to go to Europe. Just twenty-four hours before our flight, I made the choice to cancel our trip. I wanted to go so badly, not just because I had financed the majority of the trip, but to go to Europe on an adventure with the man I loved.

But I knew canceling the trip was the right thing to do. Other than the plane tickets, most of the cost of the trip was non-refundable, but to me it was worth it. Who wants to go on an amazing trip to Europe with the man you think you are in love with whose father is seriously sick? That didn't sound like much fun.

The airlines were able to credit us for our tickets: one in my name, and one in Brett's.

We'll just go next year, I thought, kind of excited about the idea that we might have another whole year together. After I canceled everything, I headed back to Aspen from Virginia, not knowing what the future was going to bring, but happy to be going home to nest for a bit.

After I got home, I talked with Brett every day. He was extremely worried about his father and very grateful to me for being willing to postpone our trip. The truth was, I felt great about my choice to accommodate gracefully. I felt empowered and believed I had made a wise choice.

After about a week in Aspen, Brett invited me to come back to Michigan, and I went. During my first two weeks there, I spent a lot of time on my own. Many days, Brett would leave the cabin early in the morning to drive the hour and a half in each direction to see his father and not return until late in the evening. I didn't have a car—and nowhere to go anyway—so I spent time in the garden, wrote, and cleaned the house. I was content, and he gave me a lot of love and attention when he was there.

One day he asked, "Would you like to come with me tomorrow to meet my dad and his wife? They'd like to meet you, and I want you to meet them."

"Of course, I'll come with you," I said, trying to hide how excited I was. "I would love to support you and meet them."

I knew Brett didn't take many women home to meet his parents, so I was secretly thrilled. The first visit was a bit awkward, but over the summer I returned many times and enjoyed spending time there. Both of his siblings were around, along with a smattering of family friends who came to visit his father as he recovered. I loved them all and grew especially fond of his brother, Matt, who not only shares Brett's passion for waterskiing but also a love of land.

One morning, Brett and I were sitting in the yard drinking our morning cup of coffee when he turned to me in between rounds of the online poker game he was playing. He grabbed my hand and said, "Honey, I think I can spend the rest of my life with you."

This was coming from a man who was a bachelor at forty-one, had run a nightclub for six years, and had previously told me not to get to set on a relationship that would last more than a maximum of eighteen months.

"Pardon me. What did you just say?" I asked, dumbfounded.

"Yeah, I can…spend the rest of my life with you. I love you."

I sat there for a few minutes taking in what I had heard and finally asked, "What made you change your mind?"

He gazed back at me. "You picked tomatoes with me."

Just as when he told me about the eighteen-month dating rule, I took a few minutes to digest this unexpected answer.

"Whoa, whoa, whoa. Just a minute." I said, laughing out loud. "You're telling me I didn't have to come see you all those times in Mexico, or take you out to dinner, or buy you all that waterski gear? All I had to do was pick some tomatoes?"

"Yep," he said.

I was having a major a-ha moment. It wasn't the money he really cared about; it was me. I'm sure the money didn't hurt, but maybe it wasn't the primary reason he was with me.

I saw light at the end of my dark tunnel. Maybe I could really be in a successful relationship as an empowered woman holding the purse strings.

We continued to work in the yard, pruning, weeding, and watering. Earlier in the summer, Brett encountered an audiobook called *Dirt to Soil* by Gabe Brown. Since we had an hour and a half drive each direction several times a week to visit his father, we listened to *Dirt to Soil* multiple times. We fell in love with Gabe's practices of regenerative farming.

For me, it was a book not just about *soil* health, but about *soul* health.

Over a period of months, the woman who had spent all those years going out every night in Aspen once the children were gone—getting dressed up in little black dresses and fancy shoes to go out, dine, and sip Chardonnay—wanted to build a farm with a garden, fruit trees, cows, goats, chickens, and a couple of dogs. I was elated but confused.

Where had Suzanne the party girl gone?

I'd been kidnapped by this amazing vision of getting back to nature.

I laughed at myself and one day said to Brett, "My next book—if I ever finish this one—is going to be called *From Campo to Camo: One Woman's Journey Back to Nature.*"

Campo di Fiori is a lovely Italian restaurant in Aspen I frequented during my Aspen years. I loved Campo, but my heart had returned to the land, gardening, and being close to nature. I even bought a UTV (although I had never heard of a UTV before that summer), a utility vehicle that allowed us to get around the property easily and be in nature.

I was returning to my love of landscaping and having my hands in the soil. I was returning home.

CHAPTER 18

If You Can't Beat Him, Join Him

Having "enough" is not an amount. It's a state of being.

–LYNNE TWIST

Brett's cabin was in a relatively remote part of Michigan, but there were a few diners nearby, and we often went out for a late lunch or dinner. The diners were far from fancy, but it was nice to get out after a long day in the garden. The menus were limited to dishes like hamburgers, jalapeno poppers, a limited selection of overcooked vegetables, salads made of iceberg lettuce, and more ranch dressing (which I found out later was—and still is—the most popular dressing in America) than you can possibly imagine.

Throughout the summer of 2019, Brett played online poker whenever he had a free minute. We would sit down at the bar of one of the local diners, order, and he would play poker.

It bothered me. I wanted him to talk to me while we were out, but poker was always on his phone screen—and seemed more important than engaging in a conversation with the woman he wanted to "spend the rest of his life with."

I wanted to say something like, *Why are you always playing that stupid game with imaginary money while I'm paying for your lunch with real money? Don't you like my company?* Or something like that.

But I didn't.

I wanted to surrender to who Brett was and not expect him to be any different. After I realized this was an ongoing behavior, I decided to experiment with a new way of being. Every time we went to a restaurant, I came prepared with my phone or computer. While we waited for our food, Brett would sip on his drink and pull out his phone—and so would I. I figured if I couldn't beat him, I'd join him, as the old expression goes. I wanted to see what would happen.

When I travel for work or fun, I have a lot of meals on my own, and I always have a computer or phone with me while I eat. I write, work, or text friends. I do it because I enjoy it. Since I often felt I was by myself during our meals together, rather than complain about it, I did what I do when I dine solo.

I was amazed at what happened.

I would be doing my thing, and 90 percent of the time, Brett would stop playing poker, lean over, touch my arm softly, and say, "Whatcha doin'?"

"Nothing," I would say, smiling. "Just messing around."

Often, his question led us into a conversation about this or that—which is what I really wanted all along. It was a valuable lesson for me, and I am proud to say I never mentioned one word about what I was experimenting with. Until he reads this book—if that ever happens—he will never know.

I got what I wanted by accepting who he was and not complaining about who I *wanted* him to be. It was another empowering moment. I took care of myself and took a stand in a different way than I would have in the past. I let go of any expectations that Brett needed to talk to me for me to feel loved. The result of him engaging with me during our meals was a bonus.

The experience of three a-ha moments in a short period of time was mind-blowing to me: choosing to postpone our trip to Europe (and not being upset over the change in plans), the recognition that Brett was not there just for the money, and now accepting someone I loved regardless of what they did were three incredible miracles.

The light at the end of the tunnel became even brighter.

After pulling weeds and picking flowers and fresh food from the garden, and learning about no-till drilling from *Dirt to Soil*, we spent many late afternoons scouting the neighborhood for deer, turkey, birds, and butterflies in the UTV.

Michigan is a huge deer hunting area. I didn't grow up deer hunting, so this was a strange land for me, where men—and women— hunt, fish, can tomatoes, wear Carhartts, and drive around in pickup trucks. This was no Ross, California, but I was loving it. I felt excited and content with my new life.

I stayed in Michigan until the middle of July. I loved gardening and looking for deer. I loved the weather. I wasn't bothered by all the bugs that were supposedly there. I loved the landscape and the simplicity of the culture—and the people.

One morning on our way to visit his father, Brett turned to me and asked, "How would you like to go waterskiing tomorrow?"

"Wow. That would be amazing. But where?"

"There's a private lake about an hour from here where we can ski. You have been so great visiting my dad and working in the garden with me. I want to do something nice for you. "What do you think? Would you like that?"

I was so excited. After leaving Virginia and canceling our trip to Europe, we had not been skiing once, and I was missing the sport I love.

"Let's do it."

We loaded up our gear the next afternoon and headed south. We arrived at the site and were greeted by a couple who owned 250 acres of farmland. They had dug a lake a few years earlier that was long enough for a waterski course. It wasn't much different than most farms in the Midwest, but to me it was the most beautiful setting ever.

After getting off the water that day, I looked at Brett and said, "I want a lake."

I'd been to many private lake sites since meeting Brett, but none had ever stirred a craving to have my own piece of property and lake. But that day I had a vision. I wanted a lake, a garden, chickens, cows, and all.

Brett looked at me with the biggest smile I had ever seen and said, "I am so excited. Building a lake is my ultimate dream. And the best part about this is it's *your* idea."

"I love you, honey," he said as we walked off the dock arm and arm. "Let's go find some land to buy."

As we walked with his arm around me and mine around his waist, I was reminded of the day we were in Mexico where he refused to hold my hand and thought, *My, how things have changed. I'm the luckiest woman in the world.*

Brett loved his cabin and wanted to buy something close to home. Land in this part of Michigan is less expensive than many parts of the United States, it's relatively flat (ideal for digging a lake), and water rights are obtainable. I loved it there as well, so off we went on days we weren't going to see his father, driving the backroads in the UTV in search of for-sale signs.

We found a real estate agent who just happened to have a brother who had built several lakes in the area. We found Jason, a civil engineer—coincidentally or not—from someone we had met on my dream lake earlier that summer, who was willing to help us. And the list went on and on of serendipitous coincidences supporting our quest to find land and build a lake. *From Campo to Camo: One Woman's Journey Back to Nature* was moving toward becoming a reality.

In the middle of July, I returned to Aspen to prepare my house for an August rental, and then headed to Lake Tahoe to spend time on the lake that had been a part of my life for as long as I could remember. And even though the children were grown and had their own lives, all three—along with girlfriends and boyfriends—came for at least part of the time. August in Tahoe was one of my favorite times of the year. The lake is beautiful—and a month with my family was always wonderful.

Since the children all had jobs or school to return to by mid-August, I found myself alone during the second half of the month. It was frustrating to be on a lake—with a boat in the driveway—and no one to go skiing with. I have friends in Tahoe, but I knew getting anyone to get up and go out on the lake early is like pulling teeth.

And after skiing so many places in warm water, the idea of jumping in fifty-eight-degree water was losing its appeal. It's refreshing to get in, but after getting out of the lake—and driving back to the dock in the cool early morning mountain air—I was often chilled to the bone.

I left Lake Tahoe the summer of 2019, and for the first time in almost six decades, I was ready to go. Although I didn't realize it at the time, the end of my long-term love affair was coming to a close. I would return to Lake Tahoe again, but my passion would never be the same.

All I wanted to do was get back to Michigan and the warm summer water and ski behind a good boat. Again, I was shocked, not knowing who this person was inhabiting my body.

I returned to Michigan at the end of August. One day, as I was looking over my credit card statement, I found myself getting upset over the long list of charges on the credit card I had given Brett. My resentment over giving him a card in the first place (in his name) was building as the months wore on. That day I hit a breaking point and realized I was going to have to come up with a different way of handling the situation. I didn't want to leave *again* because of money issues without trying everything I could possibly think of.

I prayed a lot that night for an answer.

It came.

The next morning, as we were laying in bed, I turned to Brett and said, "I can't take sorting through all these charges you are racking up on my credit card. I get so upset when I see them. This is not working.

"But rather than cutting you off completely," I continued, "I have come up with an alternative solution. You stop using my credit card, and instead I will give you a set amount of money each month. You figure out what you want to spend it on. This is how I handle money with my children, and it works pretty well, so I think we should try it."

I went over Brett's ongoing expenses like mortgage, phone bill, an approximate amount for food each month, added a bit, and settled on a set amount for the next two months until he was scheduled to go back to Mexico for work in early November. Brett agreed to my plan. I Venmoed him money that day and sat back with a sigh of relief.

I took a chance. I did something differently. I felt as good about it as I could at the time. And if this solution didn't work, I would try another one until I found one that did.

Ironically, I had a much better understanding of my mother and father's arrangement. My father gave my mother an allowance, and after covering basic expenses, she chose where to spend the money. Maybe it wasn't as bad of an option as I thought as a child. The only difference was, I was a woman giving to a man, and this man was not my husband. Whether I liked it or not, I had to get comfortable with this dynamic, because it didn't look like anything was going to change anytime soon—with or without Brett.

In return for my financial contribution, I got a great deal of support. From household chores and duties, to helping me with projects and a never-ending show of kindness, Brett's commitment to our relationship never faltered. And although I was the breadwinner, he contributed to making our lives the best they could be.

It felt like a win-win.

CHAPTER 19

Love the One You're With

Love the person with whom you are in relationship
rather than put energy into complaint and what's wrong
with them. That means loving them regardless of what
they do. It's called unconditional loving.

—JOHN-ROGER, DSS

September and October came and went, but no property. Before Brett's
declaration that we should spend the rest of our lives together, I had
been invited on two trips: one to India in October 2019 and one to
Africa in January 2020. The dates were set by the people I would be
traveling with.

Just before I left Michigan, Brett asked me, "So, why did you
decide to go on these trips anyway? You need to stay here with me so we
can keep looking for property."

"Well," I confessed, "I planned these trips a long time ago, and
I didn't know back then if we'd still be together." The truth was, if
things didn't work out, I didn't want to be sitting around waiting for

him. I wanted to ensure this time there would *not* be twenty tearful phone calls.

I was traveling to India with an Aspen-based group called Lead with Love. I only knew a couple of people in our group of nine (eight women plus Paul, our token man), but I didn't care who was going. I just wanted to go.

Because of my deep love of wildlife, I had added an extra week to our two-week trip to search for a tiger. I wasn't going to India without at least trying to see a tiger. Tigers are a bit harder to find in India than big cats like lions and cheetahs in Africa, but I was bound and determined to do my best.

Lead with Love had planned our itinerary, but it's India, so plans often end up being quite different than anticipated. I was comfortable with this type of travel from my trips to Africa. However, I also had my own personal agenda.

A new decade was approaching. I had a sense 2020 was going to bring a *radical* shift in my world. Out of the six decades I've been on the planet, three of the "zero" years (the years that begin a new decade) have been somewhat traumatic and definitely life-altering. I was born just before the start of 1960, and I believe anyone would call emerging from the comfort of my mother's belly into a bright, cold, sterile room a traumatic experience.

In 1990, I moved to New York City because Mark lost his job in California and secured a job in the Big Apple. I didn't want to leave my life and house and family to move to New York City, and I had several full-blown temper tantrums before agreeing to move.

I moved to Aspen in 2000 because my husband was moving to London with another woman, and I was forced to make a change. Maybe I had something to do with these experiences, maybe I didn't, but I do know they were traumatic all the same. Some decades came and went with no change, but these three all happened to fall on a new decade.

It seemed as if the "big shift" in 2020 was going to be building a lake and getting back to nature with the man I loved, but I was skeptical.

I tried to lay aside my fears of Brett being there for the money, but they continued to nag at me—especially after the sun went down along with a glass of wine or two. That question of *Should I stay or should I go?* from the famous song by the Clash, swam around in my head.

I asked myself on several occasions, *What significant shift was 2020 possibly meant to bring?*

So, my personal agenda while I was in India was that I was going to do my best to stay open to what the universe might offer. I was on a search for clues, and I figured India—and the incredible wisdom of the culture—was as good a place as any to look.

I arrived in India one day before the rest of the group. I wanted to feel refreshed after the long flight before we began to explore Delhi, which was our first stop. Due to a late departure out of Denver, I arrived at my hotel around 5 a.m., so I slept in and spent the day recovering.

After some rest, I went to the hotel gym for a workout and was heading out for some lunch when I ran into Lydia. Lydia was a tarot card reader. She was sitting in the lobby of my hotel between readings.

I went over to her and asked, "Are you available for a reading this afternoon?"

I had no idea whether Lydia was any good at reading tarot cards, but she was there—directly in my path.

"Of course, I am. Can you come back at three o'clock?" she said to me with a smile lighting up her beautiful face.

"I will meet you right here at three. I'm so excited!" I said, beaming from ear to ear.

I was back at exactly 3 p.m., prepared for whatever clues the tarot cards had to offer.

Lydia asked me to choose seven or so cards, which she laid out in a pattern. Lydia knew nothing about my life. I had given her zero information. All she knew was that I was a blond, fifty-something, white woman from America.

I can't remember everything Lydia said that day, as it was a lot of complicated information, but the one thing I do remember was, "I can see two options for you. I think you should take the first one. It looks better than the second."

She paused as she stared at the cards. "But there is another possibility that you still don't know about," she said thoughtfully.

I was blown away. Brett and Matt and I had seen two properties that were viable options for building a lake and creating our fantasy.

That must be it. She is talking about the properties. I guess I'm supposed to buy one of them and stick around with Brett.

I didn't know what she meant about another possibility, but maybe it meant we were supposed to wait and something better was going to come along. I thanked Lydia for her time and went back to my room.

The rest of the group arrived the next day, and we started our journey through India in Delhi. Each day was new and magical. So many people had warned me of the poverty in India and how I better be prepared. I found the poverty, the filth, the noise, and the chaos to be fascinating. Most of the people in India are happy and peaceful and live simple lives in the face of an immensely complex society. They don't care about the garbage. They walk right over it and—as far as I could tell—don't even see it.

Our second stop was Jaipur, which is famous for many things, including an astrological park with the world's largest stone sundial and beautiful architectural representations of each of the astrological sun signs. As we were getting ready to leave the park, some of the women went to the gift shop to purchase souvenirs. I was sitting on a stone wall in the shade, drinking a cold bottle of water, thinking about my experience in the park and talking with our Indian guide who was standing next to me. Our next stop, he told me, would be the holy city of Rishikesh.

Quite unexpectedly, I blurted out, "Is there a way for me to see an astrologist in Rishikesh? I want to get my chart read."

The guide looked at me and smiled, "Well, the great-grandson of the designer of this park is standing right there," he said pointing to a man who I hadn't noticed standing near us.

I had no plan of meeting with an astrologist on the trip, but kind of like the tarot card reader in the lobby of the hotel, one appeared. For those of you who don't know, an astrological chart is generated these days by putting information on the day you were born, the hour, and location of your birth into a computer program, which produces a chart. Each person has a unique chart based on their information. The chart is then interpreted by an astrologer. In America, astrology is considered pseudoscience (i.e., a false science), but in India, astrology is considered just as much of a science as biology, astronomy, and physics.

When in India . . .

As it turned out, most of my fellow travelers also wanted their charts read. We were leaving the next day for Agra to see the Taj Mahal, so we had limited time to arrange seven readings that afternoon and evening. Each reading was a short twenty minutes per person, so there was only time to get to the heart of the reading. Some of the women were not impressed with the astrologist, but for me it was incredible.

Without going into too much detail, the astrologer told me I was creative and spiritually on a quest to answer the question of what we as human beings are doing on this planet during our lifetimes. For anyone who knows me, this accurately sums up my lifelong questions of who the hell are we, and what is our real purpose in being here?

The astrologer also told me my lifelong struggle was—and always has been—successful intimate relationships. He told me the first few years of 2020 held a picture of finding and creating a relationship meant for my spiritual growth.

Mind you, like the tarot card reader, I didn't tell this man one thing about my life, except for my birth date, time, and location. He knew nothing about Brett and my desire to figure out if I should move forward in the relationship or not. I had received another clue: My astrological chart confirmed I was going to find the man of my dreams.

Our journey through India continued. The Taj Mahal was even more breathtaking than I could have ever possibly imagined. I was awed by the magnificence of this beautiful engineering feat. The Taj Mahal was commissioned in 1632 and built by the emperor at the time for his wife. It is a stunning ivory-white mausoleum inspired by love. It was the most beautiful building I had ever seen.

After our sunrise visit to the Taj Mahal, we went on an eight-hour, extremely bumpy car ride from Agra to Rishikesh. Again, I was awestruck by the chaos in every corner of India. Even in the more rural areas, the noise, the smell, and the traffic never ceased.

Rishikesh is a holy city located on the Ganges River at the base of the Himalayan foothills. It is renowned as a mecca for yoga and meditation, and like everywhere else in India, it is filled with sights, sounds, color, and chaos. During our four-day stay, in the middle of all the chaos that surrounded us, our group of nine took time to do yoga and meditate in the sanctuary of our hotel.

At one point, one of my fellow travelers mentioned she wanted to see an Ayurvedic doctor during our stay. As soon as she brought up the idea, I wanted to go as well. I didn't really know what an Ayurvedic doctor did, but given my experience with the tarot card reader and astrologer, I figured what the heck.

Thanks to Google (and somewhat decent internet), you can find anything—even in Rishikesh. We found a doctor within a five-minute walk from our hotel.

Most of the women (and Paul) wanted to go. The appointments were $20 for 20 minutes with the doctor. As it turns out, we discovered Google had led us to one of the most famous Ayurvedic doctors in all of India.

I was sitting in the waiting room with Paul, filling out some paperwork before seeing the doctor. The paperwork was six long pages of questions for the doctor to review so he could reveal my "dosha," whatever that meant. I hadn't a clue.

I now know most people see an Ayurvedic doctor to discover their dosha, which is a unique blueprint of one's life that serves as a guide to healthy dietary choices supporting overall well-being. My goal was more of a spiritual discovery rather than a health discovery.

The first page had the standard questions you find on any form: name, age, birthday, email—and that question on every intake form I have ever filled out at a doctor's office: marital status. I have been checking divorced (or single, depending on my mood) for 20 years, always wondering why my marital status was important when I went to see an eye or foot doctor—or any doctor for that matter—other than maybe a therapist.

I looked at Paul, laughing, and said, "What the hell? Why do all doctor's forms ask about my marital status? I just don't get it."

I didn't expect him to have a good answer, but I had to ask.

The rest of the questions were challenging, and I struggled with the answers. As we were finishing our six pages' worth of disclosures about things like how big the bridge of your nose is and whether your hair is brittle or thinning, two of our fellow travelers came out from seeing the doctor.

One was quite upset, thinking she had been conned, and gestured to Paul and me—with a dramatic waving of her hand in front of her neck indicating we should leave immediately. She was quite convinced the doctor was a quack and *not* to be believed. I took this with a grain of salt and the recognition that the appointment was $20 for 20 minutes. I could take what I liked and leave the rest.

My time came to see the doctor, and I followed the receptionist to another building and ascended a flight of stairs. She handed the doctor my paperwork as I sat down. The doctor took the paperwork and started flipping through the pages, barely looking at the many questions I had painfully answered. He asked me how I was doing, but other than that, he was quiet. He took my pulse briefly and went back to the paperwork—not saying a word.

Maybe this guy is a quack, I thought to myself. *I don't see much happening here.*

After what seemed like an eternity, the doctor looked at me and said with a serious face, "So why are you single at fifty-nine?"

I am pretty sure I laughed out loud. Really? This was the question he was asking me? His office was too far away from where we filled out the forms, and there was no way he could have heard me giggling with Paul in the waiting room.

"I can't believe you are asking me that."

And for the first time, I shared my burning question.

"Actually, funny enough, I came to India to figure out whether I should stay with my boyfriend or not. He is eighteen years younger than me, and I am thinking about buying some property with him, which I have to finance, and I am scared I will build it and he will leave. I don't know what to do."

I briefly shared with the doctor about my previous three major changes, all of which had fallen on a zero year, and how I knew some major change was coming in 2020.

The doctor looked at me and said, "The way to your salvation and healing is through being in an intimate, loving relationship."

"But how do I know this is the one?"

"Well, he's the one that's here, so choose him. Frankly, it doesn't really matter," he said in all seriousness.

We talked for a bit longer. He didn't offer much more advice than that, and he didn't mention my "dosha." I left my barely twenty-minute appointment feeling elated. I was not expecting—by any stretch of my imagination—this piece of advice based on checking *single* on a lengthy intake form.

I walked back to where Paul was waiting and said, "You're not going to believe what the doctor asked me."

"What?" Paul asked, seeing the huge smile on my face.

"After all that work filling out his forms, the only thing he asked me was why I was single."

We both burst out laughing.

"You're kidding, right?"

"Nope, dead serious," I said.

After Paul's appointment with the doctor, I shared more about my visit with him as we made our way back down the quiet alley laden with cow manure to our hotel. Paul also had a wonderful experience with the doctor, and we were both quite pleased. On our way out, the doctor had invited us to come back the next morning at 6 a.m. to meditate with him, so Paul and I and another one of our companions agreed to come back. The doctor emphasized the importance of us being punctual in the morning. He was very adamant.

The next morning was just as incredible. Rather than actually meditating, the doctor spoke to us about how—and why—to meditate and encouraged all three of us to meditate every morning. He explained the benefits of a strong practice and how this discipline would change our lives forever.

He shared with us how meditation allows one the internal freedom to *never* be upset about anything, no matter what is happening in the world around us. After our 45-minute talk on the benefits of meditation, the doctor gave us each time to ask a question.

I patiently waited my turn and asked the nagging question I had since meeting Brett, and certainly since the doctor's suggestion that Brett was the obvious pick: "How do I really know *this man* is the one I should choose? I really hear—and have heard from other healers I have met in India—an intimate relationship is the way to move to a higher consciousness for me in this lifetime. I get it, and I accept this is true, but I'm scared I am making a mistake. Shouldn't I be finding a sixty-year-old, like my daughter suggests I do?"

"I will repeat what I told you yesterday," he said. "He is the one who is here. So, he is the obvious choice."

The doctor continued, "All of you Western people looking for love, your soul mates, and perfect partners are insane. Love comes from dedication, discipline, commitment, and communication. If you practice these four things, everlasting love is the result. NOT the other way around," the doctor emphasized. "And I will remind you all again, meditate every day for lasting peace and joy."

I felt in the depth of my soul the doctor was right. I reflected on some of my interactions with the people I had met during our trip— guides, drivers, and others. Most were married and had been for many years, and most had arranged marriages.

Occasionally, some of them had seen a man or woman they wanted to marry—and suggested to their parents they would like to have them arrange for their hand in marriage—but I didn't meet one person who had ever spent any time with the person they were going to marry before their wedding day. Some had never even seen the person before their wedding day. Everyone I met shared they were in successful, peaceful, joyful, loving, long-term marriages.

You don't find that too often in the United States. I thought to myself. Why not?

The doctor had answered that question. The people in these marriages practiced dedication, discipline, commitment, and communication from the beginning. In the West, we think we have to find the perfect partner first, and then we'll start practicing all these things--until we decide we don't feel like it anymore.

We left the doctor after two enlightening hours. I felt elated about the possibility of creating a successful, peaceful, joyful, intimate relationship with Brett.

As we were strolling home blissfully that morning, Paul looked at me and asked, "Are you going to call your boyfriend and tell him the good news?"

"No, I think I'll wait a bit. He'll know soon enough," I said with a peaceful feeling in my heart.

In that moment, I made a commitment to myself—and to Brett—to stick around and practice loving him fully without concern of the past or future in trust and faith of the unknown.

In that moment, I also made a commitment to meditate every day. I remembered John-Roger, founder of the Movement of Spiritual Inner Awareness and the University of Santa Monica, saying, "Spiritual exercises lead to spiritual growth." The message was now very clear.

After leaving Rishikesh, a few of us traveled on to central India in search of a tiger. Many people go to India to see a tiger but have no luck. We did.

In fact, we saw two.

While we were in central India looking for tigers, we had—for the first time since arriving in India—some time to relax and enjoy some quiet reflection. This was the first place we had been that was not hectic. As I was sitting by the pool one day basking in the sunshine, I noticed an app on my phone I had signed up for months earlier. It's called The Pattern.

You put in information including your name, birthdate, and where you were born, and the app spits out messages based on the lunar cycle. I had time, so I opened the app for the first time. Apps like this are a dime a dozen, I'm sure—and maybe they all say the same thing—but this was the one I opened that day.

What did it have to say?

The way to your salvation is through an intimate relationship.

It didn't say find yourself and learn to be independent. It didn't say your career is the way to your salvation, or any hundreds of other suggestions. The Pattern told me this was my time to seek out an intimate relationship.

Not only that, it also said the partner who would best serve *me* was carefree and most likely out of the normal expected realm of possibilities. He would not be what society in general thought was acceptable. The relationship would not be conventional.

Well, I thought to myself, *Brett definitely fits the bill. He's young, wild, and carefree.*

After Lydia, the astrologist, and the Ayurvedic doctor (all of whom I had coincidentally met while in India), this fourth insight sealed the deal for me. There was no way the Universe was not sending me a very clear message.

My time in India came to a close after our last stop in the holy city of Varanasi, where people have been pilgrimaging for hundreds of years. After another magnificent experience and a strong end to an amazing trip, I headed back to the United States.

A few days before I left India, I had been speaking to Brett on the phone about my experience when he said to me, "Stop in Michigan on your way home. I want to see you."

"But I'm only home for five days before I come to Mexico to be with you for a month. I'm going to see you very soon. I need to go home."

Then I gave it some thought. In Mexico, Brett would be busy working most of the time, and I may not have the chance to share with him the important insights I received on this trip. I decided to make the detour.

I diverted my trip—I got off the plane in New Jersey, and rather than heading to Aspen, I headed to Michigan to spend two days at Brett's cabin before heading home to repack my suitcase for a month in Mexico. We spent some quiet time together, and I had a chance to share all I had learned in India—including my insights about our relationship. He was thrilled, and so was I.

After three days in Aspen, I returned to Mexico and celebrated my sixtieth birthday and the third birthday in a row I had celebrated at the resort. We spent the day skiing, releasing baby turtles into the ocean, and swimming with two beautiful porpoises. I felt loved and cared for by Brett, the other guests, my children, and a plethora of friends.

Turning 30, 40, and 50 had been challenging, and I expected 60 to be no different. It was in some ways, but overall, I was proud of making it this far, proud of my life accomplishments, and looking forward to what lay ahead.

Don't Count Your Chickens Before They Hatch

There is in you something that waits and listens for the sound of the genuine in yourself. It is the only true guide you will ever have.

–HOWARD THURMAN

I was back home in Aspen. On January 1, 2020, I pulled a medicine card. I hadn't pulled a medicine card since my declaration that 2019 was the Year of the Butterfly. I shuffled the cards carefully, even though I hadn't looked at them in a year, and, lo and behold, the Butterfly card turned up once again. Apparently, I was still in a time of immense transition, but I still wasn't sure what the "big change" was going to be.

I was off to climb Mount Kenya from January 20 through the first week in February. I hadn't seen Brett since New Year's Eve, so I visited him in Mexico for six days before my trip to Africa. I knew from experience that not seeing him for six or seven weeks was *not* a good idea.

During those six days, I had the brilliant idea of buying a waterski boat. One of the big boat dealers and his wife were guest coaches that week in Acapulco. I had never met this couple before, but it seemed fortuitous we were there at the same time. I went for it. Why not buy a waterski boat? We were, after all, building a lake.

I ordered a custom-colored boat in anticipation that it would be finished by April 20, when we were scheduled to return to Michigan. An orange, purple, or yellow boat didn't speak to me, and I already had a black, white, and gray boat, so I wanted something with a bit of pizzazz. I wanted a boat trimmed in hot pink, but hot pink was not a commonly available color selection in the boat world. So, we designed the boat in white, black, and Brett's signature color teal blue.

I left Mexico psyched about my purchase and headed home to pack once again.

My two-week trip to Africa began with visiting three camps for orphaned elephants with the David Sheldrick Foundation, followed by a challenging climb up Mount Kenya to an elevation of 16,400 feet. I was invited a year before to go on the trip with ten of my female friends (eleven of us in total, of course). I kept promising myself I would do some training for the climb, but something more interesting than hiking always seemed to come up. Plus, Michigan and the coast of Mexico are close to sea level, so training was even more difficult.

Several times I tried to back out of the trip out of fear I couldn't make it to the top, but something inside me wanted to summit a mountain that high. The top of Aspen Highland Bowl at 12,392 feet—before shushing downhill on a pair of skis—was the highest I had ever been.

On the second day of our five-day, thirty-three-mile hike, I listened to an audiobook by a woman named Nancy Levin. When I first started her book *Worthy*, although the book is well-written, I didn't feel it spoke to me—or my life—but it was recommended by someone who thought it would help me in the organization of my book, so I continued to listen.

Other than admiring the incredible scenery, I didn't have much else to do in between huffing and puffing, and the book helped me to focus on other things besides my lower back pain, which was screaming at me, *Stop and retreat. What do you have to prove?*

I listened to the entire book during our arduous eight-hour hike that day, and as I continued to listen, a deeper message began to speak to me. I realized I could choose to drop my constant questioning of whether the person with me was here for me, or my money.

The fact is, short of giving it away as I had considered years earlier, I would never know the answer, so why torture myself with the question? Do any of us ever really know why people are in our lives?

I decided to drop my fears of being used for money on Mount Kenya, knowing the mountain is one of the most beautiful and expansive places on Earth, and it was big enough to shoulder my concerns.

As we crested to the top of our long climb that day, I saw Lake Michaelson 1,000 feet below where we would be camping for the evening. It is a magical lake surrounded by flowers that grow ten times their normal size compared to anywhere else on the planet, with a view of the majestic peak of Mount Kenya in the background.

My ten cohorts and I, six guides, and thirty-three porters camped there for the night, enjoying the sun setting below the horizon as the shimmering moon rose over the lake, and the temperature dropped to well below freezing. I cuddled up in my sleeping bag and dreamed of a life free of the burden of my own wealth.

The next day we climbed the thousand feet out of the lake area and another 1,500 feet to our final campsite.

After setting up and eating a semi-hot meal, I got a decent night's rest wrapped in two heated survival blankets, a heated vest, and several layers of clothing to keep me from freezing to death as I mentally prepared for our summit to the top. We rose early the next morning and started hiking in the dark around 4 a.m. in order to reach the summit by sunrise. I was wearing a fresh eight-hour heated vest above my base layer and three other layers of clothing including a huge down jacket, two hats, and heated gloves.

During that five-day hike, until the day we summitted, we did not see another human being that was not part of our rather large group. Many people climb the famous Kilimanjaro, but few climb majestic Mount Kenya. I cannot describe the vast, raw, rugged landscape. If God has a country, Mount Kenya is part of it.

Our summit morning was challenging for me. I questioned why, if I didn't like cold—and didn't like hiking, I had ever agreed to such a ludicrous goal. On top of that, air is thin at 16,400 feet, the wind was howling, and the shale and ice on the trail were slippery. I put one foot in front of another, reminding myself I had mentally prepared—and I was *not* going home without completing this climb, no matter how hard it was.

Most of my female companions were much fitter and always in front of me, climbing like mountain goats. My ego had to take a backseat and stop comparing their progress to mine. And although those ten women are some of my favorite people on the planet—strong, empowered, beautiful women who were genuinely encouraging me—I knew I was on a solo journey, and only I could be the one to make the choice to complete my goal.

When I took my final step, I burst out crying in joy. I had done it. I made it. I was so proud of myself. I had made the choice to let go of some old, useless baggage just two days before, and I knew in my heart I could only go up (or down, given my current elevation) from here.

With my eight years of extensive world traveling, I felt complete. I didn't necessarily think my trip to Kenya would be my last adventure,

I just no longer felt the need to prioritize traveling as much as I had. I was having a challenging time doing me, life with Brett, and traveling, and I was *always* on a plane. I was over it.

I wanted to stay home more and focus on writing, self-care, putting effort into my relationship, buying property, and settling down. I would never stop going to see my children when I could, but between India in October and Kenya in January, I knew I was done with constant packing and unpacking. At least for now.

Sometime during our descent from Mount Kenya, with an extremely limited connection to the outside world, one of the women found out about this thing called the "Coronavirus," and the term "pandemic" was thrown around.

Honestly, I am not sure I even knew what an accurate definition of a pandemic was. I didn't take it seriously at all. I had traveled with many of these same women to Ethiopia in 2014 during the height of the Ebola crisis. Ethiopia was at the epicenter of the Ebola outbreak, along with East Africa, and the U.S. government had warned Americans *not* to visit.

After almost canceling our trip, we went anyway. I never thought about Ebola once during our visit—nor did we see any signs of an infectious threat to the African people or anyone else. I certainly had no concern over a disease named after a Mexican beer.

After only six days in Aspen, I headed back to Mexico for a month. It had been about five weeks since I had seen Brett, and I was excited to reconnect. Kenya was my final adventure for the foreseeable future. I was committed to allowing love and money to be easy and joyful. I was committed to Brett and our future together.

Having arrived in Acapulco safely—and easily, which always brought a sense of relief—we were inundated with post after post, flip-flopping between the seriousness of this world crisis and making fun of the clearly far-fetched possibility of a global pandemic, known as the Coronavirus.

As March 2020 went on, Europe, along with China and a few other countries, seemed to be the most impacted. The United States didn't seem to be strongly affected—and no one in Mexico had any clue about what was about to happen. It was life as usual. We sat around and drank Coronas and laughed about the absurdity of the situation.

This trip to Mexico was no different than any of the others. People continued to come from all over the country—and world—for a destination waterski vacation. Each week there was a new group, most of whom I had never met. Many of these new friends were from places like the rural Midwest—which was so foreign to me, except for my recent exposure to rural Michigan. And even though the guests came from eclectic backgrounds, waterskiers are passionate about the sport, so there was always instant common ground to begin a conversation.

After talking about ski line lengths, equipment, and the oh-so-complicated topic of various possible fin settings, conversations usually turned to a more personal nature. I shared my book topic with most guests at one point or another during the week, and as usual, everyone seemed to have something to say.

Oddly enough, in this small sector of the population, women were often the predominant earners. Whenever I came across a couple in this situation, I asked many questions of both spouses about how they managed their relationships successfully. The most important common element I heard was communication—good, clear communication.

In each case, the wives (or girlfriends) loved their jobs. They weren't jealous or upset when their husbands or partners spent time waterskiing or doing a variety of other recreational activities. Yes, the men were waterskiing, but they were all contributing in some way, and both partners valued what the other brought to the table. I noticed a theme of equality and mutual respect.

I reflected on my relationship with Brett. Our communication was limited, and although Brett seemed to value me, I often questioned if he genuinely appreciated my contributions. He attributed our lack of communication to his job as a coach and the fact that he needed to make all his clients feel special. I sometimes still felt like I was just one of his guests and not his girlfriend—or financier.

Toward the end of my month in Mexico, I got a call from a rental agent in Aspen about a family who was interested in renting my house for three weeks beginning March 10, just a few days before I was scheduled to go home.

"Why not rent it?" Brett said to me. "I would love for you to stay here with me for another three weeks."

As soon as I heard these words, all of my fears about lack of communication or anything else flew right out the window.

"That sounds amazing," I said with a big grin. "I'm gonna do it."

I made some phone calls and sent a laundry list of instructions on what needed to be done to prepare the house for the rental. Being a control freak, it was challenging for me to leave the arduous task of moving to someone else, but I would make some money, and I could stay in Mexico with Brett and ski.

Because I had extended my trip unexpectedly, I had no place to stay the first week. A group of women had rented out the villa for a birthday bash, and not only was there no bed for me to sleep in, as Brett was sharing a room with a guest coach, I was also acutely aware these fourteen women—some of whom I knew—had no interest in the "girlfriend" of the coach sticking around and ruining their fun.

It was March 14, 2020. I had booked a room at a local hotel. I was happy to have some time on my own and regroup a bit before returning to the villa for two weeks. Brett dropped me off at the Princess Hotel and left for the airport to pick up his guests. I was expecting a room overlooking the ocean, but instead I ended up in a dingy room in the back of the hotel. Within hours of arriving, my positive vibrations of basking in the quiet and beauty of the Princess Hotel started to hit the fan.

Sunday, March 15, and Monday, March 16, were two of the most upsetting days I had ever experienced in my life to that point. As I was hidden away in the back of the hotel, news of a pandemic was hitting home—and hitting Mexico. Brett was unavailable, and in my mind's movie, he was off gallivanting with fourteen women, while I was lonely and isolated. And scared.

The Princess Hotel was still open, but the checkout desks were packed with people fleeing the city. I secured myself a better room with some sunlight, but every hour, the news brought new horrors and concerns. Each of you had your own experience during this time, so I am sure you can relate to my extreme discomfort and fear of the unknown. I paced back and forth in my hotel room for what seemed like an eternity.

I called my children numerous times, trying to decide whether to come home or stay in Mexico. I still believed I had some kind of control over what was to come, and I needed to make a plan and be prepared.

When I finally did talk to Brett, his response was, "Relax, nothing has happened yet. There is no need to jump to conclusions."

That didn't make me feel any better, I was a planner, after all. I kept trying to figure out what to do. I didn't want to leave Brett in Mexico for fear of us being separated for who knows how long, but I also didn't know if I should stay.

On top of knowing next to nothing about what was going to happen anywhere on the planet, a group of six young Australians brought the Coronavirus to Aspen during the height of our spring tourist season. Alexandra was quite concerned about me returning to Aspen because I was sixty, and my mother had died of a rare lung disease. According to the experts, I was at high risk for this life-threatening virus.

"Please, Mom, *don't* come to Aspen," Alexandra said to me on one of our many phone conversations. "It's too dangerous here for you."

I talked to all three children about the possibility of staying in Mexico, and they were all supportive of whatever I decided. And if I did come back to the United States, because Aspen was a hot spot, they all agreed Michigan would be a better place for me to quarantine.

I didn't like hearing from my children—or my ex-husband who reminded me a lot—about how I was at high risk for catching a virus because it made me feel old. I finally had to tell them all to zip it, but secretly I was happy they were supportive of me going to Michigan. That's where I wanted to go anyway.

Fully aware that new decades tended to bring life-altering change for me, I was still wondering whether Brett and a lake were the "big change" I was waiting for.

Criminy, I thought, half-seriously, *I've called in a pandemic to help me figure out what my big move is in 2020.*

A pandemic certainly fit the criteria of traumatic and life-altering.

The only problem was, Brett didn't want to leave Mexico, and I had this romantic vision in the back of my mind of staying like renegades and escaping the world. We would ride out the pandemic for a couple of years, living on the beach drinking coconut water from the coconuts that fell from the trees growing beside the warm Pacific waters.

Many local friends told us we could stay with them and their families, but I had some concerns. Media brought new fears every hour, and although I had credit cards, I had no cash. The world was in crisis, and with no money if the banking system crashed (which didn't seem unrealistic at the time), no job, and no home, my carefree dream of staying didn't seem so great after all. Still at the Princess Hotel with limited ability to speak with Brett, my thoughts ran wild.

Some of the female guests at the resort left before the end of the week. They were mothers, daughters, or wives, and their families were insisting they come home. On Friday, March 20, the U.S. government announced that if all Americans abroad did not return home within twenty-four hours, there would be no guarantee they could get back in the country, even if they held a valid U.S. passport.

Camille, Carson's girlfriend, had just started a Fulbright scholarship in Buenos Aires nine days before the U.S. announced the severity of the situation. I figured if she could stay I could stay, but hours after speaking to her, Camille's program was closed, and she was told if she didn't get on a plane immediately, the only way to guarantee her reentry into the U.S. was by naval ship that could take up to three months of sea travel.

Camille boarded a plane that night.

Now what was I going to do? Even Camille had left a Fulbright scholarship.

It seemed there wasn't an hour that went by where important global occurrences were not being hurled at all of us. I begged Brett to come to my hotel that evening so we could talk. He arrived after a final dinner out with the ladies—including drinks—but I didn't care. He was there, and I finally had the chance to talk to him about what was going on.

Earlier that evening, the resort made the decision to close its doors the next morning. With nowhere to stay and after much debate about his still-sick father, all our other family members at home, and not knowing what would happen or how long we would be there, we decided to return to the U.S. the next day. I let go of the fantasy of riding out the pandemic in a foreign country. It was just too scary.

"Come with me to Michigan," Brett said to me. "Going back to Aspen is not a good idea, and besides, we need to go to the same place."

Those were the words I wanted to hear, and my children had already agreed that Michigan was a "safer" place for me to go, given everyone's concern over my age.

I made a plane reservation for the next morning on the last scheduled flight to Grand Rapids, Michigan. Without forewarning, we were leaving six weeks before the end of the season. At 5 a.m. the next morning, with no plans to return to Mexico, we packed up eleven waterskis, multiple boots and bindings, ski gear, our clothes, a SUP, and four rolls of toilet paper quickly and efficiently.

We really didn't know how radical it would have been to stay, but there were too many unknowns, and I knew the financial burden was going to fall solely on me. It was a bizarre, eerie trip home through empty airports. Brett's son picked us up at the airport, and we literally crammed all our bags into his small car and headed to Brett's cabin for the unforeseeable future.

It was cold in Michigan in March, and until I was able to get someone to send me some winter clothes, I wore Brett's. My renters had left after only four days in Aspen because of the fear of the Coronavirus. I couldn't blame them, but during their short stay they had left my house a disaster, including leaving trash everywhere for the bears to get into. It was just another thing to deal with that seemed out of my control, but I was with Brett, and I was happy.

Drinking seemed to be excessive for many people during this time, including us. We watched a lot of movies those first few cold months. I was still cleaning away, trying to make Brett's house my home. For the most part I paid for everything, but there wasn't a lot to buy. Gas, food, and liquor were our only expenses, other than Brett's household bills, which he was paying.

In between eating, drinking, and watching a lot of TV, I entertained myself with yoga classes via Zoom, daily meditation, free-form writing, working, and writing. I was keeping up with my spiritual practices, but there were still days when I was upset, unbalanced, and wondering whether this was where I wanted to be and if Brett was the best choice. I flip-flopped a lot. Brett was always there to reassure me and let me know how much he loved me.

Other than a rogue road trip to Florida to go waterskiing in mid-April where we slept in Brett's truck on our way and opened doors with our elbows when we needed gas or food, we nestled into his cabin for the next four months. As the weather got warmer, we spent our time working in the garden, wandering the back roads of rural Michigan in the UTV in search of deer and turkey, and taking in the beauty of the Upper Midwest, often followed by huge nightly bonfires in the front yard.

The first two months of warm weather came and went. Our new boat was delayed and not scheduled to be completed until the end of July due to production difficulties. The dealer was kind enough to give us another boat to use until then, so in between gardening and daily rituals, we headed to the lake we had joined an hour south of the cabin. Thankfully, the pandemic had not really affected the waterski world.

We continued our search for land, and at one point we approached Brett's neighbors who had forty acres adjacent to the land his cabin was on. If we were able to secure that piece of property, we would have enough land to build a lake.

The idea sounded amazing in the beginning until I realized half the lake I would be paying for would be on Brett's land. I started to panic.

In the back of my mind, I had been thinking that if we built a lake together and our relationship didn't work out, I would gift the land to the county and make it available for fishing and wildlife exploration if I didn't want to keep it myself. It was my comfort thought. I was too selfish to let Brett have it without me.

When talk of buying the land next door became a possibility, in which case half the lake would be on his land, not only would I lose control—he would have no reason to stay with me. From that realization forward, whenever the conversation turned toward the future, I felt sick to my stomach.

Every time I questioned our relationship (which was often at that point), Brett would say things like: "It's going to be a lot more difficult on me than you if you leave. What am I going to do for the next ten years if you aren't around? You'll be fine, but I won't have anything."

And every time he said this, the thought that ran through my head was, *Great, so you'll keep me around for ten years, and then when I need you, you'll be gone.*

Brett still didn't hide the fact that he was never going to be faithful to me or anyone else, and at that point, I was not prepared to settle for less than all of him. Many people close to me, including and especially my children, were concerned about the road I was heading down.

I didn't know what to do. I loved him and was afraid to leave, but I was also terrified to stay. It is sufficient to say there was a plethora of bright red flags, which happened to look very similar to the ones in my relationship with Greg. Sometimes I wondered if I was trying to fix what I had broken with Greg and prove I could be an empowered woman with money, but honestly all I was doing was buying love again.

I kept paying for our groceries and everything else. I had already purchased the UTV and the boat. I knew I was also on the hook to pay for any future healthcare or dental problems Brett might have, because he had no insurance. There was no end in sight.

Just as in my two previous relationships, as time went on, I got more and more angry. It was like picking up the underwear over and over again: I kept doing it, and I was getting resentful.

I felt like I had learned nothing.

My house was rented in Aspen, and even though I could have stayed in Michigan, my children and I decided to make our annual trip to Lake Tahoe. By the time August 8 came and I headed for Tahoe, my head hung low on our car ride to the airport.

I looked at Brett and said, "I'm not sure I'm coming back. I just don't know if I can do this."

Brett knew how my previous relationships had ended, so I am sure he understood what I was saying, but he didn't respond. I don't think he knew what to say.

Eventually, eyes staring down the road, Brett said, "Take some time, honey, and figure out what you want. You are welcome back anytime."

I was broken. I didn't know if I would return, but there was the brand-new boat with only twenty-two hours on it delivered just days before I left. Just like when women sleep over with a new man and "accidentally" leave their earrings on the bedside table, I had left a boat, a UTV, and my belongings. I got on the plane to Reno with tears in my eyes, wanting to run but also wanting to make this one work.

My anger and tears did not cease once I got to Tahoe. All three children arrived shortly after I did with their significant others and tried to support me the best they could, but I was inconsolable.

I didn't get up with coffee in hand to ask them to waterski. I didn't participate in family dinners. I didn't play cards, as we always had in the past.

I cried a lot.

I didn't know whether to stay with Brett or not. I did love him and our life together, but I didn't want to take care of him. It was that simple. The rules of the game had changed, just like they had with Greg.

On one of many occasions that month, while Derek was trying to talk me off the edge of the proverbial cliff, he said to me: "Why don't you just go back to Michigan and use him as much as he uses you? Enjoy your time with him."

"Not a bad idea," I replied, trying on the thought.

I knew Brett would still welcome me back whenever I wanted to come and had even invited me to go to Virginia with him for three weeks, where he had secured a coaching job in September. Maybe if I used him as much as it seemed like he was using me, we would be on a more level playing field, and our relationship issues would resolve. Maybe that's what equality would look like for us.

I booked a plane ticket that day.

After the worst summer of my life in Tahoe, I headed back to Michigan. I was bound and determined to let go of my concerns and just be happy with the man I loved; the man I was going to spend the rest of my life with in our beautiful, cute house with a magnificent garden and Scottish cows with their long bangs on the perfect waterski lake I had created in my fairy tale vision.

Part of my upset with Brett had always been that I couldn't seem to get a straight answer about what our plans were going to look like. After I arrived back to Michigan, I tried to get a date out of him about when we would leave for Virginia, but the date always seemed to change, and that was a difficult pill for a control freak to swallow. He was comfortable with not knowing an exact time frame, but the planner in me wanted to know.

I can't exactly tell you why, but I can tell you I definitely wanted to know what was going to happen in September—and over the winter.

Brett was not going to be returning to the resort, and I was prepared for us to winter in Florida and to pay our rent down there, where hopefully he could figure out how to coach clients behind our new boat. But I never got any answers.

Just a lot of, "I don't know. Why does it matter?"

This just added to my frustration. If I was going to be footing the bill, I wanted to know. It was a vicious circle. I felt he was acting like a child, and he probably thought I was acting like his mommy, telling him what to do.

I made it three days at his cabin before completely snapping.

I lost my shit.

I got up in Brett's face one afternoon and told him exactly what I thought of him. I slapped him, then punched him, and then, empowered by a few late afternoon drinks, I threw a chair across the garage. It all happened so fast. Honestly, I can't even remember what our final fight was about. More than likely, it was about money.

As horrified as I was, I had to admit this situation felt familiar. Only three times in my life had I physically lashed out at someone: once with Mark when he told me he was in love with someone else, once with Greg when I smashed his picture on the floor, and now with Brett. In all these cases, I had come to my wits' end because I hadn't set appropriate boundaries along the way. I felt taken advantage of to the point where I lost control of my temper.

I never wanted to be in this situation again.

I calmed myself down and went inside and booked a plane flight for the next day. I packed up all of *my* things. Then I packed some of the things I had bought for *our* life, like the weed eater, the edge trimmer, a suitcase (I bought for him), multiple pairs of waterski gloves *I* had purchased, the teal blue life vests, and as much stuff as I could get my hands on. I'm still mad I didn't take the salad spinner with the teal blue top, the brand-new rake, and a multitude of other household items I knew would never get used again, but even though I was grabbing everything I could find, I didn't want to seem trivial.

I couldn't take a lot of things with me, including all the work I put into the garden and the flowers I bought and planted and tended to. I knew they would all go back to weeds. It was heartbreaking.

Brett just sat there and watched me. I wanted him to say something. I wanted him to commit to me. I wanted to be his one and only woman. But he wasn't going to agree to that.

I got on the plane on August 31, devastated and feeling so low about my inability to keep my temper in check. We dropped off the new teal blue boat at the dealer on the way to the airport.

"You know I can't leave this boat with you," I said. "I would be so angry about it, you would never hear the end of it."

The brother of a friend was on his way to pick up the UTV before I left the cabin. Brett arrived home from dropping me off at the airport as it was being loaded onto a flatbed. My friend's brother told me Brett had tears in his eyes.

I wanted to believe those tears were for me.

I returned to Aspen. All three children were there to try to help me pick up the pieces.

Alexandra made me a big sign that said: "It's *not* all your fault."

I felt like it was. I sank into a deep depression. I didn't want to live. I wanted this immense heartache to go away. I wanted him back. He wouldn't speak to me or answer my emails or texts. Even the children, who bring me so much joy, couldn't pull me out of my funk.

I officially sold the UTV shortly after coming home. I wanted to keep it, but it was impractical and not allowed on the streets in Aspen. Signing over the title was a painful close to a future with Brett. The boat was safely parked in Grand Rapids with strict instructions not to release it to *anyone* except me.

How did I get myself into this very complicated mess?

I was even more upset than I had been in Tahoe. The pandemic was still in full force, and there was nowhere to go and nowhere for me to hide. No new boys to make out with. Nowhere for me to find peace.

I hired a local therapist at the request of my children. They knew I needed help. I knew I needed help. I found her online. It didn't really matter who she was. I was working on myself in between bouts of tears and therapy appointments. I did a lot of soul searching, regular meditation, yoga, and free-form writing.

I thought I had hit bottom. I didn't know where up was, but I was smart enough to remember I had recovered from Mark, I had recovered from Greg, I had recovered from Harry, and I had recovered from all the other men who had broken my heart for one reason or another. I would recover from this heartbreak too.

Within two weeks of being home, I got a text message from Jenna. She and her husband Kreg were coming through Aspen, and Kreg remembered I lived there, so they called to find out if they could stop by for a night or two. I barely knew these two legends of the waterski world, but they had been guest coaches a couple of times in Mexico, so we had some history.

I was happy to have them visit. It felt like a gift: two angels arriving just when I needed them. They parked their RV outside my house for a couple of nights, and on the first night they came in for a visit. The children were still at home pandemicing and in the kitchen making dinner.

I knew Jenna well enough—and she knew Brett—so I shared with her that I had split with him. She agreed with the children that although she thought he was great, he was not the best partner for me.

After hearing what had happened, she asked with a big smile on her face, "Well, did you love him, or do you love waterskiing?"

"Of course, I loved him, but I LOVE waterskiing," I said enthusiastically.

I shared with her my upset over attempting to plan a winter in Florida with Brett, and how frustrated I was with his lack of commitment.

"Why don't you come to Florida anyway?" Jenna asked. "Explore the waterski world. Try out a bunch of different lakes and coaches. Each lake has its own personality, and hopefully you can find a place that feels good to you. You can stay with us until you figure out where you want to be."

I didn't know what to say to this generous offer. All I really knew about Florida was from my trips with Brett and from visiting Mark's grandparents in Fort Myers Beach years earlier. Florida to me was traffic, old people, and high-rise buildings, all of which had never turned me on.

Going with Brett who knows his way around is one thing, but going by myself is a whole different game, I thought to myself.

Jenna's offer ran through my head. The idea sounded great, but how was I ever going to navigate going to Florida by myself?

I had also been flirting with the idea of returning to Mexico for a month after the first of the year. I knew Brett wouldn't be there, so I was knocking around that idea as well. I loved Aspen, but I didn't want to spend an entire winter there—especially with so many limitations due to Covid. The idea of going to Mexico and Florida gave me some hope.

I can do this without Brett. I can go to these places. I'm not scared, I thought—only partially believing what I was telling myself.

In Aspen, the pandemic was in full force. Cases were rising as Thanksgiving and colder temperatures approached, and there was no vaccine in sight. Among the children, there were different opinions about how to socialize or not socialize to keep everyone safe. The rift became deeper by the day.

I had heard an upsetting story about a family back in May through a Zoom group meeting. One of the group members had talked about the upset in his family over one of his children *refusing* to wear a mask— and the others insisting he had to if he was going to interact with the family—and how that drove their loving family apart.

At the time, I felt empathy for their situation but honestly thought it was a problem that was easily avoidable. I was appalled that a family could be split in half over a virus.

Until it happened to us.

In fact, it had been brewing beneath the surface for some time. Carson and his girlfriend Camille were concerned about being exposed to the virus and wanted the entire family to quarantine. Derek had Covid twice already, so they were not so worried about him (at the time we thought once you had Covid, you were unlikely to have it again), and I was making the choice (which was painful at times) to stay in. But Alexandra and John were less concerned about Covid and had socialized with some of their friends on several occasions just prior to Thanksgiving.

We had family discussions over how to handle the situation and whether we should even get together for Thanksgiving in the same house. Should we wear masks? Should we social distance during the evening? There were no vaccines back then and no in-home tests to take, so we were at a standstill over how to handle our family Thanksgiving dinner.

In the end we couldn't agree. Carson, Camille, Derek, and I had Thanksgiving dinner at home. I made dinner for Alexandra and John. Derek acted as a delivery man and took them food to their apartment down the street.

I was devastated. Not only was I falling apart, my family seemed to be in crisis over a virus. Carson and Camille left to go back to Bozeman the next morning. My sixty-first birthday was just days away, and I was looking forward to celebrating with all the children for the first time in years. However, because of the Covid conflict, that didn't happen.

It was now December. After five months of quarantining previously with Brett and four months of my adult children living with me (and now a visiting nephew), I needed some alone time a few nights a week. But nothing was open, so there was nowhere for anyone to go.

Because my house in Aspen is an old Victorian with quite an abnormal floor plan, my bedroom is located directly off the kitchen/ living room. Often there were nights when I would slink away to my room, just wanting to be left alone while the children were in the main room watching TV, playing cards, or shooting the breeze. Their joy only intensified my loneliness.

I tried to bite my tongue and endure the pain—knowing I could join them but not feeling up to it. On several occasions, I lost my temper out of frustration with them—and myself for not *wanting* to join in.

I didn't want the children and my nephew to leave permanently, but I was desperate for some space. I wanted to be able to sit on my couch some nights in my underwear, eat cheese and crackers, and watch *The Crown*.

Then one night, much like I did with Brett, I snapped. I said some truly terrible things that I did not mean, but they came out of mouth anyway.

The next morning, I asked Alexandra, John, and my nephew to move out and go back to their two-bedroom condo on the other side of town.

"I need some space," I told the three of them. "I'm still not doing well, and I can't take you guys being here every night. I love you all very much, but you have to go home."

I tried to be as calm and diplomatic as possible, but the damage had already been done. Words are tricky. You can't take them back.

As the three of them were taking their last load of stuff out to the car, John looked at me and said, "You sure have an odd way of showing you love us."

And he was right.

The first three nights were heaven. All I had wanted was for the children to give me a little bit of time on my own, and say, "Enjoy yourself—how about we check in with you on Monday?" Now they were barely speaking to me, and they certainly weren't coming to visit.

Everyone hated me. Mark's family (who was my nephew's family) got involved at one point, and it felt like everything I knew and everyone I loved had disappeared. I lost my boyfriend, my children, and Mark's family. No one seemed to be interested in supporting me. I wasn't in touch with my friends, partially because of the virus and partially because I had little energy to reach out and connect with others.

I thought I had hit rock bottom before. Now I knew I had.

I had never known so much pain. Everything seemed to be slipping through my fingers. Everyone I spoke to was so happy their kids were home, but I was yelling at mine. I felt like an incredible loser.

I was humbled to my knees.

I often thought to myself, *How can I be doing all of this spiritual work and life is still so hard?*

I was so sure committing to Brett was the change 2020 was meant to bring, but clearly I was wrong. The new decade had definitely brought trauma, but I had no idea what it all meant.

Although therapy was going well and my children even joined me to resolve some of our issues, I knew I needed more support, so I hired my next life coach. Now I had a therapist *and* a life coach.

As Will Rogers said, "If you find yourself in a hole, stop digging."

I threw down my shovel.

A Light at the End of the Tunnel

The light of a single candle can dispel the darkness of a thousand years.

–JOSEPH GOLDSTEIN

By the grace of God, 2020 finally ended. Even though the pandemic was still a real threat—and we were still wearing masks—2021 had dawned with the possibility of new opportunities. Yet again, I hadn't drawn a Medicine Card since last New Year's—but one morning just after the first of the year, I randomly decided to pull a card. I mixed them thoroughly again, wondering what 2021 would bring.

Lo and behold, there it was *again*: The Butterfly.

What was I needing—or wanting—to learn from this card?

I knew I wanted to come out of my chrysalis and find my beautiful wings. Although I had begun to identify what was *not* working (including love affairs with young, hot, broke athletes, and taking things personally, among others), I wasn't clear what was going to replace some of these faulty, ingrained thoughts and behaviors.

I knew if I didn't replace these thoughts and behaviors with new thoughts and behaviors (new neural pathways) I was going to end up in the same mess.

Since my breakup with Brett, I had spent time reflecting on how I wanted my life to look. For my entire life, I had been trying to prove to other people how hard I worked. I knew how hard I worked, and I knew I created work for myself. I didn't want to show up that way anymore.

I didn't want to be bothered by comments like I heard from Bob at the pharmacy years before, "Why would you ever have to work? You're rich. You don't need to work."

I still resented hearing people say things like these, but there was nothing I could do about what others were thinking or saying (like the man who told me I absolutely had 40 million dollars in the bank). I reminded myself that I had dropped my story while climbing Mount Kenya, and it was now time to replace my thoughts with new thoughts—and actions.

What if life didn't have to be so hard?

As I had told Jenna back in September, although I did love Brett, I truly loved waterskiing. My passion for waterskiing was replacing my passion for snow skiing. My longing for warmth was replacing my tolerance for cold.

On January 15, 2021, I boarded a plane headed toward Mexico for a month in the sun. I knew Brett wouldn't be there because I had double-checked with several people before committing. It would have been too uncomfortable if we were there together—mostly for me.

I arrived at the villa, sat down on the couch while I waited for my room to be ready, and struck up a conversation with a stunning brunette wrapped in a light green sarong who was sitting on the couch as I entered.

After a brief friendly introduction, I nervously shared with her, "I used to date the resident coach, and I'm feeling uncomfortable about being here. I wanted to come so badly, but I'm still nervous."

Olivia, as I found out her name was, looked at me and said, "Me too."

I thought to myself, *Me too, what? Is this another one of Brett's extracurricular flings I don't know about?*

"Can I ask who you used to date?" I asked her nervously.

Olivia looked at me and said, "I used to date Sam. He was the resident coach here a few years back."

I had heard about Sam before, and I sighed with relief.

Olivia was the first person I spoke to on this month-long journey, and I thought to myself, *Look at that. You're fine. Olivia's here. She dated Sam and she's back. I don't have to be afraid.*

I not only kept a journal of my life while I was in Mexico, I recommitted to a journal of my waterskiing. Fortunately, Covid hadn't affected the waterski world much, since we were all skiing at least thirty-two feet behind a boat—way more than the six feet of social distance recommended by the CDC. Since I had been able to ski several times during the pandemic and kept developing my skills, I had started a waterski journal in 2020. In the beginning (because I had so many bad habits), there wasn't a single coach who would even let me ski the course, but I wrote about each time I was on the water, anyway. I had fifty years' worth of bad habits to unlearn. But the pros document all their sets, so I figured I would as well.

In 2020, I made approximately 520 passes (6-8 passes per set). In those 520 passes, I made it around all six buoys successfully ten times. I know because I put a big star next to each time I made it. I didn't know how I made those ten passes so I could repeat it, but I was elated each time nonetheless. I also did the math: Ten out of 520 tries is 1.9 percent. I made the course 1.9 percent of the times I tried.

In 2021, during my first week in Mexico, I set a goal to ski six 26.7-mph passes in a row off the dock. And although 26.7 mph is quite slow in the world of waterskiing, six out of six passes off the dock (with no warm-up pass) was ambitious for me. It gave me something to work toward.

When Jenna and Kreg arrived in Mexico, I told them I was going to take them up on their offer to come to Florida. I would stay for exactly three months, from March 7 until June 7. I wanted to make those six out of six passes off the dock by the time I left Florida, giving me a solid five months of skiing to complete my goal.

I also set a longer-term goal to compete at the Women's Senior World Championship in 2026. Senior Worlds was an outlandish goal, but I didn't care. At that point making six out of six passes off the dock was an outlandish goal.

I committed to go to Florida by myself. It was a long way to drive for a 61-year-old woman, but I felt whatever would happen was going to be okay. Whether my car broke down, I got lost, or I embarrassed myself on the ski dock, I viewed this trip as a test of relying on myself.

I found a definition of a spiritual pilgrimage that said something like this: a journey to a sacred place that conscious-driven travelers embark on to let the outside world enrich and enable their hearts and minds. That perfectly described what I hoped would happen during my trip to Florida.

When I told my children I was going on a spiritual pilgrimage, one of them asked me if I was going to Mecca.

"No, I'm not going to Mecca. I'm going to Florida, from waterski lake to waterski lake, for exactly three months. It's going to be an incredible pilgrimage and very spiritual," I declared. "It's kind of like going to Mecca—just different."

I returned home from Mexico and spent three weeks in Aspen, where I shoveled snow to clear a walking path from my mudroom door to the driveway, and scraped my car daily, I also did some home repairs, saw John and Alexandra, enjoyed some snow skiing, and prepared for my trek to Florida.

I spent some time during my three weeks at home with a fun thirty-six-year-old. Although Will wasn't a serious relationship, I enjoyed hanging out with him. He was a good escape from my loneliness, and he filled a void.

One night Will texted me, "Your boy's here at Eric's Bar."

I responded with, "What boy? What are you talking about?"

"You know, the one you shouldn't be hanging out with," Will texted back.

I laughed out loud to myself and texted, "Well, that isn't narrowing it down much. Who are you referring to exactly?"

"The one who's really into teal blue. You know, the one you bought a boat for."

I hated it when anyone said I bought a boat for Brett. It made me upset.

This can't be happening. And I didn't buy a boat for him.

I had heard rumors Brett was coming to Aspen, but I thought he was coming in the summer. It was only February. I was not mentally prepared to accept he was in town.

I called Will immediately.

"Are you sure it's Brett?"

"He's wearing a teal blue jacket. Yeah, I'm sure," Will said, chuckling. "He's talking about how he's going to be running the waterski lake down valley."

Great, I thought to myself. *Really great.*

"He's trying to get me to be friends with him. I don't want to be friends with him," Will said to me.

Will and Brett had never met, but Will knew all about Brett from what I had told him, and it's safe to say he wasn't a big fan.

Why is Brett trying to make friends with the one man I am spending time with?

My ego got the best of me. I texted Brett immediately and asked him to back off.

He didn't respond. He hadn't responded to me in a year. Why would I expect him to respond now?

The same thing happened a second time a couple of nights later. I knew because Will told me.

I was angry and hurt—and honestly jealous. Even though I knew I wasn't walking off into the sunset with Will, I didn't want to lose him to Brett. Will was *my* friend, and I didn't want him to be *Brett's* friend. I could just see the two of them out on the town causing trouble while I was home on my couch—alone.

Will confirmed Brett was moving to town for the summer and was only in Aspen for a visit on his way to somewhere or another. Even though Will's news gave me some relief, I still wasn't looking forward to Brett moving back.

Why, out of all the places Brett could go—even though he had lived in Aspen before—was he moving to the teeny tiny town I lived in? Many of my friends insisted he was moving to Aspen to get me back, but I knew him too well. He definitely wasn't trying to win me back.

By March everything had returned to normal with the children. Somehow, we had weathered our pandemic storm. I hung out with Alexandra and John frequently and was in touch with the boys on a regular basis. I don't know if I could have left on my jaunt to Florida if my relationship with them had not been on the mend. We were back together as a team, even though some of us were physically separated by miles. I can't tell you exactly how this happened, but as the old adage says, time heals all wounds.

The night before I left for Florida, Alexandra and a few friends had a small send-off party for me. During the party, Carol, one of Alexandra's best friends in Aspen, said to me in her adorable Chilean accent, "I know you are going to meet the perfect man in Florida."

"Yes, mama," Alexandra chimed in. "I agree with Carol. Someone is going to appear. I know it. Someone who is *age appropriate* and perfect for you."

"You mean someone I can bring home to meet the fam?" I responded, chuckling. "Maybe you're right. Who knows. I'm open for whatever happens."

The idea was intriguing—and inspiring—but I knew in my heart my journey was not about meeting someone. It was about coming home to myself.

The next morning, I loaded up my car in preparation to leave. I took my golf clubs, bicycle, waterski equipment (of course), bowling ball (just in case), an electric piano, a printer, office supplies (so I could work while I was gone), vitamins and beauty supplies, and enough clothes to last three months. My car was *very* organized—and *very* full.

As I pulled out of my driveway, I left behind the snow and ice to head toward warmth and whatever experiences would come my way. Like climbing Mount Kenya, I consciously chose to leave behind all previous notions of what I thought worked in my life—but didn't—and prepare myself for whatever my higher power had in store.

I thought my trip to Mexico had healed me of Brett, but clearly after Will's two encounters with him—and my upset around it—Brett was still on my mind. I didn't like the feeling. Will was on my mind as well. I didn't like that feeling either. As I headed to my first stop, to have dinner with my dear friend Jamie in Denver, I committed to leaving Brett and Will and all the other young, broke, trouble-making men—and the heartache that eventually came along with those choices—behind.

Even though I am well-traveled, this solo journey was unlike any other I had ever taken. I had a plan as to where I would stop each night along the way, and I knew I would go to Jenna and Kreg's in Orlando for a week or so when I arrived. Beyond that, I would travel around Florida to wherever the wind blew me. I committed to taking everything as it came—breakdowns and breakthroughs.

As I left Denver the next morning, I looked for an audiobook and randomly chose one called *The Second Mountain: The Quest for a Moral Life* by David Brooks. My choice of book turned out to be perfect. The following recap may not necessarily reflect Brooks's main message, but it is what I got out of his words.

In *The Second Mountain,* David Brooks defines life as a two-mountain journey. On the climb up the first mountain, we focus on graduating from school, starting a career and family, and doing all those things we are "supposed" to do. We attempt to climb the mountain we think we are meant to climb. The goal of this mountain is to be a success, make one's mark, get married and raise a family, and experience personal happiness.

I could relate to this. I had gotten my degrees, been married, bought a home, and successfully raised three amazing children who were off exploring their own mountains.

Brooks goes on to speculate that often people get to the top of this first mountain, look around, and find the view unsatisfying. Sometimes, Brooks says, life has a way of pulling us off this first mountain because of illness, or divorce, or financial catastrophe, but whether one is on the top of the first mountain—or gets pulled off it for some reason or another—one realizes there is another, bigger mountain to climb.

This second mountain climb tends to be more self-actualizing. Brooks says that although self-care is important, overfocus on self-care alone can disconnect us from community—and cause us to become lonely. The goal of the second climb isn't as selfish as the first climb. The second climb is more enlightening, more fulfilling, and more satisfying.

For some strange reason, I felt like this "spiritual pilgrimage" of mine was about beginning the trek up my second mountain. I was committed to living beyond my self-imposed limits. I was committed to living a peaceful, joyous life with or without a man. I wanted to live into my joy—self-created joy, that is—with or without an intimate partner.

I had a lot of time to myself with thirty-plus hours on the road. Besides listening to audiobooks, I called friends, listened to music, got gas and snacks, and had an occasional nap on the side of the road. My car didn't break down, thankfully, but I was prepared for that as well and clear that I was going to accept *whatever* came my way.

My therapist had encouraged me to make some 4" x 6" cards for my car. Each card had a positive affirmation on it. They said things like "I bring light to myself and others," I trust in the divine," "Today I am going to make this my greatest day yet," and a big one for me: "99% of the time what other people think or say has nothing to do with me."

I was familiar with the power of affirmations. I knew from Joe Dispenza that to rewire the brain, it is necessary to replace the old neural pathways with new neural pathways. I could go on and on about what I knew, but I'm not sure until I made these cards and put them in my car that I knew how powerful affirmations really were. Either that, or I was slow and needed constant reminders. Every morning, I would shuffle the cards and draw one. The card of the day sat on my center console just below my middle display. I had lots of time to see it.

I spent some of my driving time reflecting on my relationship with Brett and all the others I had tried to buy affection from. I realized I not only tried to buy the affection of lovers, I did the same thing with my children, ex-husband, friends, and work associates.

I recalled the voice in my head that said, *Just this one last time. Next time will be different, I promise.*

I had said this same thing so many times before, but this time *was* different, and I knew it. I no longer needed to repeat the same mistake again expecting a different result. At least that is what I wanted to believe. I was sixty-one and knew I had to replace my conditioned behaviors with something different—or live with the consequences for the rest of my life.

Somewhere along my drive, I also had an a-ha moment about Brett. When I first visited him in Mexico, he had clearly told me, "Don't get too attached to me. I don't date women for more than eighteen months."

I had to admit, I thought I was going to be the one to change him. Maybe I could be the woman he stuck with forever. After May 31, 2020—exactly eighteen months after Brett and I started hanging out—I started treating him differently.

I wanted him to have a plan for the fall.

I wanted him to clean up his house.

I wanted him to get health insurance.

I wanted him to go to a proper dentist.

It was like a switch had flipped—a switch I was not aware of at the time—and I wanted him to man up.

We had made it eighteen months, so I thought we had a future together. Now that I had proven to myself *I* was good enough to keep him, now I thought he had to prove that *he* loved me. I wanted to control him, but he was very clear in the beginning—and in the end—he would not be controlled by anyone.

I argued with him, and he didn't listen.

I seduced him, and he didn't listen.

I begged him, and he didn't listen.

I finally slapped him, punched him, and threw a chair across the garage. And he still didn't listen.

As badly as I felt about my actions for so long, I recognized I had been trying anything and everything to convince him to be the way *I* wanted him to be.

I was now clear I could not control another person. The only person I could control was me.

I was still a Two—an over-giver by nature—so in order to do that, I had to take a leap of faith, slow down, and stop over-giving. I wanted to try something new.

I pulled into Jenna and Kreg's driveway and was greeted with open arms. I stealthily moved my many bags, including my electric piano, into the room they gave me, and I organized my sporting equipment in my car. You would have thought I was staying for a year. I started making plans to visit the plethora of lakes in Orlando and lake hop around Florida.

I thought I had died and gone to heaven.

Once I arrived in Orlando, in between skiing, making new friends, and working, I also got lost a lot. One time, when I tried to outsmart Siri and take a detour, I ended up in the gigantic Epcot parking lot for at least half an hour, trying to get out. Siri was probably laughing at me.

I do *not* like getting lost. It makes me feel out of control. But throughout my pilgrimage, I was lost more times than I can count. I took a lot of deep breaths, told myself I would eventually figure out where I was if I were patient, and let go of always needing to know where I was going. I went from ski site to ski site and followed my dream. I made wonderful friends—especially with my host and hostess—and I took each day as it came.

Toward the end of my stay in Florida, Jenna, Kreg, and I took an hour-and-a-half long car ride to visit some friends northeast of Orlando.

As we were driving along, Kreg pointed to his left. "That's where the Villages are."

"What are the Villages?" I asked, curious as to why he was pointing them out.

"The Villages is a fifty-five-plus retirement community and has become quite the place to retire," Kreg answered. "They have endless activities available for the residents."

"People love living there," Jenna added, giggling. "Rumor has it that it has one of the highest rates of STDs in the country."

"OMG, that is hysterical," I responded. Then I remembered something.

Following my divorce from Mark—almost two decades earlier—I had created an idea for an imaginary retirement community. It began when my friend Anne and I were discussing where we were going to live when we were older and ready to retire.

The idea was quite simple and grew over time. In my ideal vision, *my* retirement community would be in Mexico. Everyone would be welcome. The more the merrier. The community would organize communal activities like wheelchair races at 5:00 p.m., followed by margaritas at 6:00. In my original scenario, I had the cocktail hour before the wheelchair races, but thought better of serving liquor to retired elders before racing wheelchairs, so we switched up the order.

Over time, the vision included tiny houses. Everyone could have their own space, but there would be a common area to come together for some fun.

I had often wondered about my obsession with creating a retirement community—even if it were a fantasy. I wasn't sure it was what "normal" people focused on early in their lives. Maybe it was to quiet the voice in my head I had inherited from my father, which was always reminding me retirement equals death.

Maybe it was to quiet the voice in my head that I needed to find a partner and worried about what would happen if I didn't. This voice definitely believed that without a partner, I would be useless—and lonely. The retirement community solved both these possible fates: I would never be bored, and I would never be lonely.

"It's gonna be great," I often told my friends. "I'll be ninety-five hitting on seventy-seven-year-olds."

I always chuckle when I tell people that. They chuckle too, but I think they know I might be serious.

Most people want to be loved and to find the love of their lives. As far as I can tell, most of us are raised to believe we need to find our perfect partner, our soulmate, in order to "be okay" in life. We are raised to believe we have to find someone to grow old with: someone to sit beside us in our rocking chair on the porch, overlooking our white picket fence that surrounds our suburban house with the two-car garage where we raised our 2.4 children (or whatever fantasy we grew up with).

After my divorce, I started questioning whether spending my life alone or finding "Mr. Right" were my only two options. My imaginary, joyful, fun, safe retirement community provided an alternative to either having to find someone to be with or, God forbid, growing old alone. It provides an alternative—an invitation—to throw out the concept of the "white picket fence." I tell people when they are struggling to find that perfect someone, "You don't have to worry. You can come to my retirement community."

I have offered this suggestion to more people than I can count, and I have *never* had anyone turn down my imaginary offer. I have asked young and old, friends, family, strangers, cashiers, bus drivers, and bartenders, and once they hear the idea, they are all in. Their delight (and often immense relief) showed me I was not alone in my fear of dying alone—or doing whatever it took to find someone so I didn't die alone. A partnership seemed an insurance policy against loneliness.

In short, I had talked about the idea of a retirement community for decades, and here it was in living color. The Villages had become a gathering place for not only older people but younger adults as well. It was a booming small metropolis, and for the first time, I saw my vision in full swing.

I wonder if they have wheelchair races at 5:00 and margaritas at 6:00, I thought, amused.

Shortly after that, Carson came to visit me for a week. For my sixtieth birthday present, he had promised a week-long visit to Mexico for a mother-son ski week, but since the pandemic had prevented our trip to Mexico, his visit to Orlando was a make-up for that trip. I was thrilled when he told me he was coming. I suggested we spend five days in Orlando and then drive to Charleston to surprise Derek for the weekend. Carson thought the idea was great.

Derek has had a chip on his shoulder for years that no one in the family—except for me—had ever visited him at boarding school or college when he had gone willingly (or been dragged unwillingly) to visit his two siblings at every school they had ever been to. Everyone in the family was supposed to come to his college graduation in 2020, but because of the pandemic, even that had been canceled. In my view, Derek was rightfully disappointed.

Meanwhile, my three months in Florida were coming to an end, and I would be headed back to Aspen soon. Charleston was a bit out of the way, but not by much. And it was a bonus having Carson help me load my bags and sporting equipment in preparation for my journey home.

As Carson and I pulled out of Orlando on our way to Charleston, I reflected on my previous assumptions about Florida (i.e., traffic, old people, and high-rise buildings). Those things were all true, but they were not the impression I was leaving with. I left with memories of beautiful lakes (complete with the occasional alligator), good friends, warm temperatures, and loads of sunshine.

When we pulled into Derek's garage after our six-hour road trip from Orlando, Derek was there to greet me.

When I rolled down the window on the passenger side, Derek looked in, about to say, *Who did you bring with you?* But what came out of his mouth was, "Oh my God, Carson, what are you doing here? This is incredible."

Needless to say, I was elated, and we spent a wonderful weekend together enjoying the late spring in South Carolina.

I had not yet met my waterskiing goal. So, after Carson left, I went out twice to a waterski lake near Charleston to give that goal a last chance to come to fruition before returning to Aspen.

On my last day in Charleston, I managed to ski four out of six passes in one set, and then five out of seven in the next. I was getting closer, and the percentage of time I was skiing the course had risen from 1.9 percent to over 60 percent. I still wanted to meet my goal, but 60 percent was certainly nothing to be ashamed of.

I left Charleston happy and mentally satisfied. I was climbing my second mountain and was on my way to the summit, no matter what it took to get there.

––––––––––––––

My next stop was Michigan, to finally pick up the teal blue boat I hadn't seen since the previous September. I had no idea what I was going to do with it once I got it back to Aspen, but it seemed to be the next right step. On my way to pick up the boat, I thought about how I left Brett and how I insisted on taking all those things with me, including the boat. I took back what was mine—knowing I looked greedy and would probably be despised for it.

It was different from the way I had behaved in the past. When my father was on the edge of bankruptcy and needed the trust he put in my name to settle his debts, I could have claimed what was mine and let my father go broke, kept the trust, and paid for my parents' expenses for the rest of their lives. Instead, I bailed him—and my mother—out. I could have gone to court with Mark for our divorce. Instead, I settled our divorce out of court because I didn't want to fight anymore. With Greg, I tried to get the money back I had been naïve enough to give to him, but there was no getting it back.

I also realized many of the people I knew who received a large windfall burned through the money until it was gone. Both my parents and Greg went through all the money—just like most lottery winners do. Even my brother, whom I rarely spoke to, went through all his inheritance.

Somehow I managed to double what I received.

Maybe I should give myself some credit for my skills in this area.

I had been smart enough to put the boat and the UTV in only my name when we bought them. I had obviously learned something: At least I wasn't going to lose those assets like I had lost my house in Ross, the cash, or countless other items along the way.

I arrived at the Grand Rapids airport just in time to hand my car keys to Ben, who works for me in Aspen. I could have picked up the boat and driven it back to Aspen, but I knew my spiritual pilgrimage was over. It was time to go home. Ben had flown from Aspen to Grand Rapids to pick up the car and the boat and drive them home, and I got on an airplane headed to Aspen that night.

I arrived home safely. I sat down in my backyard and took in the beauty of my home. Ben, the car, and the boat arrived a day and a half later.

The following evening, I had dinner with Alexandra, John, and Alexandra's friend Carol and filled them in on my amazing adventure.

"Sorry girls, no new man."

"That's okay, Mama. It sounds like you had an incredible time," Alexandra said while she squeezed my arm gently. "We love you."

I melted.

I reflected on my journey. No words can authentically capture my pilgrimage completely. I had driven just over 6,000 miles—most of them on my own. I was proud of myself for taking a chance and going to Florida. I didn't meet my waterskiing goal, but I was proud of my success. I didn't finish my book, but I was proud of my writing accomplishments. No new man was in my life, but I felt at peace. My cup felt full, and it felt amazing.

———————

Just after the Fourth of July, I made a trip to Farmer City, Illinois, to visit some friends I met in Mexico who were big water skiers and had their own lake.

As I had said to them at the dinner table one evening in Mexico, "I want to go to Farmer City. I want to come to see where you people live."

"What do you mean by *you people?*" they responded.

"You know," I said, laughing out loud, "You people who live in the Midwest and sit around and watch the corn grow."

I didn't mean to insult them. It honestly just came out. After my experience in Michigan—worlds apart from my life growing up in California—I loved the Midwest and the simplicity of life there. I loved the people I had met, and I wanted more of it.

I booked a ticket.

My plane was delayed, and I thought I would be too late to ski that afternoon by the time I arrived, but five minutes after I got to the lake in Farmer City, I was told to "suit up."

I was going skiing. I ran one pass off the dock without a warm up, which is not what I would normally do. For some reason, I went straight into the course and delightedly made all six buoys. I ran another and another and another, all successfully. In the end, I ran six out of six passes off the dock back-to-back.

I started to cry. I had reached my goal. It was like my final step on Mount Kenya. I can't describe the overwhelming feeling of joy and accomplishment I felt. Again, skiing six out of six passes at 26.7 miles per hour is not exactly a goal worthy of distinction among true skiers, but for me, it had taken commitment, dedication, and unwavering enthusiasm to get there.

I had watched video after video of myself skiing. It always felt like a rerun of the same movie, just with different boats and different bathing suits, on different bodies of water, but I had stuck with it. Even though I couldn't see each individual tiny change, I had gone from being able to run a pass successfully 1.9 percent of the time to 100 percent—at least for that day.

The success I had that glorious July afternoon gave me an enormous amount of confidence. Maybe if I kept doing the work in my life like affirmations, rewiring, free-form writing, and all of my other practices, even though I couldn't see enormous change on a daily basis, the change would occur if I stuck with it. I often thought of the ten-thousand-hour rule Malcolm Gladwell wrote about in his book *Outliers*: Success does not usually come quickly; it comes with perseverance and practice.

Not only was waterskiing a worthy physical and mental challenge for me, but doing what I loved brought me new friends and new adventures.

As I always told my children when they were younger, "Don't play soccer just because your friends are playing soccer. Play soccer because you love soccer. When you find your passion, friends and connections will come. And even if they don't, you will still find joy in playing soccer."

Waterskiing, for me, is a dance on the water. It is a place where perfection is difficult to find. It takes grit and determination, and a willingness to right yourself when somehow you are out of balance. It will always be a place for me to practice course correction, humility, and grace.

Your Guess Is as Good as Mine

To be a person of integrity, you will come to the realization that you will not compromise yourself or the truth within you any longer.

–JOHN-ROGER, DSS

There had been quite a bit of wine consumed. It was close to midnight. I had come to visit my ex-mother-in-law and her boyfriend in France for the weekend. My ex-husband, Mark, his wife Natasha, and their five-year-old twin girls had also come to visit. We spent a beautiful, cozy afternoon playing games and having quality time together.

Natasha and I were doing the dishes after dinner. Our day and evening had been peaceful and lovely. Natasha and I have a solid relationship built on years' worth of work to maintain a loving family. As she handed me the last of the glasses on the dining room table, the conversation shifted and she brought up the topic of my book.

"If you tell *your* truth in your book," she said, "you're going to have to live with the ramifications of your actions forever."

I believe she had no malicious intent and said this out of love, and a desire to protect me as well as others. So at first, I felt empowered and confident in my response. I explained I was writing an inspirational memoir—a journey of my life in service to women and men learning to maneuver through the challenges of love and money. I had concerns about sharing my personal life, but I told her, "I am writing it anyway. I don't have control over how anyone interprets it.

"It's not my intention to upset anyone," I continued. "I do my best to make any difficulties I share in this book to be of my doing, not anyone else's. Everyone involved is simply an actor in the movie of *my* life."

Natasha and I went back and forth on this point.

"Maybe the family you hold in such high regard will no longer love you if you tell your story," Natasha finally said. "And that could include Mark, his mother, me, and possibly your children."

Natasha's comments, especially after the third or fourth time, were difficult for me to swallow. Was she right? My worst nightmare would become a reality. No one would love me if I shared my truth. They would all think I was just out for spiteful revenge. I would have no family, no friends, and no possibility of a future suitor. I would die miserable and alone.

"You're right," I said to Natasha tearfully. "I won't write it. No one will love me."

I don't know if it was the tears or something else, but Natasha turned to me and humbly said, "Write your book. Tell your truth."

After our good nights, I went to my room to jot this story down so I wouldn't forget my perception of what happened. Yet again, I was potentially giving up something I had worked so hard on because someone else didn't think it was a good idea. The tears didn't flow like they had in the past, but I had still cried.

We've all heard that if six people witness a single car crash, the police officer on the scene will hear six different versions of what happened. Our minds remember what they grasp in the moment, and if there are missing pieces, we tend to fill in the blanks with what we think happened—or expected to happen.

The truth is there is nothing I can say that won't possibly make someone mad. We all remember the past differently.

I am grateful to Natasha because she helped me face my fears. I am writing my truth anyway. Tears and all, I am willing to take a leap of faith and stand up for the idea that it is okay for me to write what I remember. It is okay to have an opinion. I do not have to back down. My intention has always been to come from love—for myself as well as others.

In the prologue, I mentioned three challenges that caused me to write this book:

1. Being a Woman on Top (a woman who has more resources than most)
2. Habitually saying and thinking things that keep me stuck without being aware I am saying or thinking them
3. Being without a soulmate in a world that seems obsessed with finding "the one"

I began my "research project" to find answers about how I could solve the problems I was having dating men when I was wealthier than they were (which seemed to be always).

As it turns out, although that was my outer journey, I realized my inner journey was even more important. The way I dealt with money in my intimate relationships became *my* lens for spiritual growth.

What is my truth now after writing this book?

- I still sometimes struggle with being a Woman On Top.
- I still sometimes say and think things that keep me stuck.
- I still wonder if I will ever find—or need to find—a soulmate.

And even though my spiritual curriculum will continue throughout my life, here are the lessons I have learned so far.

- Simplifying everything is truly the greatest gift. The simpler things become, the less likely things go astray, and the easier it is to clarify what is important.
- Self-care is of the utmost importance. The more I simplify, the more I have time to take care of my needs.
- Acting with integrity is a crucial part of building an honest, healthy relationship—with your partner, yourself, and anyone else you come into contact with.
- I am working on giving generously and joyfully with no expectation in return. I want to be the best Two I can be. If I receive generosity of heart, love, or money from others in return, it is a bonus. Rather than give, give, give and then shout fuck you, now I just give. If I want to spend money, I do. If I don't, I don't.
- I take personal responsibility for the assets I have generously been given rather than feeling ashamed for receiving them.
- I continue to work on not taking things personally. I have an ego, which sometimes gets the best of me, but my spiritual practices help keep it in check.

- Spiritual exercises lead to spiritual growth, as many wise teachers have said throughout time.
- According to Malcolm Gladwell, we need ten thousand hours of experience to reach mastery. That means we also need patience. Sometimes it looks like we are going backwards, but if we stick to our practices, we will move forward.
- Viktor Frankl said, "Between stimulus and response there is a space. And in that space lies our freedom and power to choose our responses." Before I respond, I now ask myself, *Is what I am about to say or do in line with who I am and how I want to be?*
- Hire Slowly, Fire Quickly. I strive to eliminate everything that doesn't work in my life as fast as possible and take my time when making new commitments.
- I don't have to be a lotus flower. Sometimes I want to be a cactus. A cactus is beautiful—and badass.
- To set healthy boundaries with people (especially men I am in a relationship with), I must be clear about what I truly want and need, and then communicate it. Men won't change for us, but they might change because of us.
- I am letting go of past resentments. Brett and I have had closure and are on friendly terms. The same is true with Greg, Harry, and many others.
- I'm watering and fertilizing my own lawn instead of looking over everyone else's fence and wondering why their grass looks so green.
- I have spent so much of my life working so hard, trying to convince my father, my kids, my friends, and myself that I am *not lazy.* I'm done proving.

- I still have little sticky notes everywhere that I use to write down my to-do's and cross off finished things (with an immense amount of satisfaction). I used to believe I needed to get to a place where I had no more sticky notes. Well, I know now that's never going to happen. I still make new clean sticky notes each week—and sometimes more often—because sticky notes bring me joy.
- Other than my children, my north star has always been to seek a connection with the divine. This has been true since I was old enough to understand the idea. I have been pulled away from this connection often during my life, getting sidetracked by the belief that if I were popular or loved by a man, I would experience the ultimate state of bliss. I'm clear now the ultimate state of bliss is found in loving myself first and continuing to rewire my brain with positive, loving thoughts allows me to connect to my source.
- We need people. My relationships with family, friends, and lovers are wonderful and very satisfying. People (especially those who push my buttons) are a reflection of me, and without them I wouldn't have a mirror.
- I don't have to try to convince others to follow the path I have chosen. Two ears, one mouth, as Alexandra reminds me. There has become less reason to talk and more reason to listen. People will see my actions for themselves, and if what I'm doing is helpful for them, they will want more of whatever I am dishing out.
- Waterskiing is a metaphor for my Spiritual Growth. Determination, patience, and follow through are everything. Practice, practice, practice leads to success.

I will never know if the Indian doctor or the Gods held some truth for me. Both experiences were fascinating (and comical), and I think of them often. I know the Indian doctor's advice on meditation is absolutely valid, but who really knows what each of our individual paths are to spiritual growth? Is it spending two years on my own to then find a partner? Is it committing to the partner I am with, no matter who they are?

But what if I'm not with a partner, for whatever reason? Is there then no path to learning whatever I need to learn on this planet?

I talked with a woman recently at an event. She is bright, talented, beautiful, wealthy—and lonely. She is approaching sixty. She wants to find a partner. She has wanted to find a partner since her divorce more than five years ago. I know she has tried, but she hasn't found that perfect one. Maybe she is too picky, and maybe not.

I looked at her with compassion and said, "What if he never shows up? Then what? How do you want to spend the rest of your life?"

Life can be lonely sometimes—whether you are with someone or not.

Even if we find our perfect mate, no one lives forever. Dying, in my opinion, is the ultimate break up. It happens with couples all the time. It's just part of life. There is usually nothing we can do to prevent it.

So, even though I believe we definitely need people for connection and spiritual growth, I think believing we have to have a partner to be complete is a dead-end road with no opportunity for personal growth. If someone comes along, great, but if not, I can still live a joyous, full, wonderful life.

What if Christian is right? What if nothing ever changes? What if I keep attracting young, hot, broke men? My definition of young might change over time, but what if this path *is* my spiritual curriculum?

The one thing I know that I did not know when I started writing this memoir is I am okay just the way I am. Life is okay just the way it is.

What is right for me is enjoying the journey and loving my children, friends, and everyone else who enters into my sphere. Spiritual growth is not necessarily about doing anything differently; it's about changing my perspective—which usually results in a new outcome. For me—at least for now—I don't *need* a relationship with one man. I am able to get my intimacy needs met with a lot of different people—most importantly myself.

I hope reading my story has been helpful for you. Writing it has been a godsend for me. Thanks to the fact I wrote my journey down, I know how much I have grown over the years.

On one of my trips to Uganda, I met up with my friend Tony. Tony and I live in different cities, so we don't see each other often, but when we do we always find time to chat about our personal lives.

Over a glass of wine overlooking the skyline of Kigali, Rwanda, Tony shared, "Miriam and I are living together, as you know, and we have been for a few years, but that just doesn't seem to be enough for her. She is pressuring me to make a commitment and marry her. Two weeks ago, she went so far as to threaten to leave if I can't move forward and propose to her."

I knew from previous conversations that Miriam was a paralegal. She was good at her job and made a solid living, but her work didn't come close to fulfilling her purpose and passion. Tony was a musician and performer who had a huge personality and lived his purpose and passion to the fullest.

"I just can't stand it when she complains about her job. She is just not that much fun to be around. I don't understand why she doesn't quit if she doesn't like it. I don't want to spend the rest of my life with a person who is so unhappy," Tony told me.

"I just can't seem to pull the trigger and marry Miriam. The thought of marrying someone who is not satisfied leaves me feeling like a deer in the headlights. I love her, but her lack of enthusiasm is more than I am willing to take on."

I loved the fact that Tony had clear boundaries, but I left our conversation in Kigali feeling sad for Miriam. It was clear they loved each other and there was not a lot I could say to console him.

A few months later, I saw Tony at a board meeting in Denver, and he was beaming.

He pulled me aside and said with a huge smile, "Guess what? Miriam and I are getting married. I am so excited."

I was happy for him, but surprised. "Last time I saw you, you weren't keen at all on marrying Miriam. What happened to change your mind?"

"She found her purpose and passion," Tony said with delight. "She quit her job as a paralegal and has gone into business for herself renting and selling pet costumes."

"Pet costumes?" I said, trying not to laugh. "That's so wonderful."

"She knows who she is and what she wants to do. She started her own business. She loves it and it is booming." I could see the joy in his eyes. "She has found what fills her up and it changed everything for me. I love this woman and I'm so proud of her."

Renting and selling pet costumes was not anything I had ever considered to be a viable business, but I became a convert then and there. Miriam found her very unique purpose and passion. The next time I saw her, I could visibly see the shift in her demeanor and attitude and feel her sense of delight in doing something she found meaningful. I could see what Tony saw.

I was so happy for them. Tony knew what he wanted, and when Miriam discovered what she wanted, they found true love.

No, we don't need a partner to be complete. But no matter where we live or who we are, when we take a stand for ourselves, take a risk, and live into our purpose and our passion, we live our dream—and become more attractive to others.

After meeting my waterski goal in Farmer City, I decided on a whim to draw a medicine card. To my true and utter disbelief, I drew the Butterfly Card again.

I was curious about the odds of picking the same card so many times in a row, so I did the math. One out of fifty-two (cards) is a 1.9 percent chance. That was exactly the same odds as my waterskiing in 2020. I was blown away by the coincidence.

Later that night, with the Medicine Cards still sitting on my bedside table, I decided to try one more time. This time I didn't shuffle the cards. I was tempted to pull the top card, but I wasn't sure if I might have put the Butterfly Card on the top of the stack, so I opted for the second card.

There it was again. I had pulled the Butterfly Card twice in one day.

This is beginning to get really weird, I thought to myself.

I am still pulling medicine cards, and the Butterfly Card doesn't come up as often as it did before. But for me, it will always be the Year of the Butterfly. My journey will never end. I'm always going to be spreading my wings and learning to fly.

And if none of this works, there's always my imaginary retirement community.

Acknowledgments

Heartfelt gratitude to my mother and father, who unknowingly sacrificed so much to create an environment for me to be able to see the light and share my experience with others.

To the many men in my life who taught me so much.

To my three children, Alexandra, Carson, and Derek, for putting up with their mother's desire to finish a book, embracing my journey, and allowing me to patiently—sometimes painfully slowly—learn a new, more peaceful way of being.

To the many people who helped me write this book and share it with the world, including Amanda Rooker at Split Seed Media, author Michael Conniff, Amber Vilhauer and her team at NGNG, and Ashley Bunting and her team at Merack Publishing. I also give thanks to my friend and mentor Gabriella Taylor who allowed me to share her "love print" model in this book.

Finally, I would like to express my heartfelt gratitude to the many people who took time out of their lives to read my story and offer feedback before publication.

I love you all along with so many others!

About the Author

Suzanne Leydecker is an author, speaker, global philanthropist, and proud mother. She builds unshakable women who reclaim their worth and fall in love with their lives. She encourages and supports women to find their purpose and passion, practice self-care, and set appropriate boundaries in love and life.

Suzanne received her master's in marriage and family counseling from the California Institute for Integral Studies and a certificate in Spiritual Psychology from the University of Santa Monica. She is incredibly proud of her three children, Alexandra, Carson, and Derek, who are now young adults living their own lives. She travels often, and lives in Aspen, Colorado, and Orlando, Florida.

Suzanne speaks on podcasts and provides personalized trainings and retreat experiences for professional teams and social groups. Visit www. suzanneleydecker.com to connect!